AQA GCSE Foundation

¡Mira!

Anneli McLachlan

Leanda Reeves

www.heinemann.co.uk

✓ Free online support
✓ Useful weblinks
✓ 24 hour online ordering

0845 630 33 33

Part of Pearson

Heinemann is an imprint of Pearson Education Limited, a company incorporated in England and Wales, having its registered office at Edinburgh Gate, Harlow, Essex, CM20 2JE. Registered company number: 872828

www.heinemann.co.uk

Heinemann is a registered trademark of Pearson Education Limited

Text © Pearson Education Limited 2009

First published 2009

13 12 11
10 9 8 7 6 5 4

British Library Cataloguing in Publication Data
A catalogue record for this book is available from the British Library.

ISBN 978 0 435395 92 6

Edited by Naomi Laredo
Designed by Ken Vail Graphic Design, Cambridge
Typeset by Ken Vail Graphic Design, Cambridge
Original illustrations © Pearson Education Ltd.
Illustrated by Beehive Illustration (Mark Ruffle), Stephen Elford, Graham-Cameron Illustration (David Benham), Ken Laidlaw, NB Illustration (Ben Swift), Sylvie Poggio Artists Agency (Rory Walker)
Cover design by Wooden Ark Studio
Picture research by Caitlin Swain and Susi Paz
Cover photo © Masterfile/Radius Images
Printed in China (GCC/04)

Acknowledgements
We would like to thank Liliana Acosta da Uribe, Elena Alegre, Iñaki Alegre, Ione Ascanio Green, Nicky Barrett, Clive Bell, Gillian Eades, Clare Farley, Elaine Harnick, Alex Harvey, Chris Lillington, Ana Machado, Esther Mallol, Ruth Manteca, Philippa McFarland, Judith O'Hare, Vicki Orrow-Whiting, Diana Reed, Daniel Reeves, María Rodríguez, Siobhan Snowden, Caitlin Swain, Carolyn Tabor, Alison Thomas, Ron Wallace and Melissa Wilson for their invaluable help in the development and trialling of this course. We would also like to thank the pupils at the Instituto de Edcuación Secundaria López Neyra (Córdoba) and Isabel Teresa Rubio; the pupils at the Colegio Europa Internacional (Sevilla), Pedro de Lorenzo and Setmaní Valenzuela; Lucentum Digital and all those involved with the recordings.

The authors – Anneli McLachlan and Leanda Reeves (née Reed) – and publisher would like to thank the following individuals and organisations for permission to reproduce photographs:

Pearson Education Ltd/Mind Studio pp **7** (David), **9**, **10** (d), **15**, **22**, **24** (3–8, 10–11), **26** (a–e, 3–6), **27**, **28** (shop, a, b, d, f), **30** (food), **31**, **33**, **35** (María, Lía), **36**, **45–55**, **58**, **63**, **65** (woman), **83** (actor), **85**, **86**, **89**, **90**, **96**, **102**, **105** (girl), **113**, **116** (girl), **124** (b, c), **126**, **134**, **143**, **150**, **153**, **160**, **161** (volunteers, girl, boy), **162**, **164**, **174–182**, **186**, **187**, **191**, **195**; Photodisc pp **7** (Eiffel, skier), **26** (2); Yurchyks/Shutterstock p **7** (sunbathing); Photolocation 3/Alamy p **7** (ruins); Everynight Images/Alamy p **10** (a); blickwinkel/Alamy p **10** (b); imagebroker/Alamy p **10** (c); Johan Furusjö/Alamy p **11**; Ron Buskirk/Alamy p **16**; Philip Lewis/Alamy p **18** (tent); Buzzshot/Alamy p **18** (pool); Headline Photo Agency/Alamy p **24** (1); Barry Mason/Alamy p **24** (2); Pedro Diaz/Alamy p **24** (9); James Goldsmith/Alamy p **26** (f); Pearson Education Ltd/Clark Wiseman p **26** (1); Juan Monino/iStockphoto p **28** (c); Pearson Education Ltd/Ben Nicholson pp **28** (e), **105** (objects); John Warburton-Lee Photography/Alamy p **30** (bar); Pearson Education Ltd/Gareth Boden p **35** (Marcelo); Louise Batalla Duran/Alamy p **35** (Diwali); David Young-Wolff/Alamy p **35** (piñata); Robert Harding Picture Library Ltd/Alamy p **35** (Feria); Pearson Education Ltd/Jules Selmes pp **38** (girl), **166**; Photolink pp **38** (tree), **158** (1); Stockbyte p **56**; Photodisc/Kevin Peterson pp **65** (man), **145**; Nick Hanna/Alamy pp **72**, **74**; Squint/Alamy p **76**; i love images/Alamy p **83** (cashier); Iberia p **83**; Medical Doctor Nurse Dentist Pharmacist/Alamy p **87**; Allstar Picture Library/Alamy pp **88** (Cruz, Shakira), **142** (García, Hayek); Dimitrios Kambouris/WireImage/Getty Images p **88** (Moss); James Devaney/WireImage/Getty Images p **88** (Beckham); Dave Hogan/Getty Images Entertainment p **88** (Madonna); Behrouz Mehri/AFP/Getty Images p **88** (Nadal); Getty Images pp **91**, **183**; BWAC Images/Alamy p **94**; Daniel Berehulak/Getty Images p **101**; Robert Fried/Alamy p **106**; Alex Livesey/Getty Images Sport p **107**; Tequila gang/WB/The Kobal Collection p **110**; Vario Images GmbH & Co. KG/Alamy pp **114**, **156** (f); Brand X Pictures/Burke Triolo Productions p **116** (popcorn); Vera Bogaerts/iStockphoto p **124** (a); Ken Welsh/Alamy p **124** (d); Content Mine International/Alamy p **124** (e); Eandro Hermida/Alamy p **125** (top); Igor Marx/iStockphoto p **125** (bottom); Loic Bernard/iStockphoto p **127** (city); Image Source Ltd/Beth Neal p **127** (country); Nickos/iStockphoto p **132**; Wendell Teodoro/WireImage/Getty Images p **142** (Baras); Imagestate/John Foxx Collection p **144** (chips, smoking); Digital Vision pp **144** (eating), **158** (2–4); Darko Novakovis/Shutterstock p **148**; Jose Manuel Vidal/epa/Corbis p **156** (a); Jon Mikel Duralde/Alamy p **156** (b); Steven May/Alamy p **156** (c); PCL/Alamy p **156** (d); Andrew Reese/iStockphoto p **156** (e); Mark Eveleigh/Alamy p **156** (g); Jan Martin Will/Shutterstock p **158** (5); Fancy/Veer/Corbis p **159**; AP Photo/Paul White/Empics p **161** (a); AFP/Getty Images p **161** (b); Chris Wayatt/Alamy p **161** (c); Mike Finn-Kelcey/Alamy p **161** (d); Lalo Yasky/WireImage/Getty Images p **185**; Finca Bellavista p **189**.

Every effort has been made to contact copyright holders of material reproduced in this book. Any omissions will be rectified in subsequent printings if notice is given to the publishers.

Websites
The websites used in this book were correct and up-to-date at the time of publication. It is essential for tutors to preview each website before using it in class so as to ensure that the URL is still accurate, relevant and appropriate. We suggest that tutors bookmark useful websites and consider enabling students to access them through the school/college intranet.

Contenidos

Contenidos

- Talking about where you went on holiday
- Using the preterite

Repaso ¿Adónde fuiste?

De vacaciones

1

1 Escucha y escribe las letras correctas. (1–5)

Ejemplo: **1** b, i,…

¿Cuándo fuiste de vacaciones?	¿Adónde fuiste? Fui a...	¿Con quién fuiste? Fui...	¿Qué hiciste?	¿Qué tal lo pasaste?
a El año pasado…	**f** Grecia	**k** con mis amigos	**p** Escuché música. Tomé el sol.	**u** Lo pasé mal.
b El verano pasado…	**g** Estados Unidos	**l** con mis padres	**q** Fui de excursión y visité monumentos.	**v** Lo pasé fenomenal.
c El invierno pasado…	**h** Francia	**m** con mi familia	**r** Mandé mensajes. Esquié.	**w** Lo pasé genial.
d Hace dos años…	**i** la República Dominicana	**n** solo	**s** Bailé. Jugué al voleibol.	**x** Lo pasé bien.
e Hace cinco años…	**j** la India	**o** sola	**t** Monté en bicicleta. Saqué fotos.	**y** Lo pasé regular.

G The preterite ⟳196

Use the preterite (simple past tense) for completed actions in the past.

	escuchar (to listen)	comer (to eat)	salir (to go out)	ir/ser (to go/to be)
(yo – I)	escuché	comí	salí	fui
(tú – you)	escuchaste	comiste	saliste	fuiste
(él/ella – he/she)	escuchó	comió	salió	fue

Some verbs have spelling changes in the 'I' form of the verb:

Infinitive   **Preterite**

jugar → jugué (*I played*)

sacar → saqué (*I took [photos]*)

6   seis

leer 2

What did David do on holiday? Write down the four correct letters.

a played volleyball
b danced
c went on a bike ride
d skied
e took photos
f went swimming
g sunbathed
h visited monuments

El verano pasado fui a Argentina de vacaciones. Fui solo. Primero fui a Buenos Aires y luego a las montañas (Los Andes). ¡Lo pasé fenomenal! Bailé el tango en la ciudad pero fue un poco aburrido. Después visité monumentos y también saqué muchas fotos. Finalmente esquié en las montañas. Fue impresionante. ¡Viva Argentina! **David**

hablar 3

Look at the photos below and imagine one of the holidays in detail. Then have a conversation about it with your partner.

- ¿Cuándo fuiste de vacaciones?
- ■ Fui…
- ¿Adónde fuiste?
- ■ Primero fui a… luego fui a…
- ¿Con quién fuiste?
- ■ Fui…
- ¿Qué hiciste?
- ■ Hice muchas cosas, por ejemplo…
- ¿Qué tal lo pasaste?
- ■ Lo pasé…

⭐ In your speaking and writing, use sequencers (first…, then…, after that…) to extend your sentences and add extra detail. This will help you to aim for a C Grade. Look at how David uses these words in his text to do this.

primero	first
después	afterwards
luego	then
también	also
finalmente	finally

a

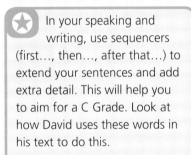

Francia – París – las montañas

b

España – la playa – las ruinas de Mérida

escribir 4

Escribe un correo sobre tus vacaciones. Utiliza las frases siguientes.

El verano pasado fui a…
Primero fui a…, luego fui a…
Lo pasé…
Hice muchas cosas, por ejemplo…
Después… y también…
Finalmente…
Fue impresionante/fenomenal/un desastre.

1 ¿Qué tal tus vacaciones?

 1 Escucha y escribe la letra correcta. (1–10)

Ejemplo: **1** a

 a Descansé.

 **b** Nadé.

 c Hice yoga.

 **d** Di una vuelta en bicicleta.

 e Vi lugares de interés.

 f Monté a caballo.

 g Patiné.

 h Esquié.

 i Hice alpinismo. ¡No tuve miedo!

 j Hice vela.

> ★ tener miedo = *to be scared*
> tuve miedo = *I was scared*
> no tuve miedo = *I wasn't scared*
> These expressions don't translate word for word into English – you just have to learn them.

 2 Escucha otra vez y escribe la letra correcta. (1–10)

Ejemplo: **1** d

 a ¡Lo pasé genial! **b** ¡Lo pasé bien! **c** ¡Lo pasé bastante bien!

 d ¡Fue regular! **e** ¡Fue un poco aburrido! **f** ¡No me gustó nada!

G The preterite: irregular verbs ➲196

Some common verbs are irregular in the preterite.
Note that, unlike regular preterite verbs, these have no accents.
Ver *(to see)* is almost regular in the preterite, apart from not having any accents.

	hacer *(to do)*	tener *(to have)*	ver *(to see)*	dar *(to give)*
(yo – *I*)	hice	tuve	vi	di
(tú – *you*)	hiciste	tuviste	viste	diste
(él/ella – *he/she*)	hizo	tuvo	vio	dio

> ★ Keep an eye on words and phrases that mean the same thing. A variety of expressions may be used in your reading or listening exam. For example:
> hacer patinaje = patinar = ir a la pista de hielo
> Keep a list of these throughout your GCSE course to help you remember them.

 3 *Match up the sentences which mean the same thing.*

1 Hice ciclismo.
2 Un día patiné y luego nadé.
3 Fui a la piscina y también monté a caballo.
4 Un día hice equitación y otro día hice esquí.

a Hice natación y también hice equitación.
b Di una vuelta en bicicleta.
c Un día fui a la pista de patinaje y luego a la piscina.
d Un día monté a caballo y otro día esquié.

4 Escucha. Copia y completa la tabla en inglés. (1–6)

	weather	activity	opinion
1	hot	climbing	great

> When you are listening, pay attention – some of the weather expressions may have **no** in front of them, which means the weather wasn't like that!
>
> **No** nevó.   It **didn't** snow.
>
> Negatives like **no** can change the meaning of a whole sentence, so listen out for them.

¿Qué tiempo hizo?

Hizo buen tiempo.

Hizo mal tiempo.

Hizo calor.

Hizo frío.

Hizo sol.

Hizo viento.

Hubo niebla.

Hubo tormenta.

Llovió.

Nevó.

5 Lee los textos y contesta a las preguntas.

El verano pasado fui de crucero por las islas Griegas. Hice natación y vela. Hizo mucho calor excepto un día que hubo niebla. ¡Qué raro! Me gustó mucho, lo único malo fue que no pude hacer windsurf. ¡Qué pena! **José**

El año pasado fui a Argentina de vacaciones y lo pasé fenomenal. Hicimos esquí en Catedral y a veces tuve miedo porque hizo mucho viento. Nevó mucho pero también hizo sol. Fue una experiencia inolvidable. **Alicia**

ir de crucero = *to go on a cruise*

1 Who had sunny weather?
2 Who had windy weather?
3 Who went sailing?
4 Who had some fog?

5 Who was scared at times?
6 Who had hot weather?
7 Who had an unforgettable experience?
8 Who was disappointed by something?

6 Escribe un texto sobre tus vacaciones. Contesta a las preguntas en español.

- ¿Adónde fuiste de vacaciones?
  El año pasado fui a…
- ¿Qué hiciste?
  Primero…, después…, luego…
- ¿Qué tiempo hizo?
  Hizo… /Hubo… /Llovió./Nevó. Pero no…
- ¿Qué tal lo pasaste?
  Lo pasé… Fue una experiencia…

> To aim for a Grade C in writing:
>
> - Use time expressions: **el verano pasado** (last summer), **el año pasado** (last year).
> - Extend your sentences with sequencers: **Primero**…, **después**… etc.
> - Give details and join ideas together with **y** (and), **también** (also), **pero** (but).
> - Include opinions: **lo pasé fenomenal** (I had a great time), **fue una experiencia inolvidable** (it was an unforgettable experience).

2 Vacaciones para todos

 1 Escucha y escribe la letra correcta. (1–5)

¿Dónde te quedaste? | *Me quedé en…* | *¿Dónde te alojaste?* | *Me alojé en…*

a un camping

b un hotel de lujo

c un parador

d una pensión

e un albergue juvenil

 2 Escucha otra vez y completa la tabla en inglés. (1–5)

	location	description	facilities
Mónica	Portugal, in town	old but comfortable	bar, no restaurant
Adrián			
Laura			
Ibrahim			
Jorge			

Estaba…
en la costa   en el campo
en la montaña   en la ciudad

Era…   No era (nada)…
antigu**o/a**   barat**o/a**
modern**o/a**   animad**o/a**
bonit**o/a**   ruidos**o/a**
fe**o/a**   tranquil**o/a**
car**o/a**   cómod**o/a**

Tenía…   Había…
No tenía ni… ni…
(un) bar
(un) gimnasio
(un) restaurante
(una) discoteca
(una) piscina climatizada
(una) sauna
(una) cafetería

G   The imperfect tense   ⟹ **198**

The imperfect tense is used to describe what something *was* like.

*The campsite **was** in the mountains.*
El camping **estaba** en la montaña.
*It **had** an impressive swimming pool.*
Tenía una piscina impresionante.

	estar *(to be)*	**tener** *(to have)*	**ser** *(to be)*
(yo – *I*)	est**aba**	ten**ía**	era
(tú – *you*)	est**abas**	ten**ías**	eras
(él/ella – *he/she/it*)	est**aba**	ten**ía**	era

hay – there is/there are → *había – there was/there were*

escuchar **3** Escucha y lee las preguntas. Escribe la letra correcta.

Ejemplo: **1** f

1 ¿**Cuándo** fuiste de vacaciones?
2 ¿**Adónde** fuiste?
3 ¿Con **quién** fuiste?
4 ¿**Dónde** te alojaste?
5 ¿**Cómo** era el hotel?
6 ¿**Qué** tiempo hizo?
7 ¿**Qué** hiciste durante tus vacaciones?
8 ¿**Qué tal** lo pasaste?

a What did you do during your holiday?
b Where did you stay?
c How was the hotel?
d What was the weather like?
e Where did you go?
f When did you go on holiday?
g What sort of time did you have?
h Who did you go with?

hablar **4** *Using the questions from exercise 3 and these notes, have a conversation with your partner about a holiday. Remember to answer each question with a full sentence.*

1 hace dos años
2 Gran Canaria
3 con mis amigos
4 hotel de lujo

5 cómodo, moderno, pero ruidoso; discoteca, gimnasio
6 buen tiempo y mucho sol
7 canté karaoke, bailé
8

leer **5** Lee el texto y contesta a las preguntas en inglés.

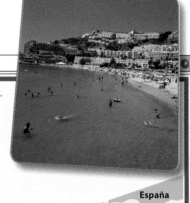

En febrero fui a Gran Canaria con mis hermanos. Pasé una semana allí.

Mi hotel estaba en la costa. **Era** muy moderno y animado. Pero también era caro porque era de lujo. **Tenía** un restaurante fantástico y también un gimnasio.

El primer día hizo frío y llovió un poco, **pero después** hizo sol. A mí me encanta el calor.

Todos los días jugué al baloncesto y al tenis en el hotel, e hice windsurf y vela en la playa. ¡Fue muy divertido!

El último día, el viernes, fue un día estupendo. **Primero** di una vuelta en bicicleta. **Luego** bailé en la discoteca y fui a una fiesta muy divertida. **Por fin** vi un concurso de fuegos artificiales.

Para mí Gran Canaria es un lugar ideal para ir de vacaciones. **Fue una experiencia** inolvidable. Espero volver el año que viene porque me encanta. ¡Un abrazo! **Jorge**

España

Marruecos

Islas
Canarias

1 When did Jorge go to Gran Canaria?
2 How long did he spend there?
3 What was the hotel like? (4 details)
4 What was the weather like? (3 details)
5 What activities did he do every day?
6 What did he do on his last day?
7 What does he say about next year?

★ Use Jorge's text as a model for exercise 6. Finish the phrases in blue with your own ideas. Include:
● Time expressions: **el año pasado**…
● The imperfect: **el hotel era**…
● The preterite: **nadé en el mar**…
● Sequencers: **primero**…, **después**…
● A general opinion: **fue una experiencia**…

escribir **6** Describe tus vacaciones.

3 En el hotel

1 Match the booking forms to the hotel guests. Then read the booking forms and note down:

- Date of arrival
- Number of nights
- Details of rooms requested

1

Apellido	Smith
Correo electrónico	jsmith@gmail.com
Fecha de llegada	9 ▼ diciembre ▼
Número de noches	2 ▼
Habitación doble	0 ▼
Habitación individual	1 ▼
Con balcón	✓ ▼
Con vistas al mar	✓ ▼
Cama de matrimonio	✗ ▼
Preguntas/Comentarios	
¿Hay gimnasio en el hotel?	

2

Apellido	Collyns
Correo electrónico	acgs@hotmail.com
Fecha de llegada	21 ▼ junio ▼
Número de noches	5 ▼
Habitación doble	1 ▼
Habitación individual	0 ▼
Con balcón	✓ ▼
Con vistas al mar	✓ ▼
Cama de matrimonio	✓ ▼
Preguntas/Comentarios	
Nos gustaría una habitación con un ambiente romántico	

3

Apellido	Lupinov
Correo electrónico	alov@yahoo.com
Fecha de llegada	2 ▼ mayo ▼
Número de noches	9 ▼
Habitación doble	1 ▼
Habitación individual	1 ▼
Con balcón	✓ ▼
Con vistas al mar	✓ ▼
Cama de matrimonio	✓ ▼
Preguntas/Comentarios	
¿Se admiten perros?	

2 Listen and read the conversation and fill in the grid. Then listen and fill in the grid for the other conversations. (1–4)

	type of room	with	nights + dates	cost
1	double	bath, balcony, sea view		

> ⭐ The reception desk of a hotel is a place where conversation takes place in a polite way. Use **usted** rather than **tú** in these situations. The **usted** part of the verb is the same as the 'he/she' part of the verb: ¿**Quiere** una habitación con baño? *(Do you want a room with a bath?)*

- ● ¿En qué puedo ayudarle?
- ■ Quiero reservar <u>una habitación doble</u>.
- ● ¿Quiere una habitación con baño o sin baño?
- ■ <u>Con baño y con balcón</u>, y con <u>vistas al mar</u>, por favor.
- ● ¿Para cuántas noches?
- ■ Para <u>cuatro noches</u>, del <u>16</u> al <u>20</u> de <u>agosto</u>. ¿Cuánto es, por favor?
- ● Son <u>doscientos</u> euros.

3 Con tu compañero/a, haz dos diálogos utilizando el diálogo del ejercicio 2 como modelo.

a , 5th–11th April – 140€

b , 24th–29th July – 160€

4 Escucha y escribe los nombres. (1–6)

Ejemplo: **1** RODRÍGUEZ

5 Lee y empareja las preguntas con los dibujos correctos.

1 ¿Hay servicio de habitaciones?
2 ¿Hay conexión a Internet?
3 ¿Hasta qué hora se sirve el desayuno?
4 ¿A qué hora cierra la recepción?
5 ¿Hasta qué hora está abierto el restaurante?
6 ¿Se admiten perros?

6 Escucha. Copia y completa la tabla en inglés. (1–6)

	name	question	answer
1	Watson	Until what time is restaurant open?	11 pm

7 Con tu compañero/a, haz el diálogo. Luego haz otros diálogos cambiando las palabras subrayadas.

● Dígame.
■ Tengo una reserva para esta noche.
● ¿Su apellido, por favor, señora?
■ <u>Yang</u>.
● ¿Cómo se deletrea?
■ <u>Y-A-N-G</u>.
● Vale. <u>Una habitación doble con vistas al mar</u>. Aquí está su llave.
■ Gracias. <u>¿Se admiten perros?</u>
● <u>Sí, señora. Se admiten perros</u>.

> Hasta las… horas.
> Sí, señor/señora. Hay conexión a Internet.
> Sí, señor/señora. Se admiten perros.
> Por desgracia no, señor/señora.
> El desayuno se sirve hasta las…
> El restaurante está abierto hasta las…
> La recepción cierra a las…

1 *Anderson*

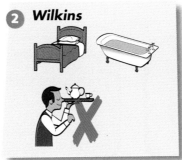

2 *Wilkins*

3 *Douglas*

11:30 pm

4 Reclamaciones

1 Escucha y lee la canción. Escribe las letras en el orden correcto.

Estribillo
¡Ay, este hotel!
Este hotel me vuelve loca.
Quiero quejarme ahora.
¡Quiero un descuento ya!

3 Me hace falta una pastilla
de jabón.
¿Qué vamos a hacer Ramón?
Quiero cambiar de habitación.
Esa es mi intención.

[Estribillo]

1 La habitación no está limpia.
Hay insectos en la cama.
El aire acondicionado está roto.
Y la luz no funciona.

[Estribillo]

4 En el suelo hay cucarachas.
En el baño no hay toallas.
El mar, ¿dónde está?
Aquí no hay buenas vistas.

[Estribillo]

2 El aseo no está limpio.
No hay papel higiénico.
El baño está sucio.
Y también hay mucho ruido.

[Estribillo]

5 Necesito un secador.
No funciona el ascensor.
Quiero hablar con el director.
¡Ay! ¡Qué horror! ¡Qué horror!

[Estribillo]

2 Busca estas frases en español en la canción.

a I want to complain now.
b I want a discount now!
c The air conditioning is broken.
d The toilet isn't clean.
e And also there is a lot of noise.
f I want to change room.
g There are cockroaches on the floor.
h The lift doesn't work.

> ⭐ The song contains words that will be new to you. As you do exercise 1:
> - Look for cognates to help you match the text to the pictures. For example: **insectos** = *insects*. Can you see a picture with insects in it?
> - Look for words that you have already met. For example, the words **baño** (bath) and **cama** (bed) should help you.

3 Escucha y escribe los problemas en inglés. (1–3)

Ejemplo: **1** dirty toilet,…

¿Qué le pasa, señor/señorita? Quiero quejarme…
El baño no está limpio
El aseo está sucio
La habitación no está limpia
Hay mucho ruido

El ascensor/El aseo/ La luz/La ducha	no funciona
Me hace falta	papel higiénico jabón un secador
Me hace**n** falta	toallas

4 Listen to these longer conversations. What does each customer ask for and how does the receptionist react? (1–3)

	customer's request	receptionist's reaction
1	discount	will clean room and give discount

Quiero un descuento.
Quiero cambiar de habitación.
Quiero hablar con el director.

Lo siento mucho.
El hotel está casi completo.
Voy a llamar al ingeniero.
Vamos a limpiar la habitación.
Tengo una habitación libre con vistas al mar.
Le voy a dar un descuento/toallas.

G **Me hace falta**

A useful phrase to say what you need is **me hace(n) falta**…
This behaves like **me gusta(n)**.

For singular nouns:
Me hace falta papel higiénico.
I need toilet paper.

For plural nouns:
Me hacen falta toallas.
I need towels.

5 Con tu compañero/a, haz diálogos.

● ¿Qué le pasa, señor/señorita?
■ …
● Lo siento mucho. …

1 ■ lift not working – want discount
● will give discount

2 ■ light not working, need towels – want to change room
● hotel almost full, will phone engineer

3 ■ dirty toilet, need toilet paper – want to change room
● hotel almost full, will clean room and give discount

6 Lee el texto y completa las frases en inglés.

El año pasado fui de vacaciones a Barcelona y lo pasé muy mal. Me alojé en una pensión cerca de la Plaza Real. Era barata pero no era nada cómoda. Estaba sucia y era vieja.
No había jabón en el cuarto de baño y no había toallas. Por la noche había mucho ruido porque estaba cerca de una calle con mucho tráfico. También había cucarachas enormes. ¡Qué asco! Por eso no dormí mucho.
El año que viene voy a ir de camping. Por lo menos allí no habrá cucarachas. **Rafa**

por lo menos = *at least*

1 Rafa's holidays in Barcelona were…
2 He stayed…
3 There was no…, no… and a lot of… at night.
4 There were also enormous…
5 Next year Rafa is going to…
6 At least there won't be any…

7 Describe unas vacaciones horrorosas. Utiliza las palabras en azul del ejercicio 6.

Prueba oral

Holidays

You are going to have a conversation with your teacher about holidays. Your teacher could ask you the following:

- Where do you normally go on holiday?
- What do you like doing on holiday?
- Describe your last holiday.
- What did you do?
- How was it?
- What was the weather like?

Remember that you will have to respond to an unexpected question that you have not yet prepared.

 1 You are going to listen to Tom, an exam candidate, taking part in the above conversation with his teacher. Listen to part 1 of the conversation and match the beginnings and ends of these sentences.

¿Adónde vas de vacaciones normalmente?   ¿Qué te gusta hacer cuando estás de vacaciones?

1 Cada año voy de…

2 Normalmente voy a España pero a veces voy…

3 Me gusta mucho ir de vacaciones a España porque…

4 Cuando estoy de vacaciones me…

5 Me encanta…

6 También me gusta escuchar música en la playa y descansar pero…

a …hace mucho sol y también hace calor.

b …no me gusta nada leer. ¡Qué aburrido!

c …a Grecia.

d …gusta mucho nadar y tomar el sol.

e …vacaciones con mi familia.

f …sacar fotos.

 2 Listen to part 2 of Tom's conversation and note down the words that fill the gaps.

luego	hice	me quedé	pasé	fue	nadé	muchas veces	fui	después	me alojé

– Describe tus vacaciones del año pasado.

– El verano pasado **(1)** ▨ de vacaciones al sur de España, a Andalucía. Fui con mi familia. **(2)** ▨ en la costa, en Estepona, y **(3)** ▨ en un hotel de lujo de tres estrellas. **(4)** ▨ una semana allí. El hotel tenía una piscina y una discoteca – ¡qué guay!

– ¿Qué hiciste durante tus vacaciones?

– **(5)** ▨ muchas cosas, por ejemplo fui a la playa **(6)** ▨. Primero descansé, **(7)** ▨ hice vela en el mar y **(8)** ▨ jugué al voleibol. También **(9)** ▨. Un día, di una vuelta en bicicleta y vi lugares de interés. **(10)** ▨ estupendo.

 3 Now listen to part 3 of Tom's conversation. In which order does he use these phrases?

a Pues, en invierno voy a hacer esquí.

b ¡Qué horror! No me gustó nada.

c …después hizo sol. A mí me encanta el calor.

d En verano, creo que voy a volver a España.

e Por lo general, fue muy divertido y lo pasé genial…

f El primer día llovió un poco y escribí unas postales…

4 *What was the unexpected question that Tom was asked in part 3 of the conversation? Which tense did he use to answer it?*

5 *Now it's your turn! Prepare your answers to the task and then have a conversation with your teacher or partner.*

- Use the Grade Studio and Tom's answers to help you plan.
- Adapt what Tom said to talk about yourself but add your own ideas.
- Prepare your answers to the task questions and try to predict what the 'unexpected' question could be. The examiner might base this question on something you have already said, or ask something totally new!
- Record the conversation. Ask a partner to listen to it and say how well you performed.

> *Award each other one star, two stars or three stars for each of these categories:*
> - *Pronunciation*
> - *Confidence and fluency*
> - *Range of tenses*
> - *Variety of vocabulary and expressions*
> - *Using longer sentences*
> - *Taking the initiative*
>
> *What do you need to do next time to improve your performance?*

GradeStudio

Make sure you cover the basics.

- Use **simple structures** correctly, e.g. *voy* (I go), *hace sol* (it's sunny), *hace mucho calor* (it's very hot), *fui* (I went).
- Include **simple opinions**, e.g. *Me gusta mucho* + infinitive. *Me gusta mucho nadar y tomar el sol.* (I really like to swim and sunbathe.) *Me encanta* + infinitive. *Me encanta sacar fotos.* (I love to take photos.)
- Join your sentences with **connectives**. Tom uses *y* (and), *pero* (but) and *también* (also).

To reach Grade C, show that you can use different tenses and sequencing words correctly.

- Use **the present tense** to describe where you go on holiday and what you like to do on holiday, e.g. *Normalmente voy a España.* (Normally I go to Spain.)
- Use **the preterite** to say what you did and what the weather was like, e.g. *Hizo sol e hice natación… fui de excursión… vi unos monumentos muy interesantes.* (It was sunny and I swam… I went on a trip… I saw some very interesting monuments.)
- Use **lo pasé** to give your opinion of how it was. Tom uses *Lo pasé genial.* (I had a great time.) What other adjectives could you use with *lo pasé*?
- Use **the near future tense** to say what you are going to do, e.g. *En invierno voy a hacer esquí.* (In winter I am going to go skiing.)
- Include **sequencing words**, e.g. *Primero descansé, luego hice vela en el mar y después jugué al voleibol.* (First I relaxed, then I went sailing on the sea and afterwards I played volleyball.)

To increase your marks:

- Use **exclamations** like *¡Qué aburrido!* (How boring!) *¡Qué guay!* (Cool!) *¡Qué horror!* (How awful!) and expressions such as *Fue un desastre.* (It was a disaster.)
- Use the **imperfect tense** to describe the campsite/hotel and the facilities. Tom uses *El hotel **tenía** una piscina y una discoteca.* (The hotel had a swimming pool and a disco.)
- Try using the following **time expressions**: *un día* (one day), *el primer día* (on the first day), *el último día* (on the last day), *en verano* (in summer) and *en invierno* (in winter).

Prueba escrita

De vacaciones 1

1 Read the text and put these headings into the order of the text.

a **Dancing the night away**   b **Better weather**   c **Time to relax**

d **A European tour**   e **Good facilities**   f **The campsite from hell**

Me encantan las vacaciones porque me gusta descansar. Por lo general no hago mucho. Primero desayuno, luego hago natación y después hago vela o voy de excursión. Por la noche bailo en la discoteca. ¡Qué guay!

El verano pasado fui de vacaciones a Francia con mi familia. Primero fui a un camping cerca de Dinard y lo pasé fatal. ¡Fue un desastre! El camping era muy feo y no había piscina. Además, no hizo buen tiempo. Hizo frío todo el tiempo. Un día hizo viento y otro día llovió. ¡Qué pena! Fue una experiencia horrorosa.

Carlos

Después fui a Fougères. Aquí el camping era caro pero era tranquilo y cómodo con un restaurante. También había una piscina climatizada. Hizo sol e hice natación todos los días en la piscina. Hice muchas cosas, por ejemplo, el viernes fui de excursión con mis padres y vi unos monumentos muy interesantes. Saqué unas fotos buenas. Fue impresionante.

Al final lo pasé bien en Francia pero el año que viene creo que no voy a ir de camping. Voy a hacer un viaje por Europa: España, Italia, Alemania y Francia, y me voy a quedar en albergues juveniles. ¡Lo voy a pasar bomba!

2 Find the equivalent of these expressions in Spanish in the text. Copy them out.

1 First I have breakfast, then I go swimming…
2 …and afterwards I go sailing or on an excursion.
3 Last summer I went on holiday to France with my family.
4 It was a disaster.
5 There was also a heated swimming pool.
6 I did a lot of things, for example…
7 I took some good photos.
8 In the end I had a good time…
9 …next year I think that I am not going to go camping.
10 I am going to have a great time.

3 Look at the sentences you found in exercise 2. Make a note of which tense they are in: present, preterite, imperfect or near future.

4 *Answer the following questions in English.*

1 What was the campsite in Dinard like? (2 details)
2 What was the weather like in Dinard? (3 details)
3 What did Carlos do every day in the second campsite?
4 What did he do on the Friday? (3 details)

5 Which countries is he going to visit next year?
6 Where is he going to stay?

 5 *You might be asked to write about your holidays as a controlled assessment task. Use the Grade Studio to help you prepare your account.*

⭐ GradeStudio

Make sure you cover the basics.

● Show that you can use **basic structures**. Carlos uses *hago* (I do), *no hago* (I don't do), *voy* (I go), *desayuno* (I have breakfast), etc.
● Give **simple opinions**. Carlos uses *me encantan* (I love) and *me gusta* (I like).
● Join your sentences with **connectives** such as *y* (and), *pero* (but), *o* (or) and *también* (also).

To reach Grade C, show that you can use different tenses and sequencing expressions.

● Use **the present tense** to describe what you normally do on holiday, e.g. *por lo general no hago mucho, hago natación, bailo en la discoteca.*
● Use **the preterite** to say what you did and what the weather was like, e.g. *hizo sol e hice natación, fui de excursión, vi unos monumentos.*
● Use **voy a + infinitive** to say what you are going to do, e.g. *voy a hacer un viaje por Europa y me voy a quedar en albergues juveniles.*
● Use **lo pasé** to give your opinion of what it was like. Carlos uses *lo pasé fatal* (I had a terrible time) and *lo pasé bien* (I had a good time). What other *lo pasé…* phrases could you use?
● Add **sequencing expressions**, e.g. *Primero desayuno, luego hago natación y después hago vela.*

To increase your marks:

● Use **the imperfect tense** to describe the campsite/hotel and the facilities. Carlos uses *el camping era muy feo y no había piscina.*
● Use **other connectives** such as *además*, e.g. *Además, no hizo buen tiempo.*
● Use **creo que** (I think that) to give an opinion, e.g. *creo que no voy a ir de camping.*
● Create longer sentences using **contrasting adjectives**, e.g. *el camping era caro pero era tranquilo y cómodo con un restaurante.*

 6 *Now write a full account of your holidays.*

- Adapt Carlos's text and use language from Module 1.
- Structure your text carefully. Organise what you write in paragraphs.

General points about holidays

Do you like holidays?
What do you normally do when you are on holiday?

Main paragraph

Where did you go on holiday last year?
Who with?
Give details of your hotel/campsite and its facilities (what there was and wasn't).
Say what the weather was like.
Give details about what you did.

Conclusion

Say whether you enjoyed the holiday.
Describe your holiday plans for next year.

 7 *Check carefully what you have written.*

- tenses (preterite, imperfect, present, near future)
- accents on words like *después* and *también*
- punctuation, e.g. exclamation marks at both ends of expressions like *¡Qué pena!*

Palabras

¿Adónde fuiste de vacaciones? *Where did you go on holiday?*

Fui a…	*I went to…*	¿Qué hiciste?	*What did you do?*
Alemania	*Germany*	Bailé.	*I danced.*
Argentina	*Argentina*	Escuché música.	*I listened to music.*
Escocia	*Scotland*	Esquié.	*I skied.*
España	*Spain*	Fui de excursión.	*I went on a trip.*
Francia	*France*	Jugué al voleibol en	*I played volleyball on the beach.*
Gales	*Wales*	la playa.	
Grecia	*Greece*	Mandé mensajes.	*I sent texts.*
India	*India*	Monté en bicicleta.	*I rode a bike.*
Inglaterra/Gran Bretaña	*England/Great Britain*	Saqué fotos.	*I took photos.*
Irlanda	*Ireland*	Tomé el sol.	*I sunbathed.*
Italia	*Italy*	Visité monumentos.	*I visited monuments.*
Portugal	*Portugal*	¿Qué tal lo pasaste?	*How was it?*
República Dominicana	*Dominican Republic*	Lo pasé…	*It was…*
Estados Unidos	*USA*	bien	*good*
¿Cuándo fuiste de	*When did you go on holiday?*	regular	*nothing special*
vacaciones?		fenomenal	*wonderful*
el año pasado	*last year*	genial	*brilliant*
el verano pasado	*last summer*	bastante bien	*quite good*
el invierno pasado	*last winter*	mal	*rubbish*
hace dos/cinco años	*two/five years ago*	primero	*first*
¿Con quién fuiste?	*Who did you go with?*	después	*afterwards*
Fui…	*I went…*	luego	*then*
con mi familia	*with my family*	también	*also*
con mis padres	*with my parents*	y	*and*
con mis amigos	*with my friends*	pero	*but*
solo/a	*alone*	finalmente	*finally*

¿Qué tal tus vacaciones? *How were your holidays?*

Descansé.	*I rested.*	Hizo buen tiempo.	*The weather was good.*
Monté a caballo.	*I went horse riding.*	Hizo mal tiempo.	*The weather was bad.*
Nadé.	*I swam.*	Hizo calor.	*It was hot.*
Patiné.	*I skated.*	Hizo frío.	*It was cold.*
Esquié.	*I skied.*	Hizo sol.	*It was sunny.*
Hice yoga.	*I did yoga.*	Hizo viento.	*It was windy.*
Hice alpinismo.	*I went climbing.*	Hubo niebla.	*It was foggy.*
Hice vela.	*I went sailing.*	Hubo tormenta.	*It was stormy.*
Di una vuelta en bicicleta.	*I went for a bike ride.*	Llovió.	*It rained.*
Vi lugares de interés.	*I visited places of interest.*	Nevó.	*It snowed.*
¿Qué tiempo hizo?	*What was the weather like?*		

Vacaciones para todos *Holidays for everyone*

Me alojé en…	*I stayed in…*	moderno	*new*
Me quedé en…	*I stayed in…*	cómodo	*comfortable*
un hotel de lujo	*a luxury hotel*	bonito	*nice*
un albergue juvenil	*a youth hostel*	feo	*ugly/horrible*
un camping	*a campsite*	caro	*expensive*
un parador	*a parador*	barato	*cheap*
una pensión	*a B&B*	animado	*lively*
Estaba…	*It was…*	tranquilo	*quiet*
en la costa	*on the coast*	ruidoso	*noisy*
en la montaña	*in the mountains*	Tenía…	*It had…*
en el campo	*in the countryside*	Había…	*There were…*
en el centro de la ciudad	*in the centre of the city*	No tenía ni… ni…	*It had neither… nor…*
Era…/No era nada…	*It was…/It wasn't … at all*	un bar	*a bar*
antiguo	*old*	un gimnasio	*a gym*

un restaurante	a restaurant
una discoteca	a disco
una piscina climatizada	a heated pool
una cafetería	a café
una sauna	a sauna

Pasé una semana.	I spent a week.
el primer día	the first day
el último día	the last day
Fue una experiencia inolvidable.	It was an unforgettable experience.

En el hotel   *At the hotel*

Quiero reservar…	I would like to reserve…
una habitación individual/doble	a single/double room
para… noches	for… nights
sin balcón	without a balcony
con vistas al mar	with sea views
con baño	with a bath
con cama de matrimonio	with a double bed
¿Para cuántas noches?	For how many nights?
¿Quiere una habitación con baño o sin baño?	Do you want a room with or without a bath?
¿Cuánto es?	How much is it?
¿Hay servicio de habitaciones?	Is there room service?

¿Hay conexión a Internet?	Is there internet access?
¿Hasta qué hora se sirve el desayuno?	Until what time do you serve breakfast?
¿A qué hora cierra la recepción?	What time does reception close?
¿Hasta qué hora está abierto el restaurante?	Until what time is the restaurant open?
¿Se admiten perros?	Are dogs allowed?
por desgracia no	unfortunately not
apellido	surname
¿Cómo se deletrea?	How do you spell it?

Reclamaciones   *Complaints*

¿Qué le pasa, señor/señora/señorita?	What is the matter, sir/madam?
Me hace falta…	I need…
papel higiénico	toilet paper
jabón	soap
un secador	a hairdryer
Me hacen falta toallas.	I need towels.
(no) está	it is (not)
…no funciona	the… doesn't work
no hay…	there is/are no…
el ascensor	the lift
el aseo	the toilet
la luz	the light
la ducha	the shower
La habitación no está limpia.	The room isn't clean.
El baño no está limpio.	The bath isn't clean.

El aseo está sucio.	The toilet is dirty.
Hay mucho ruido.	There's a lot of noise.
Quiero quejarme.	I want to complain.
Quiero un descuento.	I want a discount.
Quiero cambiar de habitación.	I want to change room.
Quiero hablar con el director.	I want to speak to the manager.
Lo siento mucho.	I'm very sorry.
El hotel está casi completo.	The hotel is almost full.
Voy a llamar al ingeniero.	I am going to call the engineer.
Vamos a limpiar la habitación.	We are going to clean the room.
Tengo una habitación libre.	I have a free room.
Le voy a dar un descuento.	I am going to give you a discount.

Repaso 1 *Mi vida*

De paseo por Sevilla 2

Escucha y lee los textos. Escribe las letras correctas para Antonio y Julieta.

Ejemplo: Antonio – d,…

1 Me llamo Antonio y soy de España y vivo en Salamanca. Tengo diecisiete años. Me encanta la informática. Todos los días chateo con mis amigos. También descargo música y los fines de semana escribo un blog de música rock. Siempre voy de vacaciones a la playa. Me encanta tomar el sol.

2 ¡Hola! ¿Qué tal estás? Me llamo Julieta. Vivo en Sevilla con mi familia, pero soy de Guatemala. Tengo quince años. A veces salgo con mis amigos y vamos de compras. También voy al cine una vez a la semana pero nunca veo películas de terror. Los fines de semana me gusta leer. Leo libros y revistas. A menudo voy de vacaciones a Nueva York.

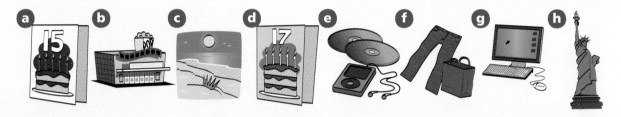

a b c d e f g h

Read the texts again. What do the phrases in blue mean? Use them to help you answer the questions below.

1 What does Antonio do at weekends?
2 Where does he always go on holiday and why?
3 Which activities does he do every day?
4 What does Julieta do once a week?
5 What does she do sometimes?
6 What does she never do?

Look out for these adverbs of frequency.
siempre – *always*
todos los días – *every day*
a menudo – *often*
a veces – *sometimes*
de vez en cuando – *from time to time*
los fines de semana – *at weekends*
los sábados – *on Saturdays*
una vez a la semana – *once a week*
nunca – *never*

G *The present tense* ➲192

For the present tense you change the endings like this:

	escuchar *(to listen)*	leer *(to read)*	vivir *(to live)*
(yo)	escucho	leo	vivo
(tú)	escuchas	lees	vives
(él/ella/usted)	escucha	lee	vive

Some verbs are stem-changing, like **jugar** (u → ue) and **tener** (e → ie).

Some verbs, like **hacer** and **tener**, are irregular in the first person ('I' form) only. Others, like **ser**, are more irregular.

	jugar *(to play)*	hacer *(to do/make)*	tener *(to have)*	ser *(to be)*
(yo)	juego	hago	tengo	soy
(tú)	juegas	haces	tienes	eres
(él/ella/usted)	juega	hace	tiene	es

3 Escucha y apunta la pregunta y la respuesta en inglés. (1–5)

Ejemplo: **1** How old are you? – 15

 4 *With a partner, ask these questions and answer them for Antonio or Julieta. Then answer them for yourself.*

- ● ¿Cuántos años tienes?
- ■ Tengo… años.
- ● ¿De dónde eres?
- ■ Soy de…
- ● ¿Dónde vives?
- ■ Vivo en…
- ● ¿Qué haces en tu tiempo libre?
- ■ Todos los días… De vez en cuando…
- ● ¿Adónde vas de vacaciones?
- ■ Siempre voy de vacaciones a…

> ⭐ Try to include the adverbs of frequency you saw in exercise 2. This will gain you marks for variety of language in speaking and writing assessments.
>
> Chateo con mis amigos **de vez en cuando**.
> *From time to time* I chat with my friends.

> Chateo con mis amigos.   Juego al fútbol.
> Salgo con mis amigos.   Voy de compras.
> Descargo música.   Voy al cine.
> Juego con el ordenador.   Leo libros y revistas.

 5 Escucha. ¿Qué tiempo hace? Escribe las letras correctas. (1–7)

Ejemplo: **1** j, b, d

> ¿Qué tiempo hace?
> Hace buen tiempo.
> Hace mal tiempo.
> Hace calor.
> Hace frío.
> Hace sol.
> Hace viento.
> Hay niebla.
> Hay tormenta.
> Llueve.
> Nieva.

 6 Describe la rutina de Pepe.

> ⭐ **Cuando…** *When…*
>
> Cuando hace sol, voy a la piscina.
> *When it's sunny, I go to the swimming pool.*

> esquiar = *to ski*

1 Cuando  ,

2 En invierno, cuando ,

3 Cuando 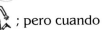 ; pero cuando  ,

4 Cuando  ; pero cuando   ,

5 Si ; pero si  ,

- Talking about means of transport
- Using adjectives to give opinions on travel

Repaso 2 *En ruta*

1 Lee y empareja las fotos con los medios de transporte.

a el autobús
b el avión
c el tren
d el monopatín
e la bicicleta
f el barco
g a pie/andando
h el autocar
i el coche
j la moto
k el tranvía

2 Escucha y lee. Copia y completa la tabla en inglés. (1–10)

	mode of transport	reason/opinion
1	bus	

1 Normalmente cojo el autobús porque **no es caro**.

2 Prefiero ir a pie porque **es sano**.

3 Normalmente cojo un taxi porque **es rápido**.

4 Generalmente voy en monopatín porque **es barato**.

5 No me gusta nada viajar en autobús porque **no es cómodo**.

6 Generalmente voy en moto porque **es rápido**.

7 Normalmente cojo la bici porque **es ecológico**.

8 Prefiero ir en tren porque **es limpio**.

9 Para distancias largas prefiero ir en avión pero **es caro**.

10 Para distancias largas no voy en autocar porque **es muy lento**.

> ★ When you use **en** to say how you travel, remember to leave out the definite article **el** or **la**, e.g. Voy **en** autobús. *I go by bus.*
>
> When talking about going on foot, say: Voy **a** pie or Voy **andando**.

3 ¿Cómo prefieres viajar? Escribe estas frases.

Ejemplo: **1** Normalmente prefiero ir en autocar porque es barato.

1 Normalmente  porque ✓

2 Generalmente  porque

3 Cuando  , porque

4 Cuando  porque

5 Todos los días porque ✓

6 Nunca porque  **!!!**

> Prefiero ir a pie
> Prefiero ir en…
> porque …
> (no) es barato
> (no) es caro
> (no) es cómodo
> (no) es ecológico
> (no) es lento
> (no) es limpio
> (no) es rápido
> (no) es sano

 4 Escucha y escribe la hora correcta. (1–8)

| 20:57 | 09:10 | 19:03 | 12:40 |
| 10:25 | 06:14 | 22:32 | 13:50 |

> ⭐ In travel situations, you will hear clock times given in the 24-hour clock. From 1 pm onwards you'll need to listen for numbers higher than 12!
> las trece — 13:00
> las catorce cero tres — 14:03
> las quince treinta y cuatro — 15:34
> las dieciséis treinta — 16:30

 5 **Listen and read the conversation. Copy and fill in the grid.**
Then listen to two more conversations and fill in the grid for those. (1–3)

- ● Buenos días. ¿Qué quiere?
- ■ Quiero <u>dos</u> billetes para <u>Madrid</u>, por favor.
- ● ¿De ida o de ida y vuelta?
- ■ <u>De ida y vuelta</u>. ¿A qué hora sale el tren?
- ● Sale a las <u>ocho diez</u>.
- ■ ¿De qué andén sale?
- ● Sale del andén <u>7</u>.
- ■ ¿A qué hora llega?
- ● Llega a las <u>trece veinte</u>.
- ■ ¿Es directo?
- ● <u>No, hay que cambiar</u>.

> De ida. →
> De ida y vuelta. → ←
> Hay que cambiar.
> Es directo.

	¿cuántas personas?	destino	→ → ←	salida	andén	llegada	¿directo?
1							

 6 Con tu compañero/a, haz tres diálogos. Cambia los datos del ejercicio 5.

¿cuántas personas?	destino	→ → ←	salida	andén	llegada	¿directo?
2	Sevilla	→ ←	13:20	3	15:05	✓
1	Málaga	→	10:20	6	12:25	✗
3	Granada	→ ←	18:05	4	20:10	✓

1 ¿Qué vas a hacer?

España

• Sevilla

1 Escucha y escribe la letra correcta. (1–6)

Ejemplo: **1** d

a

el Alcázar

b

la catedral y la Giralda

c

la plaza de España

d

el parque de María Luisa

e

la plaza de toros

f

el centro comercial Plaza de Armas

> ⭐ Before listening, think of the sound of each place name. It will then be easier to spot when you hear it. As you listen, try to pick out key phrases which identify the place each person is talking about.

2 Lee las frases y empareja las actividades con las fotos.

1

2

3

4

5

6

a Voy a sacar fotos.
b Voy a comprar recuerdos.
c Voy a ver vistas espléndidas.
d Voy a dar un paseo.
e Voy a tomar unas tapas.
f Voy a ver una corrida.

3 Escucha a las personas del ejercicio 1 otra vez. Escribe la letra correcta del ejercicio 2.

Ejemplo: **1** d

4 *What are you going to do in Seville? Write a short text. Make sure you use the sequencers you saw in Module 1:* **primero** *(first),* **después** *(after that),* **luego** *(then).*

> Primero voy a..., también voy a...
> Luego voy a... y después voy a...

G *The near future tense* ➡ **200**

For the near future tense use the present tense of **ir + a + infinitive**:

(yo)	voy		**comprar**
(tú)	vas	a	**comer**
(él/ella/usted)	va		**descubrir**

¿Qué **vas a hacer** en Sevilla?
*What **are you going to do** in Seville?*
En Sevilla **voy a comprar** recuerdos.
*In Seville **I'm going to buy** souvenirs.*

5 Escucha y lee la conversación. Contesta a las preguntas.

María: Hola Juan. ¿Qué tal?

Juan: Hola María. Fenomenal, gracias.

María: ¿Qué vas a hacer hoy?

Juan: Pues… voy a visitar Sevilla. Primero voy a ir al Alcázar. Voy a sacar muchas fotos y comprar recuerdos también.

María: ¿Cómo vas a ir al Alcázar?

Juan: Voy a ir a pie porque hace buen tiempo.

María: ¿A qué hora abre el Alcázar?

Juan: Abre a las nueve y cierra a las seis de la tarde. Después voy a tomar unas tapas en un bar.

María: Y luego ¿qué vas a hacer?

Juan: Luego voy a ir a la plaza de toros. ¡Voy a ver una corrida! ¿Quieres venir conmigo?

María: ¡Ay! Va a ser horrible. No, gracias. Odio las corridas.

1 What is Juan going to do today? (4 details)
2 How is he going to travel and why?
3 What are the opening times of the first place he is going to visit?
4 What does he ask María?
5 Why does María say no? (2 details)

 6 Escucha. Copia y completa la tabla en inglés. (1–3)

	places to visit	activities mentioned	transport & reason	opinion
1				

 7 Now write a conversation about a trip to Seville or another destination and perform it with your partner. Use the conversation in exercise 5 for ideas.

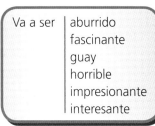

Va a ser	aburrido
	fascinante
	guay
	horrible
	impresionante
	interesante

● ¿Qué vas a hacer hoy?
■ Pues, voy a visitar… Primero voy a… Luego voy a…
● ¿Cómo vas a ir al/a la…?
■ Voy a ir en…/a pie porque…
● ¿A qué hora abre…?
■ Abre a las… y cierra a las… ¿Quieres venir conmigo?
● Sí/No, gracias. Va a ser…

go for a walk
take photos

9:30 → 18:30

see a bullfight
buy souvenirs

16:00 → 21:00

2 Comprando recuerdos

Escucha y escribe la letra correcta y el precio correcto. (1–6)

Ejemplo: **1** d 20€

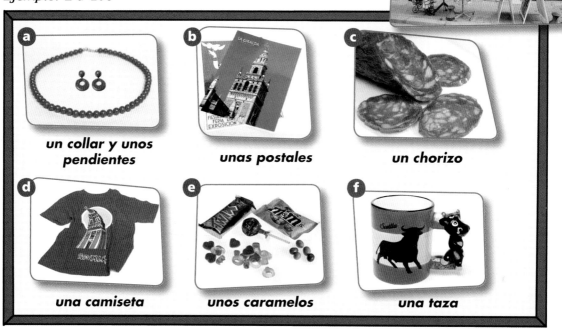

a un collar y unos pendientes

b unas postales

c un chorizo

d una camiseta

e unos caramelos

f una taza

Escucha y escribe la letra del ejercicio 1 y la(s) tienda(s) correcta(s). (1–6)

Ejemplo: **1** b – el quiosco/el estanco

el supermercado

el quiosco

la carnicería

la confitería

la farmacia

la joyería

la tienda de recuerdos

la tienda de ropa

el estanco

Con tu compañero/a, pregunta y contesta por los objetos del ejercicio 1.

- ● ¿Dónde se puede comprar un collar?
- ■ En la joyería o en la tienda de recuerdos.

o = or

> As you do exercise 3, take care over your pronunciation. Listen and repeat this rhyme first, paying attention to how you say the letters in bold.
>
> A mí me gustar**í**a
> Ir contigo a Sevi**ll**a.
> Al**lí** hay una carnicer**í**a
> Y también una **j**oyer**í**a.
> En Sevi**ll**a te voy a comprar
> Un cho**r**i**z**o y un co**ll**ar.

4 Escucha y lee. Empareja las frases con los dibujos.

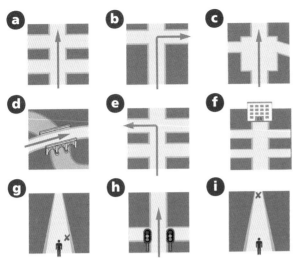

1 Está cerca.
2 Está lejos.
3 Sigue todo recto.
4 Cruza la plaza.
5 Cruza el puente.
6 Pasa los semáforos.
7 Toma la primera calle a la derecha.
8 Toma la segunda calle a la izquierda.
9 Está al final de la calle.

 5 Lee los mensajes y mira el mapa. ¿Adónde van? Escribe el nombre de la tienda.

1 Mira. Está muy cerca. Primero sigue todo recto. Luego pasa los semáforos y después toma la primera calle a la derecha. Está al final de la calle.

2 A ver. Está lejos. Primero sigue todo recto. Cruza la plaza, luego cruza el puente. Está a la derecha.

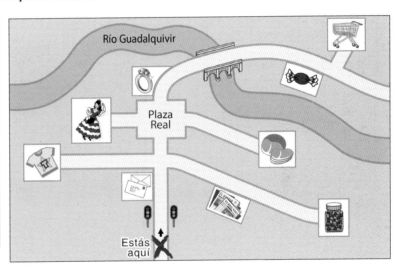

 6 Escucha las direcciones y mira el mapa. Escribe la tienda correcta del ejercicio 5. (1–9)

 ¿Por dónde se va al/a la…?

 Primero… Luego…

 7 Write a question for your partner. Your partner looks at the map and writes down how to get there.

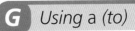

¿Por dónde se va al supermercado?
Primero… Luego… Después…

G *Using a (to)*

¿Por dónde se va a…? *How do you get to…?*
a + el = al   ¿Por dónde se va **al** supermercado?
a + la = a la   ¿Por dónde se va **a la** farmacia?

- Ordering in a restaurant
- Using **me gusta** + the definite article

3 Tomando tapas

1 Escucha y lee. ¿Qué significa?

Ejemplo: **1** gazpacho = gazpacho soup…

Restaurante La Alhambra

Menú del día – 15€

Primer plato
gazpacho
lentejas con chorizo
jamón serrano
tortilla de patatas

Segundo plato
paella
chuleta de cerdo con verduras
filete de ternera
calamares
merluza

Postres
flan
helados de fresa, vainilla
y chocolate
tarta de queso

+ pan + bebida

2 Escucha y escribe los platos mencionados. (1–2)
Escucha otra vez. ¿Les gusta 🖤 o no les gusta 💔?

Ejemplo: **1** tortilla de patatas –

3 Con tu compañero/a, pregunta y contesta.

- ¿Qué te gusta comer?
- ¿Qué no te gusta comer?

- ■ Me gusta el/la…
- ■ Me gustan los/las…
- ■ No me gusta el/la…
- ■ No me gustan los/las…

💬 Practise these sounds and then pay attention to your pronunciation as you do exercise 3:

ga**z**pacho	*th*
espe**c**ialidad	*th*
torti**ll**a	*y*
lente**j**as	*h* (back of throat!)

Listen and repeat:
Nuestras espe**c**ialidades son el ga**z**pacho, la torti**ll**a y las lente**j**as con chori**z**o.

G *The definite article* ➲**208**

When using **me gusta(n)** followed by a noun, you need the definite article.
(No) Me gusta **el** jamón/**la** paella.
(No) Me gustan **los** calamares/**las** sardinas.

Should you use **el**, **la**, **los** or **las** with each of the items on the menu above?

4 Escucha y lee. Busca estas frases en español en el texto.

a What are you going to have?
b And to drink?
c I'm thirsty.
d I'm going to have…
e Have a good meal.

f Anything else?
g I'm hungry.
h For the first course…
i For dessert…

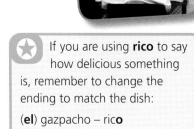

Camarero: ¿Qué va a tomar?
Valeria: Tengo hambre. De primer plato voy a tomar <u>gazpacho</u>.
Camarero: ¿Y de segundo plato?
Valeria: De segundo, voy a tomar <u>filete de ternera</u>, y de postre <u>tarta de queso</u>, por favor.
Camarero: Muy bien. ¿Y para beber…?
Valeria: Ah… sí. También tengo sed. Me pone <u>agua mineral, pero sin gas</u>.
Camarero: Muy bien.
…
Camarero: ¡Que aproveche!
Valeria: <u>El gazpacho</u>, ¡qué <u>rico</u>!
…
Valeria: Todo está muy bueno.
Camarero: ¿Algo más?
Valeria: No, nada más. ¿Me trae la cuenta, por favor?

> ⭐ If you are using **rico** to say how delicious something is, remember to change the ending to match the dish:
>
> (**el**) gazpacho – ric**o**
> (**la**) paella – ric**a**
> (**los**) calamares – ric**os**
> (**las**) lentejas – ric**as**

⊕ ZONA CULTURA

¿El servicio está incluido?

In Spain, service is normally included. You don't need to ask.

You may wish to leave a tip, **una propina**, even so.

5 Con tu compañero/a, haz tres diálogos cambiando las frases subrayadas del ejercicio 4.

6 Escucha. Copia y completa la tabla en inglés. (1–5)

> Lo siento, señor/señorita.
> Aquí tiene./Aquí tiene un (plato) limpio.

	food/drink ordered	problems
1	lentils with sausage, hake, lemonade	b

a Me falta un tenedor.

b Me falta un cuchillo.

c Me falta una cuchara.

d No hay sal.

e No hay aceite.

f No hay vinagre.

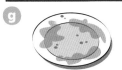
g El plato está sucio.

h El vaso está sucio.

7 *Write a dialogue in the restaurant. Use exercise 4 as a model, but make sure you include two problems from exercise 6.*

4 En Sevilla

Escucha y escribe las letras correctas. (1–6)

¿Adónde fuiste?

Fui a Sevilla.

Ejemplo: **1** d

1 ¿Cuánto tiempo pasaste en Sevilla?

a Pasé cinco días allí.

b Pasé dos días en Sevilla.

c Pasé dos semanas en Sevilla.

d Pasé una semana allí.

2 ¿Qué hiciste?

e Subí a la Giralda y fui de compras.

f Fui de excursión y visité monumentos.

g Di un paseo por el barrio de Santa Cruz.

h Vi vistas espléndidas y saqué muchas fotos.

3 ¿Qué tal lo pasaste?

i Lo pasé fenomenal.

j Lo pasé mal.

k Me gustó mucho.

l No me gustó nada.

4 ¿Qué compraste?

m Compré una camiseta.

n Compré una taza para mi madre.

o Compré unas postales.

p No compré nada.

5 ¿Cómo visitaste la ciudad?

q Visité la ciudad a pie.

r Cogí un autobús turístico.

s Monté en bicicleta.

6 ¿Qué comiste durante tu visita?

t Comí gazpacho.

u Comí paella.

v Comí jamón serrano y tortilla de patatas.

w Comí calamares.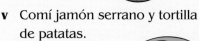

G The preterite ⤳196

The preterite is used for a completed action in the past. In the interview in exercise 1 you can hear the 'I' form of some regular preterite verbs.

-ar verbs	-er/-ir verbs	irregular preterites
compr**é** *(I bought)*	cog**í** *(I caught (a bus))*	(dar) → **di** un paseo *(I walked)*
mont**é** en bici *(I cycled)*	com**í** *(I ate)*	(ir) → **fui** *(I went)*
pas**é** *(I spent)*	sub**í** *(I climbed)*	(hacer) → **hice** *(I did)*
visit**é** *(I visited)*		(ver) → **vi** *(I saw)*

hablar 2

With your partner, imagine a visit to Seville and have a conversation about it.

- ● ¿Adónde fuiste?
- ■ Fui a…
- ● ¿Cuánto tiempo pasaste allí?
- ■ Pasé…
- ● ¿Qué hiciste?
- ■ Primero… Luego…
- ● ¿Qué tal lo pasaste?
- ■ Lo pasé… Me gustó mucho./No me gustó nada.
- ● ¿Qué compraste?
- ■ Compré… y también… pero no compré…
- ● ¿Cómo visitaste la ciudad?
- ■ Visité…, monté… Un día cogí…
- ● ¿Qué comiste?
- ■ Comí… y también… La comida (no) me gustó mucho.

leer 3

Lee los textos y contesta a las preguntas en inglés.

Who…
1. didn't like the food?
2. liked the cathedral?
3. was there for a week?
4. wasn't impressed by the sights?
5. had a great time?
6. lost their passport?

Fui a Sevilla de vacaciones y fue un rollo. Pasé dos días allí y llovió mucho. Lo malo fue que todo era muy caro. Hay tiendas con muchos recuerdos, pero no compré nada. Además el estado de los monumentos daba pena. ¡Son ruinas! ¿Y la comida? La comida no me gustó nada – ¡buagh! **Carlos**

Pasé una semana en Sevilla. La ciudad es preciosa. Hay muchos sitios fascinantes (paseos, bares, parques, monumentos) y la historia es muy interesante. Lo que me gustó más fue la Giralda con sus vistas espléndidas. Subí a la torre y saqué un montón de fotos. También compré muchos recuerdos. Lo pasé fenomenal. Para mí fue una experiencia inolvidable. **Pablo**

Pasé cinco días en Sevilla y me encantó. Vi unos monumentos increíbles – el Alcázar y la plaza de España, por ejemplo. Lo que me gustó más fue la catedral – es muy bonita e impresionante. También comí en restaurantes muy buenos. Mi plato favorito es la paella – ¡qué rica! Pero, por desgracia, un día perdí mi pasaporte. Fue un desastre. **Isabel**

leer 4

Lee los textos otra vez. Busca estas frases en español.

> lo que… = *the thing that…*
> lo que me gustó más = *the thing I liked most*

1. there are a lot of fascinating sights
2. it was a drag
3. it was an unforgettable experience
4. everything was very expensive
5. I saw some incredible monuments
6. I loved (it)

escribir 5

Write a paragraph about your holiday in Seville (or another city). Use the questions from exercise 2 to help you structure your writing.

5 Las fiestas

 1 Escucha y lee la entrevista. Contesta a las preguntas en inglés.

1 Which celebration does Samir like best?
2 When does it take place?
3 What happens during Ramadan?
4 What does he say about the feast?
5 What do people buy for friends or children?

Eid al Fitr

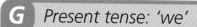

– ¿Cuál es la mejor fiesta, en tu opinión?
– Me gusta mucho Eid al Fitr. Es una fiesta muy importante para nosotros los musulmanes.
– ¿Cuándo tiene lugar?
– Al final del mes lunar del Ramadán.
– ¿Qué pasa durante el Ramadán?
– No comemos ni bebemos durante el día.
– ¿Cómo es la fiesta del Eid al Fitr?
– Preparamos una cena deliciosa. Es el día más feliz del año. Compramos dulces para la familia y los amigos y traemos regalos para los niños. Hay un ambiente muy especial y emocionante y lo pasamos fenomenal.

> **G** Present tense: 'we' ➲190
>
> The 'we' (**nosotros/as**) form of present-tense verbs is very useful when describing festivals.
>
> | | **celebrar** | **beber** | **vivir** |
> |---|---|---|---|
> | | *(to celebrate)* | *(to drink)* | *(to live)* |
> | (yo) | celebr**o** | beb**o** | viv**o** |
> | (tú) | celebr**as** | beb**es** | viv**es** |
> | (él/ella) | celebr**a** | beb**e** | viv**e** |
> | (nosotros/as) | celebr**amos** | beb**emos** | viv**imos** |
>
> How many verbs in the 'we' form can you spot in the interview? What do they mean in English?

¿Cuál? = Which?
no... ni... = neither... nor...

 2 Escucha y escribe la letra de la festividad correcta. (1–3)

a

b

c

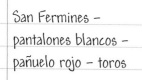

San Fermines –
pantalones blancos –
pañuelo rojo – toros

El día de los Muertos –
altares para los muertos

Nochevieja –
uvas de la suerte –
doce campanadas

 3 *Listen again and answer the questions for each of the three festivals.*

● When does the festival take place?
● What do people do? Can you work it out from the pictures and descriptions?
● Which adjectives does the speaker use to describe the festival?

4 Lee los textos. Copia y completa la tabla.

	festival	time of year	decorations	food eaten	other details
Marcelo					

Marcelo

El Diwali es una fiesta religiosa hindú conocida como el festival de las luces. Es la entrada del año nuevo hindú, en octubre o noviembre, y una de las noches más importantes del año.

Durante la fiesta decoramos las casas con lámparas de colores y guirnaldas. Cocinamos unos platos muy ricos y unos dulces buenísimos. Hacemos regalos a la familia y a los amigos. La gente lleva ropa nueva y hace explotar petardos y fuegos artificiales.

María

Para nosotros la Navidad es una fiesta importante y la celebramos el veinticuatro de diciembre. En casa decoramos un árbol de Navidad y ponemos un belén. Asistimos a la Misa de Navidad, luego nuestros amigos vienen y cenamos pavo.

Lía

La Feria de Abril es la fiesta de los sevillanos. Hay un ambiente muy especial. Llevamos trajes tradicionales de flamenco, bailamos sevillanas, cantamos, comemos y bebemos. En la Feria es típico comer pescaito con una copa de fino. Todas las tardes hay corridas de toros. El año pasado fui con unos amigos y lo pasamos fenomenal.

pescaito = *fried fish*
fino = *dry sherry*

 5 Con tu compañero/a, habla de la fiesta que prefieres.

- ¿Cuál es la mejor fiesta, en tu opinión?
- Me gusta mucho… Es una fiesta (divertida).
- ¿Cuándo tiene lugar?
- Tiene lugar en…
- ¿Qué pasa durante la fiesta?
- Llevamos…, preparamos… y traemos regalos para… Además cantamos/bailamos. Es típico comer…
- ¿Cómo es?
- Hay un ambiente (especial). Lo pasamos fenomenal.

You will gain marks by using a variety of adjectives to describe your experiences. Try to use these when speaking and writing about your favourite festival:
importante (*important*)
especial (*special*)
divertido/a (*fun*)
fascinante (*fascinating*)
impresionante (*impressive*)
emocionante (*exciting*)
increíble (*incredible*)

 6 Escribe un texto sobre tu festividad preferida.

- Use the questions from exercise 5 to help you structure your text.
- Remember to use present-tense verbs in the 'we' form.
- Extend your sentences as much as possible with connectives: **también** (*also*), **además** (*as well*), **y** (*and*).
- Use a variety of adjectives.

Travelling abroad

You are going to play the role of a tourist who has recently visited a popular city and your teacher will play the role of the interviewer. Your teacher could ask you the following:

- Where did you go?
- What is the city like?
- How long did you stay?
- What did you do?
- How did you visit the city?
- What did you eat?

Remember that you will have to respond to an unexpected question that you have not yet prepared.

1 *You are going to listen to Barney, an exam candidate, taking part in the above conversation. Which of the following do you think Barney will use to answer the first three questions? Listen and check.*

1 ¿Adónde fuiste?　**2** ¿Cómo es Sevilla?　**3** ¿Cuánto tiempo pasaste en Sevilla?

a Sevilla es una ciudad muy impresionante.

b Es una ciudad animada y fascinante con mucho que ver.

c A ver… pasé dos semanas en Sevilla. Me gustó mucho.

d Hay muchos lugares de interés y muchos monumentos.

e Fui a Sevilla. Fui en avión con mi familia.

f Me encanta porque es una ciudad antigua y muy interesante y me gusta la historia.

2 *Listen to part 2 of Barney's conversation and fill each gap with the correct word from the box.*

luego	es	saqué	visité	primero	qué	subí	fui	cogí	después

– ¿Qué visitaste?

– Visité monumentos, **(1)** _____ a la Giralda, por ejemplo. Lo que me gustó más fue el Alcázar porque me encanta visitar monumentos. **(2)** _____ a la plaza de España y también di un paseo por el parque de María Luisa. ¡**(3)** _____ bonito! Un día visité la ciudad. **(4)** _____ fui a la plaza de toros y **(5)** _____ a un museo. **(6)** _____ compré unas postales. Vi unas vistas maravillosas y **(7)** _____ muchas fotos.

– ¿Cómo visitaste la ciudad?

– Por lo general la **(8)** _____ a pie porque cuando hace sol me gusta ir a pie, pero el viernes **(9)** _____ un autobús turístico y el domingo cogí un taxi. Normalmente no me gusta viajar en taxi porque **(10)** _____ muy caro pero es rápido.

3 Now listen to part 3 of Barney's conversation and rewrite the jumbled words in bold in each sentence. What is the unexpected question that Barney is asked?

1 Comí en **tresauratens** muy buenos.
2 Comí **doescap**. ¡Qué rico!
3 Me gusta mucho comer sardinas y **saalmecar**.
4 El **oña** que viene **yov** a volver a Sevilla.
5 …y voy a **isarvit** la catedral y la Giralda **rota** vez.
6 Y voy a comer **rissadna** y calamares todos los días. ¡Va a ser **yagu**!

¿Qué comiste?

4 Now it's your turn! Prepare your answers to the task and then have a conversation with your teacher or partner.

- Use the Grade Studio and your answers to exercises 1–3 to help you plan.
- Adapt what Barney said to talk about yourself but add your own ideas.
- Prepare your answers to the questions and try to predict what the unexpected question could be. The examiner might base this question on something you have already said, or ask something totally new!
- Record the conversation. Ask a partner to listen to it and say how well you performed.

Award each other one star, two stars or three stars for each of these categories:
- *Pronunciation*
- *Confidence and fluency*
- *Range of tenses*
- *Variety of vocabulary and expressions*
- *Using longer sentences*
- *Taking the initiative*

What do you need to do next time to improve your performance?

⭐ GradeStudio

Make sure you cover the basics.

- Use **simple structures** correctly, e.g. *fui* (I went), *es* (it is), *me gusta* (I like), *me encanta* (I love), *hay* (there is/are), *hace sol* (it's sunny).
- Try to include a **simple negative**, e.g. *no me gusta viajar en taxi* (I don't like travelling by taxi).
- Use **simple connectives**. Find where Barney uses *y* (and), *pero* (but) and *también* (also).

To reach Grade C, show that you can:

- Use **adjectives** to describe things. Can you find five examples of adjectives Barney uses to describe Seville?
- Use **sequencing expressions** to lengthen your sentences, such as *primero* (first), *luego* (then) and *después* (afterwards).
- Use **the present tense** to describe a place, e.g. *Es una ciudad animada y fascinante.* (It is a lively and fascinating city.)
- Use **the preterite** to say what you did, e.g. *Vi unas vistas maravillosas.* (I saw some great views.)
- Use **the near future** to say what you are going to do, e.g. *Voy a volver a Sevilla y voy a visitar la catedral.* (I'm going to return to Seville and visit the cathedral.)

To increase your marks:

- Express **more detailed opinions** like *lo que más me gustó fue …* (what I liked most was …). How could you finish this sentence?
- Use some of Barney's **phrases**: *Fue una experiencia inolvidable.* (It was an unforgettable experience.) *¡Va a ser guay!* (It's going to be cool.) What other adjectives could you use with *Va a ser*? *Cuando hace sol me gusta ir a pie.* (When it's sunny, I like to go on foot.) Think of another way of finishing this sentence.

Read the text and put these topics into the order of the text.

    a   Christmas in Madrid
    b   I love Christmas
    c   Midnight Mass
    d   Christmas in Lanzarote
    e   Father Christmas brings presents

Mi fiesta preferida

En Gran Bretaña la Navidad es una fiesta muy importante. A mí me gusta mucho porque hay un ambiente especial. En mi opinión es la mejor fiesta. Tiene lugar en diciembre cuando generalmente hace mal tiempo. Ponemos un árbol y a veces un belén también. Normalmente Papá Noel trae regalos para todo el mundo. Es típico comer pavo. También comemos pudin. A mí no me gusta nada el pudin. ¡Buagh! ¡Qué asco! Prefiero helado o fruta. Después de la cena, si hace buen tiempo, siempre voy de paseo. Luego veo una película de James Bond con mi familia. ¡Lo pasamos fenomenal!

Para los españoles la Navidad es una fiesta importante también. El año pasado en Navidad pasé dos semanas en Madrid con la familia de mi amiga, Sonia. Vi unos árboles de Navidad preciosos. El veinticuatro de diciembre – la Nochebuena – fui a misa y luego cené ternera asada con la familia de Sonia. Después de la cena fuimos a ver los fuegos artificiales. Fue increíble. ¡Lo pasamos guay!

El año que viene voy a visitar Lanzarote con Sonia y sus padres. Voy a ver cómo celebran la Navidad allí. ¡Va a ser genial!

Naomi

Find these expressions in Spanish in the text.

    1   …a very important festival.
    2   …there is a special atmosphere.
    3   It takes place in December…
    4   It is traditional to eat turkey.
    5   …if it's nice weather…

    6   We have a great time!
    7   …I spent two weeks in Madrid…
    8   …I had beef for dinner…
    9   It was incredible.
    10   It will be great!

Find six adjectives in the text that Naomi uses to describe festivals or atmosphere.

4 *Choose the four sentences which are correct.*

1 In Naomi's opinion, Christmas is the best festival.
2 Naomi's family never put up a crib.
3 Naomi doesn't like turkey.
4 Naomi prefers ice cream to Christmas pudding.
5 She goes for a short walk after the Christmas meal.
6 In Spain, she went to Mass on Christmas Day.
7 Sonia's family ate lamb for dinner.
8 Next year she is going to spend Christmas in Lanzarote.

 5 *You might be asked to write about a celebration as a controlled assessment task.*
Use the Grade Studio to help you prepare your account.

 ## ✪ GradeStudio

Make sure you cover the basics.

● Use **simple structures** correctly, e.g. *es* (it is), *hay* (there is), *prefiero* (I prefer) and *veo* (I watch).
● Give a **simple opinion**. Naomi uses *A mí me gusta mucho…*, *No me gusta…* Can you find the phrase 'in my opinion' in the text?
● Use **connectives** to make longer sentences, e.g. *y* (and), *o* (or) and *también* (also).

To reach Grade C, show that you can:

● Use **the present tense** to talk about what normally happens, e.g. *Voy de paseo. Veo una película.*
● Use **the preterite** to say what you did, e.g. *Pasé dos semanas en Madrid. Fui a misa. Fue increíble.*
● Use **the near future tense**. Naomi uses this to say where she is going to go next year with Sonia. *El año que viene voy a visitar Lanzarote.*
● Use *porque* to give reasons.
● Use **adverbs of frequency**, e.g. *siempre* and a *veces*. Can you think of three others?
● Use **simple adverbs**, like *normalmente* (normally) and *generalmente* (generally).

To increase your marks:

● Use the **'we' form** of the verb, e.g. *Ponemos un árbol. Comemos pudin.*
● Use *si* (if) + **weather** + **activity**, e.g. *Si hace buen tiempo, voy de paseo.*
● Use *va a ser* + **adjective** to say what something is going to be like, e.g. *¡Va a ser genial!*

 6 *Now write a full account of your favourite celebration.*

● Adapt Naomi's text and use language from Module 2 to help you.
● Structure your text carefully. Organise what you write in paragraphs.

 7 *Check carefully what you have written.*

● Are your verb endings correct?
● Have you included accents on verbs in the preterite?
● Have you included all the parts of *ir* + *a* + **infinitive** to talk about the near future?

Introduction
Say what your favourite festival is. Why?
What normally happens? When?

Main paragraph
Explain how you celebrated this festival last year
Describe what you did and what it was like
Give details about food, traditions, etc.
Say whether you enjoyed the celebration

Conclusion
Talk about plans for next year

leer 1

Read this welcome message on the TV in your hotel bedroom. Answer the questions. (2 marks)

> ¡Bienvenidos al Hotel Central!
> Esta semana se puede usar la piscina.
> En este momento no tenemos gimnasio.
> No se puede fumar en las habitaciones o en el bar.
> Está permitido fumar en el jardín del hotel.

⭐ Questions generally ask for one piece of information, e.g. one sports facility. If more than one is mentioned in the text, be careful when you give your answer. Check for negatives like *no*, which mean that a facility, for example, is not available.

1 What sports facility is available in the hotel this week?

2 Where can hotel guests smoke?

leer 2

Look at the list below of activities in Seville. Which would most interest each tourist? Write a letter for each person. (1 mark for each person)

1 Antonio: I would like to see a dance show.

2 Cristina: I'm very interested in new films.

3 Teresa: I really like classical music.

4 Felipe: I want to learn about the city.

5 María: I like going on trips into the country.

6 Vicente: I love local handicrafts and souvenirs.

⭐ You need to link general words in English, such as 'dance', with more specific words in Spanish, such as *flamenco*, and the other way round, e.g. 'local handicrafts' with *arte español*. Be prepared for some unfamiliar vocabulary but try to spot words that look similar in Spanish and English and mean the same thing.

Esta semana en Sevilla

a Excursión en autocar al Parque Nacional de Doñana
El precio incluye el viaje y la comida.

b Corrida de toros: seis toros y tres matadores famosos
Plaza de toros de la Real Maestranza

c Concierto de guitarra: Orquesta Sinfónica de Sevilla
Teatro de la Maestranza

d Espectáculo de flamenco y baile flamenco español
Palacio Andaluz

e Paseo por la ciudad: historia, cultura y monumentos
Con guía. Información y comentarios en español

f Concurso de fuegos artificiales
Al lado del puente y del río Guadalquivir

g Exposición de arte español: abanicos y collares de oro
Sala de Exposiciones Río Grande de Sevilla

h Festival de cine: comedias nuevas
En varios cines por toda la ciudad

3 *Listen to Miguel talking about his holiday in Seville. Answer the questions. (6 marks)*

1 When did Miguel go on holiday?
2 How long did he go for?
3 Who did he go with?
4 Where did he go on the first day?
5 How long did he spend in the museum?
6 Where was his favourite restaurant?

> ⭐ Don't panic if you don't understand the first time. You will hear each item twice and get enough time to write your answer!

4 *Listen to Miguel giving more information about his holiday. Choose the correct letter. (3 marks)*

1 How did Miguel travel to Seville?

 a    b   c

2 What did he think of the journey?

a    b   c

3 What was the weather like when he arrived?

a   b   c

> ⭐ The recording may contain extra information that can be distracting, so always listen to the whole item before finalising your answer. The correct information could be at the start or end of what is said. A negative statement might help you to reject a piece of information.

5 *Listen to four people, Andrés, Beatriz, Carlos and Diana, talking about their hotel in Seville. What is each person's opinion of the hotel? Write P (positive), N (negative) or P+N (positive and negative). (1 mark for each person)*

1 Andrés   3 Carlos
2 Beatriz   4 Diana

> ⭐ Statements are likely to contain some material that you will not need to answer the questions. Remember that negative opinions don't always contain the word *no*.

Palabras

Mi vida   *My life*

Me llamo…	*My name is…*
¿Cuántos años tienes?	*How old are you?*
Tengo (16) años.	*I'm (16) years old.*
¿De dónde eres?	*Where are you from?*
Soy de Inglaterra.	*I'm from England.*
¿Dónde vives?	*Where do you live?*
Vivo en…	*I live in…*
¿Qué haces en tu tiempo libre?	*What do you do in your free time?*
chateo con mis amigos	*I chat (online) with my friends*
descargo música	*I download music*
juego al fútbol	*I play football*
juego con el ordenador	*I play on my computer*
leo libros y revistas	*I read books and magazines*
salgo con mis amigos	*I go out with my friends*
voy al cine	*I go to the cinema*
voy de compras	*I go shopping*
¿Adónde vas de vacaciones?	*Where do you go on holiday?*
Siempre voy de vacaciones a…	*I always go on holiday to…*
siempre	*always*
todos los días	*every day*
a menudo	*often*
a veces	*sometimes*
de vez en cuando	*from time to time*
los fines de semana	*at weekends*
los sábados	*on Saturdays*
una vez a la semana	*once a week*
nunca	*never*

¿Qué tiempo hace?   *What's the weather like?*

Hace buen tiempo.	*The weather's good.*
Hace mal tiempo.	*The weather's bad.*
Hace calor.	*It's hot.*
Hace frío.	*It's cold.*
Hace sol.	*It's sunny.*
Hace viento.	*It's windy.*
Hay niebla.	*It's foggy.*
Hay tormenta.	*It's stormy.*
Llueve.	*It's raining.*
Nieva.	*It's snowing.*
Cuando… pero cuando…	*When… but when…*

En ruta   *En route*

el autobús	*bus*
el autocar	*coach*
el avión	*plane*
el barco	*boat*
el coche	*car*
el monopatín	*skateboard*
el tranvía	*tram*
el tren	*train*
la bicicleta	*bicycle*
la moto	*scooter*
a pie/andando	*on foot*
prefiero ir en…	*I prefer to go by…*
porque es…	*because it is…*
barato	*cheap*
caro	*expensive*
cómodo	*comfortable*
ecológico	*'green', environmentally friendly*
lento	*slow*
limpio	*clean*
rápido	*fast*
sano	*healthy*
¿A qué hora sale el tren?	*What time does the train go?*
¿De qué andén sale?	*Which platform does it leave from?*
¿A qué hora llega?	*What time does it arrive?*
Quiero dos billetes para (Madrid), por favor.	*I want two tickets to (Madrid), please.*
De ida	*Single*
De ida y vuelta	*Return*
¿Hay que cambiar?	*Do I have to change?*
Es directo.	*It's direct.*

¿Qué vas a hacer?   *What are you going to do?*

¿Cómo vas a ir al/a la…?	*How are you going to get to the…?*
¿A qué hora abre?	*When does it open?*
¿A qué hora cierra?	*When does it close?*
Abre a la(s)…	*It opens at…*
Cierra a la(s)…	*It closes at…*
primero	*first*
luego	*then*
después	*afterwards*
Voy a…	*I'm going to…*
comprar recuerdos	*buy souvenirs*
dar un paseo	*go for a walk*
sacar fotos	*take photos*
tomar unas tapas	*eat some tapas (snacks)*
ver una corrida	*see a bullfight*
ver vistas espléndidas	*see some splendid views*
¿Quieres venir conmigo?	*Do you want to come with me?*
Va a ser…	*It's going to be…*
aburrido	*boring*
fascinante	*fascinating*
guay	*great*
impresionante	*impressive*

Comprando recuerdos *Buying souvenirs*

¿Dónde se puede comprar un collar?	Where can you buy a necklace?
una camiseta	a T-shirt
un chorizo	a Spanish sausage
una taza	a mug
unas postales	some postcards
unos caramelos	some sweets
unos pendientes	some earrings
el estanco	tobacconist's
el quiosco	kiosk
el supermercado	supermarket
la carnicería	butcher's
la confitería	sweet shop
la farmacia	chemist's
la joyería	jeweller's
la tienda de recuerdos	souvenir shop
la tienda de ropa	clothes shop

¿Por dónde se va al/a la…? *How do you get to…?*

Cruza la plaza.	Cross the square.
Cruza el puente.	Cross the bridge.
Pasa los semáforos.	Pass the traffic lights.
Toma la primera calle a la derecha.	Take the first street on the right.
Sigue todo recto.	Go straight ahead.
Está a la izquierda.	It's on the left.
Está al final de la calle.	It's at the end of the street.
Está cerca.	It's close.
Está lejos.	It's a long way.

Tomando tapas *Eating tapas*

Tengo hambre.	I'm hungry.
Tengo sed.	I'm thirsty.
Me gusta comer…	I like eating…
No me gusta comer…	I don't like eating…
el gazpacho	gazpacho (chilled soup)
las lentejas con chorizo	lentils with sausage
el jamón serrano	serrano ham
la tortilla de patatas	potato omelette
la merluza	hake
la paella	paella
la chuleta de cerdo con verduras	pork chop with vegetables
el filete de ternera	fillet of veal/beef
los calamares	squid
el flan	crème caramel
helados de…	…ice creams
la tarta de queso	cheesecake
el agua mineral con gas	sparkling mineral water
De primer plato…	For starter…
De segundo plato…	For main course…
De postre…	For dessert…
Voy a tomar…	I'm going to have…
Me pone…	I'll have…
¿Y para beber?	And to drink?
¿Algo más?	Anything else?
Nada más.	Nothing else.
¿Me trae la cuenta, por favor?	Could I have the bill, please?
¡Que aproveche!	Enjoy your meal!
el menú (del día)	(today's) menu
No hay sal/aceite/vinagre.	There's no salt/oil/vinegar.
El plato/vaso está sucio.	The plate/glass is dirty.
Me falta un cuchillo/una cuchara/un tenedor.	I haven't got a knife/spoon/fork.
Aquí tiene un (vaso) limpio.	Here's a clean (glass).

En Sevilla *In Seville*

Fui a…	I went to…
Pasé dos semanas allí.	I spent two weeks there.
Lo pasé fenomenal/mal.	I had a fantastic/bad time.
Me gustó mucho.	I liked it a lot.
No me gustó nada.	I didn't like it at all.
Comí…	I ate…
Compré…	I bought…
Di un paseo por…	I went for a walk round…
Fui de excursión.	I went on an excursion.
Saqué… [fotos]	I took… [photos]
Subí a la torre…	I went up the…tower.
Visité monumentos.	I visited historic monuments.
¿Cómo visitaste la ciudad?	How did you visit the city?
Visité la ciudad a pie.	I visited the city on foot.
Cogí un autobús turístico.	I took a tour bus.
Monté en bicicleta.	I cycled.

Las fiestas *Festivals*

¿Cuál es la mejor fiesta, en tu opinión?	Which is the best festival, in your opinion?
Es una fiesta divertida.	It's a fun festival.
Es emocionante.	It's moving.
Bailamos y cantamos.	We dance and sing.
Celebramos.	We celebrate.
Cenamos…	We eat… for dinner.
Cocinamos…	We cook…
Decoramos un árbol de Navidad.	We decorate a Christmas tree.
Hacemos regalos.	We give presents.
Llevamos trajes tradicionales.	We wear traditional costumes.
Es típico comer…	It's traditional to eat…
Hay un ambiente muy especial.	There's a very special atmosphere.
los fuegos artificiales	fireworks

1 Escribe la palabra para cada dibujo.

Ejemplo: **a** – la educación física

> **Las asignaturas**
> el comercio
> el dibujo
> el español
> el francés
> el inglés
> el teatro
> la educación física
> la geografía
> la historia
> la religión
> la tecnología
> las ciencias
> las matemáticas

2 Lee las frases. Identifica si la opinión es positiva (P) o negativa (N).

Ejemplo: **1** P

1 Me gusta el inglés porque es entretenido.
2 Odio la historia porque es aburrida.
3 No me gustan las ciencias porque son complicadas.
4 Me encantan las matemáticas porque no son difíciles.
5 Me gusta mucho el comercio porque es muy práctico.
6 Me encanta el teatro porque es divertido.

me encanta	el francés
me gusta (mucho)	el dibujo
no me gusta (nada)	la educación física
odio	
me encanta**n**	las matemáticas
me gusta**n** (mucho)	los idiomas
no me gusta**n** (nada)	la geografía **y** la historia
odio	el francés **y** el español

3 Escucha. Copia y completa la tabla. (1–5)

	subject	opinion (🙂/🙁)	why (adjectives used)
1	maths	🙁	boring, very difficult

G   *Using adjectives*

➡️*210*

Adjectives are very useful to help you express opinions.

aburrido = *boring*   interesante = *interesting*
difícil = *difficult*   fácil = *easy*
práctico = *practical*   entretenido = *entertaining*
divertido = *fun*   útil = *useful*

Remember to change the adjective ending to match the subject you are describing.

	el español	**la** música	**los** idiomas	**las** ciencias
-o	aburrid**o**	aburrid**a**	aburrid**os**	aburrid**as**
-e	interesant**e**	interesant**e**	interesant**es**	interesant**es**
consonant	útil	útil	útil**es**	útil**es**

4 **Con tu compañero/a, pregunta y contesta.**

- ● ¿Cuándo tienes <u>tecnología</u>?
- ■ Tengo <u>tecnología</u> <u>los miércoles y los viernes</u>.
- ● ¿Qué opinas de <u>la tecnología</u>?
- ■ Me gusta <u>la tecnología</u> porque **es** <u>divertid**a**</u>.

- ● ¿Cuándo tienes <u>ciencias</u>?
- ■ Tengo <u>ciencias</u> <u>los lunes y los jueves</u>.
- ● ¿Qué opinas de <u>las ciencias</u>?
- ■ No me gusta**n** <u>las ciencias</u> porque **son** <u>difícil**es**</u>.

> **Los días**
> lunes = *Monday*
> martes = *Tuesday*
> miércoles = *Wednesday*
> jueves = *Thursday*
> viernes = *Friday*
> sábado = *Saturday*
> domingo = *Sunday*

5 **Lee el correo de Luis y contesta a las preguntas.**

1 What is Luis's favourite subject?
2 Why does he feel this way?
3 What is his opinion of languages and why?
4 How does Rafa feel about sciences and languages?
5 What is it about art and music that he prefers?

¡Hola! Me llamo Luis y mi mejor amigo se llama Rafa. Mi asignatura preferida es la biología porque es interesante y porque me encanta el mundo animal. A mí me gustan también los idiomas (estudio francés e italiano) porque me interesan otras culturas. A Rafa no le interesan las ciencias ni los idiomas. Él prefiere las asignaturas prácticas como el dibujo o la música.

> ⭐ While speaking, remember:
>
> - ● Use **el/la/los/las** after **me gusta** etc.
> - ● Don't use **el/la/los/las** after **tengo** or **estudio**.
> - ● Make sure you use the *correct endings* for the opinion adjectives to get good marks.

G *Verbs of opinion* (gustar, encantar, interesar) **➲206**

In Spanish some verbs of opinion, e.g. **gustar**, need a pronoun (**me**, **te**, **le**) before them.

me gusta(n)	*I like*
te gusta(n)	*you like*
le gusta(n)	*he/she likes*

Encantar and **interesar** work in the same way.

me encanta(n)	*I love*
me interesa(n)	*I'm interested in*

Odiar and **preferir** do not need **me**, **te**, **le**.

Odio las matemáticas.	*I hate maths.*
Prefiero el inglés.	*I prefer English.*

6 ***Write a paragraph in Spanish giving your opinions of school subjects.***

> ⭐ Make sure you:
>
> - ● Give details about when you have certain subjects:
>   **Tengo (matemáticas) los (martes) y los (viernes).**
> - ● Express a variety of opinions:
>   **Me encanta(n)…   Odio…   Me gusta(n)…   Prefiero…**
> - ● Extend your phrases with **porque es** or **porque son**
> - ● Use a variety of adjectives (and make them agree!):
>   **divertidos, entretenidas, útil, interesante**
> - ● Try to include your friends' opinions too:
>   **A mi amigo/a le gusta…, prefiere…, odia…**

Repaso 2 *En clase*

Escucha y lee el texto. Completa las frases.

1 In winter Catarina goes to school by...
2 She walks to school in...
3 She doesn't like going by...
4 She goes by train with her friend Felipe in...
5 Her sister often goes to school by...
6 Her sister goes by bus in...

Por la mañana en invierno voy al instituto en autobús, pero en verano voy andando cuando hace buen tiempo. Nunca voy en metro porque no me gusta. Por la tarde vuelvo a casa en tren con mi amigo Felipe. Él siempre coge el tren y es divertido. Mi hermana va al instituto en bicicleta a menudo, pero en invierno va conmigo en autobús.

Las estaciones – *The seasons*

la primavera

el otoño

el verano

el invierno

Write a paragraph about how you get to and from school. Use the questions and answers below to help you structure your writing.

- ¿Cómo vas al colegio?
- ¿Cómo vuelves del colegio?
- ¿Te gusta ir en bici/en autobús/a pie?
- ¿Qué medio de transporte prefieres?

Normalmente / Por la mañana / Por la tarde
Siempre / A menudo / Nunca
En invierno / primavera / verano / otoño

voy al instituto/colegio **vuelvo** del instituto/colegio		en	autobús/metro tren/bicicleta moto/coche
		a pie	autocar
Me gusta Prefiero	ir en autobús ir en coche ir a pie/andando	cuando	hace buen tiempo hace mal tiempo llueve
		porque es	cómodo rápido barato

Listen and write down the correct letter. (1–6)
Listen again. What happens at each time?

Ejemplo: **1** a – classes start

⭐ Clock times may come up in reading and listening exams, so make sure you understand them.

a la una = *at 1 o'clock*
a las dos = *at 2 o'clock*
... y diez = *ten past...*
... y cuarto = *quarter past...*
... y veinte = *twenty past...*

... y media = *half past...*
... menos veinte = *twenty to...*
... menos cuarto = *quarter to...*
de la mañana = *in the morning (am)*
de la tarde = *in the afternoon (pm)*

4 Lee y completa el diálogo con palabras del cuadro.
Luego escucha y comprueba tus respuestas.

Pablo: ¿A qué hora empiezan tus clases?
María: Muy temprano… Empiezan a las (1)_____ de la mañana.
Pablo: ¿Qué (2)_____ en clase normalmente?
María: (3)_____ escucho al profe, pero también hablo con mis amigos.
Pablo: ¿Qué tienes que llevar a clase?
María: Siempre llevo mi (4)_____, unos bolígrafos y una regla.
También necesito mis cuadernos y mis (5)_____.
Pablo: ¡Claro! ¿Qué haces a la hora de comer?
María: Todos los (6)_____ voy al club de ajedrez, y a veces juego al fútbol en el patio.
Pablo: ¿Qué haces después del (7)_____?
María: De vez en cuando voy al club de (8)_____, y hago mis deberes.

> siempre   estuche   informática   ajedrez   libros
> haces   instituto   ocho   miércoles   juegas

 5 Escucha. Copia y completa la tabla en inglés. (1–5)

	topic	details
1	A	goes swimmimg on Thursdays

 **A** after school
 **B** start of classes
C activities in class
D items brought to class
E activities at lunch

 6 Con tu compañero/a, pregunta y contesta.

● ¿Cómo vas al colegio?
■ En verano voy al colegio
● ¿A qué hora empiezan tus clases?
■ Mis clases empiezan… 9:00 AM / 8:30 AM
● ¿Qué haces en clase normalmente?
■ En clase siempre…
● ¿Qué haces en el recreo?
■ En el recreo a menudo…
● ¿Qué haces a la hora de comer?
■ A la hora de comer…
● ¿Qué haces después del instituto?
■ Después del instituto…

en clase…
escucho al profe/a la profe
hablo
leo
uso el diccionario
escribo mucho

a la hora de comer…
en el recreo…
en verano/invierno…

juego al tenis/al fútbol
hago natación
voy al club de ajedrez
voy al club de idiomas
canto en el coro
toco en la orquesta

1 ¿Cómo es tu insti?

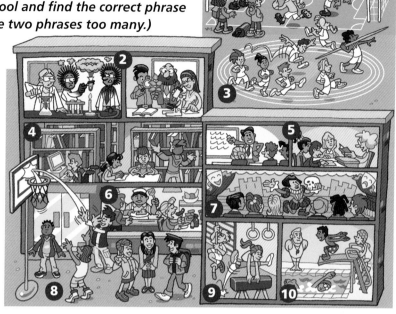

leer 1 Look at the plan of the school and find the correct phrase for each number. (There are two phrases too many.)

Ejemplo: **1** h

a unos laboratorios

b un patio

c unas aulas

d un comedor

e un gimnasio

f una biblioteca

g una sala de profesores

h un campo de fútbol

i una piscina

j una pista de atletismo

k un salón de actos

l unos vestuarios

escuchar 2 ¿Qué se menciona? Escucha e identifica las dos letras correctas del ejercicio 1. (1–5)

escuchar 3 Escucha otra vez. ¿Positivo (P), negativo (N) o positivo y negativo (P+N)? (1–5)

Ejemplo: **1** P

Lo bueno es que	hay	campo de fútbol	bueno
Lo malo es que	no hay	gimnasio	malo
	tenemos un	comedor	grande
	no tenemos	patio	pequeño
		salón de actos	antiguo
			moderno

⭐ Listen out for negative opinions and statements:

No me gusta…	*I don't like…*
Odio…	*I hate…*
Lo malo es…	*The bad thing is…*
No hay…	*There isn't a…/ There aren't any…*
No tenemos…	*We don't have a/ any…*

leer 4 Lee la página web de Mónica. Busca estas frases en español.

1 There are approximately 400 pupils.

2 It was built in the sixties.

3 My school used to be very bad.

4 The bad thing is that…

5 It's a shame!

6 My school is an ecoschool.

7 We recycle a lot of paper.

Me llamo Mónica y voy a un colegio mixto. Es público y está especializado en deportes. Hay cuatrocientos alumnos aproximadamente. Estoy en cuarto de la ESO. Fue construido en los años sesenta. Antes mi colegio era muy malo pero ahora no.
En mi cole hay buenas instalaciones, por ejemplo, los laboratorios son grandes y las aulas modernas. Lo malo es que no tenemos piscina. ¡Es una lástima! Pero lo bueno es que mi colegio es una 'ecoescuela' y reciclamos mucho papel.

leer **5** Decide whether these statements are true (T), false (F) or not mentioned (NM) in Mónica's text.

1 There is a swimming pool.
2 It's a specialist school with modern classrooms.
3 There are too many school rules.
4 Mónica doesn't like wearing uniform.
5 It's a mixed state school.

escuchar **6** Listen and note down the information Juan gives about the following topics. (1–3)

1 The school   2 The facilities   3 His opinion

hablar **7** Con tu compañero/a, haz un diálogo.

- ● ¿Cómo es tu instituto?
- ■ Voy a un colegio femenino / masculino / mixto. Es privado / público.
  Está especializado en deportes / ciencias / idiomas / teatro.
- ● ¿Qué hay en tu instituto?
- ■ Hay… y… pero no tenemos…
- ● ¿Qué opinas de tu instituto?
- ■ Me gusta mi instituto porque es…/
  No me gusta porque es…
  Lo bueno es que… Lo malo es que…

> **"99"** Some Spanish words are the same or similar in English, but they are pronounced very differently. Take care over how you say them.
>
> | | |
> |---|---|
> | **gimnasio** | heem – nah – see – yo |
> | **atletismo** | aht – leh –teess – mo |
> | **laboratorio** | lah – bo – rah – to – ree – o |
> | **moderno** | mo – derr – no |
>
> Listen to this rhyme and repeat:
> En el **gimnasio** hacemos **atletismo**.
> Los **laboratorios** son muy **modernos**.

leer **8** Lee las frases. Escoge la palabra correcta.

1 Juan **voy** / **va** al colegio en coche.
2 **Soy** / **Es** un colegio mixto con quinientos alumnos y sesenta profesores.
3 Mi colegio **es** / **eres** bastante moderno.
4 **Tienes** / **Tenemos** buenas instalaciones.
5 Cada aula **tienes** / **tiene** cuatro ordenadores y una pizarra interactiva.

G The present tense ⟹**192**

To improve your grade, make sure you use present-tense verbs correctly.

	ir (to go)	ser (to be)	tener (to have)
(yo)	voy	soy	tengo
(tú)	vas	eres	tienes
(él/ella)	va	es	tiene
(nosotros/as)	vamos	somos	tenemos

escribir **9** Escribe un blog de tu colegio.

Mi colegio **se llama**…
Mi cole **es** público/privado y femenino/masculino/mixto.
Está especializado en…
Estudio…
Las clases **empiezan/terminan** a las…

Mi colegio **fue construido** en…
Antes mi colegio **era**…

Lo bueno es que **hay**…
Lo malo es que **no hay**…
Los profesores **son**…
La comida **es**…

2 ¿Qué llevas en el cole?

1 Escucha. ¿Quién habla? (1–6)

Ejemplo: **1** Gustavo

Silvia Gustavo Maya Carlos

2 Escucha otra vez y escribe los colores en inglés. (1–6)

Ejemplo: **1** grey, white

En el cole…
llevo/tengo que llevar…

un vestido – *a dress*
un jersey – *a jumper*

una blusa – *a blouse*
una camisa – *a shirt*
una camiseta – *a T-shirt*
una chaqueta – *a jacket*
una chaqueta de punto –
    a cardigan
una corbata – *a tie*
una falda – *a skirt*
una gorra – *a (baseball) cap*
una sudadera – *a sweatshirt*

unos pantalones – *trousers*
unos vaqueros – *jeans*
unos calcetines – *socks*
unos zapatos – *shoes*

unas botas – *boots*
unas zapatillas de deporte –
    trainers
unas medias – *tights*

---

rojo		morado
blanco		
	verde	
negro		marrón
	gris	
amarillo	naranja	
azul	claro/oscuro	rosa

G Adjectives of colour ⊃210

Remember to make your adjectives of colour agree with the noun they describe. In Spanish, the adjective usually comes after the noun.

	masc sing. (el, un)	fem. sing. (la, una)	masc. pl. (los, unos)	fem. pl. (las, unas)
-o	negr**o**	negr**a**	negr**os**	negr**as**
-e	verd**e**	verd**e**	verd**es**	verd**es**
consonant	azul	azul	azul**es**	azul**es**
Exceptions	ros**a**	ros**a**	ros**as**	ros**as**
	naran**ja**	naran**ja**	naran**jas**	naran**jas**
	marrón	marrón	marr**ones**	marr**ones**

A colour adjective followed by **claro** (*light*) or **oscuro** (*dark*) takes the masculine form even if describing a feminine or plural noun:

unos pantalones **azul oscuro**   *some dark blue trousers*
unas zapatillas de deporte **azul claro**   *some light blue trainers*

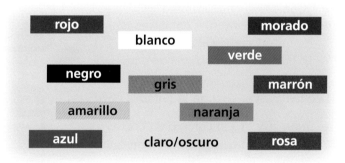

3 Using the pictures, have conversations with your partner about what you wear and what you would like to wear.

- ¿Qué llevas en el cole?
- ■ Tengo que llevar…
- ¿Qué te gustaría llevar todos los días?
- ■ Me gustaría llevar…

> Use these phrases with the infinitive to add variety to what you say:
> **Tengo que** + **infinitive** = *I have to*
> Tengo que **llevar** unos pantalones grises.
> *I have to wear grey trousers.*
> **Me gustaría** + **infinitive** = *I would like to*
> Me gustaría **llevar** vaqueros **todos los días**.
> *I would like to wear jeans **every day**.*

 4 Lee los blogs y escribe las frases en español.

a It's mega ugly.
b It's so old-fashioned.
c How embarrassing!
d but I'm not bothered
e It's also cheap.
f Cool!
g I hate it!
h It's not comfortable.

1 Hola. ¿Qué tal? Llevo uniforme y es superfeo. Tengo que llevar una falda azul, una blusa naranja y unas medias grises. Los zapatos tienen que ser negros o marrones. Es tan anticuado. ¡Qué vergüenza! 😒

2 ¡Hola amigos! En mi instituto tenemos que llevar uniforme, pero a mí no me importa porque es práctico. También es barato y fácil. Llevamos unos pantalones negros, una camisa blanca y una chaqueta roja. No tenemos que llevar corbata. ¡Qué guay! 😊

3 En mi colegio llevamos uniforme. ¡Lo odio! No es cómodo. En verano tengo que llevar un vestido a rayas y una chaqueta de punto verde oscuro. En invierno todos tenemos que llevar unos pantalones grises y una sudadera amarilla. ⚡

 5 Lee los blogs del ejercicio 4 otra vez. Copia y completa la tabla en inglés.

	uniform items	adjectives used
1	blue skirt,…	very ugly,…

 6 Copy the grid from exercise 5. Listen and fill it in again. (1–5)

| anticuado | cómodo | fácil | incómodo |
| barato | elegante | feo | práctico |

 7 Write a paragraph about your uniform or what you wear to school.

> En el cole tengo que llevar…
> Me gusta porque es (elegante).
> No me gusta porque es (feo).
> Me gustaría llevar… ¡Qué guay!

> Exclamations make your Spanish sound more authentic. To form them, use **Qué** + adjective or noun.
> ¡Qué feo! *How ugly!*
> ¡Qué guay! *(How) cool!*
> ¡Qué horror! *How awful!*
> ¡Qué suerte! *What (good) luck!*
> ¡Qué vergüenza! *How embarrassing!*

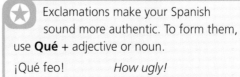

Describing school rules and problems at school

Using phrases with the infinitive

3 Las normas del insti

escribir 1 Escribe una norma para cada dibujo.

Ejemplo: **a** – Se debe escuchar en clase.

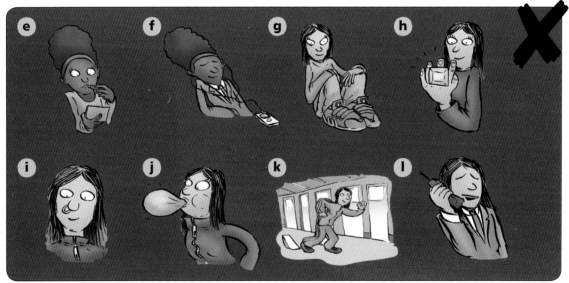

escuchar 2 Escucha y escribe las letras correctas del ejercicio 1. (1–5)

Ejemplo: **1** b, h

hablar 3 Con tu compañero/a, pregunta y contesta.

● ¿Qué se debe hacer en tu colegio?
■ En mi colegio…

● ¿Qué *no* se debe hacer en tu colegio?
■ En mi colegio…

> Se debe …/No se debe…
> comer chicle
> correr en los pasillos
> escuchar en clase
> escuchar música en clase
> hacer los deberes
> llegar a tiempo
> llevar joyas/maquillaje/ piercings/zapatillas de deporte
> llevar uniforme
> usar el móvil en clase

4 Read the Spanish school rules. Does your school have these rules? Write ✔ or ✘ for each one.

1 Está prohibido **escuchar** tu MP3 en clase.
2 Está prohibido **leer** correos electrónicos en la sala de informática.
3 No se permite **mandar** mensajes en clase.
4 No se permite **salir** del instituto durante la jornada escolar.
5 No se debe **ser** desobediente.
6 Los alumnos tienen que **ser** puntuales y amables.

> ⭐ When describing rules, try to vary the phrases you use. All of these are followed by the **infinitive**.
>
> | Está prohibido | **llevar** |
> | (No) se permite | **usar** |
> | (No) se debe | **mandar** |
> | | **comer** |

5 Escucha y escribe la letra correcta. (1–3)

a

b

c

Tengo mucho estrés porque hay muchos exámenes.

El acoso escolar es un problema serio.

Mi amigo hace novillos.

6 Listen again and note down in English what will happen in the future. (1–3)

En el futuro	voy a	tener problemas
El año que viene	vas a	ver ataques físicos
	va a	en el patio
	vamos a	tener muchos exámenes
El estrés	va a	continuar

G *The near future tense* ➲*200*

The near future tense is often used with time phrases which refer to the future.
En el futuro… *In the future…*
El año que viene… *Next year…*

Remember, to form it use **ir a** + **infinitive**.
Voy a **tener** problemas.
I'm going to have problems.
Vamos a **ver** ataques físicos.
We are going to see physical attacks.

7 Write a paragraph about the rules and problems in your school.

Las normas	Los problemas	El futuro
En mi colegio hay muchas normas. Por ejemplo:	También hay problemas en el colegio. Tengo mucho estrés porque…	En el futuro… El año que viene…
(No) Se debe…	Además…	
(No) Está prohibido…		
(No) Se permite…		

4 ¡Los profesores!

1 Look at the list of words below. What do they mean?
Look up any that you don't understand in the Vocabulario section.
How would you describe each of these teachers in Spanish?

paciente   trabajador(a)   antipático/a
listo/a   impaciente   raro/a
pesimista   normal   perezoso/a   simpático/a
tolerante   aburrido/a   severo/a
optimista   tonto/a   divertido/a

> ★ There are several cognates here – words that mean the same and look almost the same in English and Spanish. For example:
>
> paciente = *patient*
>
> But be careful! Although they look similar, cognates are often pronounced very differently in the two languages.

2 Look at the words in exercise 1 again and find 6 pairs of opposites.

Ejemplo: paciente/impaciente

3 Escucha y escribe las asignaturas y la descripción del profesor/de la profesora. (1–6)

Ejemplo: **1** matemáticas – paciente

4 Escribe frases sobre tus profes.

Ejemplo: Mi profesor de matemáticas es muy severo.
Mi profesora de…

> ★ The speakers in exercise 3 use these qualifiers to add more detail to their descriptions:
>
> demasiado – *too*
> muy – *very*
> bastante – *quite*
> un poco – *a bit*
> poco – *not very*
>
> They are used before the adjective each time. Can you spot any as you listen?

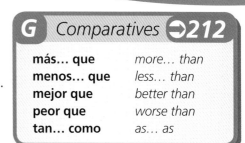

5 Escucha y completa las frases. (1–4)

1 Mi profesor de inglés es más ____ que mi profesor de matemáticas.
2 Mi tutor es más ____ que mi profesor de ciencias.
3 Mi profe de matemáticas es menos ____ que mi profe de inglés.
4 Mi profe de español es tan ____ como mi profe de francés.

G *Comparatives* ➔212

más... que	*more... than*
menos... que	*less... than*
mejor que	*better than*
peor que	*worse than*
tan... como	*as... as*

6 Copia y completa las frases del ejercicio 5 con *tus* opiniones.

7 *Read the text and answer the questions in English. Look at the text again. What do you think the phrases in bold type mean?*

Lalo: Hola, Jade. No estoy muy contento porque tenemos una profesora nueva de informática, la señora Torres. Es un poco severa y **creo que** es bastante antipática. Mi amiga Fernanda piensa que es lista pero **no estoy de acuerdo** con ella.

Odio sus clases porque es demasiado impaciente. Por ejemplo, el martes pasado hablé con mi compañero y se enfadó conmigo y me quedé sin recreo. Creo que la señora Torres es más perezosa que el señor López (el profesor de informática de antes). **Estoy harto de** sus clases porque la señora Torres es una tía paliza y es la peor profesora del instituto.

Jade: Hola, Lalo. ¡Creo que tu nueva profesora de informática es tan tonta como mi profesor de dibujo!

1 Who is señora Torres?
2 How does Lalo describe señora Torres? (2 details)
3 Why did señora Torres get cross with Lalo last Tuesday?
4 What punishment did Lalo get?
5 How does señora Torres compare to their old teacher?

se enfadó = *she got angry*
sin = *without*
de antes = *from before*
tía paliza = *annoying woman*
la peor profesora = *the worst teacher*

8 Escucha. Copia y completa la tabla. (1–5)

	Who are the teachers talking about?	Do they agree or disagree? (A/D)
1	geography teacher	A

✔ Estoy de acuerdo. ¡Claro!
✘ No estoy de acuerdo. ¡Qué va!

9 ¡A debate! Habla con tu compañero/a de tus profesores.

● ¿Qué opinas del profesor de matemáticas?
■ Creo que es divertido y bastante inteligente.
● No estoy de acuerdo. En mi opinión es muy aburrido. Es más aburrido que el profesor de inglés.

> **School life**
> You are going to have a conversation with your teacher about your school life. Your teacher could ask you the following:
>
> - What do you study at school?
> - Which subjects do you like? Why?
> - Which subjects do you dislike? Why?
> - What extra-curricular activities do you take part in and when?
> - What clubs did you go to last year?
> - What rules are there at your school and what do you think of them?
> - What activities are you going to do next year?
>
> Remember that you will also have to respond to an unexpected question that you have not yet prepared.

 You are going to listen to Jason, an exam candidate, taking part in the above conversation. Which of the following do you think Jason will use to answer the examiner's first three questions? Listen and check.

1 ¿Qué estudias en el instituto?
2 ¿Qué asignaturas te gustan?
3 ¿Qué asignaturas no te gustan?

a Siempre hay problemas con Internet. ¡Qué rollo!
b Es muy divertido pero a veces es un poco difícil.
c Estudiamos idiomas. Estudio español y francés.
d Odio la informática porque es muy aburrida.
e La historia es mi asignatura preferida porque me interesan los castillos antiguos.
f Estudio nueve asignaturas en total.

 Listen to part 2 of Jason's conversation and fill each gap with the correct word from the box.

martes	encanta	muy	juego	voy	hora	mucho	al	divertido	también

– ¿Qué haces después de clase? ¿Eres miembro de algún club?
– Me gusta **(1)** ▓▓▓ hacer muchas actividades diferentes porque siempre es **(2)** ▓▓▓ aprender cosas nuevas. Los lunes **(3)** ▓▓▓ al club de ajedrez con mi amigo Tom y los jueves voy **(4)** ▓▓▓ club de teatro con mi hermana. **(5)** ▓▓▓ hago algunas actividades a la **(6)** ▓▓▓ de comer. Por ejemplo, los **(7)** ▓▓▓ voy al club de idiomas. ¡Estudiamos japonés, italiano y alemán! Los viernes **(8)** ▓▓▓ al baloncesto en el gimnasio. Me **(9)** ▓▓▓ jugar al baloncesto porque es **(10)** ▓▓▓ fácil y bastante divertido. Lo malo es que tenemos un gimnasio muy pequeño.

3 *Now listen to part 3 of Jason's conversation and note down the order in which Jason uses these phrases. What is the unexpected question that Jason is asked?*

a …fui al club de tenis y me gustó mucho.
b No se permite mandar mensajes de texto…
c Tengo que llevar unos pantalones grises…
d En mi opinión las reglas son tontas.
e Toqué en la orquesta y también canté en el coro.
f …voy a practicar atletismo porque me encantan los deportes.

> ¿Qué actividades hiciste el año pasado?

> ¿Tienes muchas reglas en tu instituto?

> ¿Qué actividades vas a hacer el año que viene?

 4 *Now it's your turn! Prepare your answers to the task and then have a conversation with your teacher or partner.*

- Use the Grade Studio and your answers to exercises 1–3 to help you plan.
- Adapt what Jason said to talk about yourself but add your own ideas.
- Prepare your answers to the questions and try to predict what the unexpected question could be. The examiner might base this question on something you have already said, or ask something totally new!
- Record the conversation. Ask a partner to listen to it and say how well you performed.

> *Award each other one star, two stars or three stars for each of these categories:*
> - *Pronunciation*
> - *Confidence and fluency*
> - *Range of tenses*
> - *Variety of vocabulary and expressions*
> - *Using longer sentences*
> - *Taking the initiative*
>
> *What do you need to do next time to improve your performance?*

⭐ GradeStudio

Make sure you cover the basics.
- Use **simple structures** correctly, e.g. *estudio* (I study), *es* (it is), *hago* (I do) and *voy* (I go).
- Include **simple opinions**, e.g. *me encanta(n)* (I love), *me gusta(n)* (I like), *odio* (I hate).
- Use **simple connectives** to make longer sentences, e.g. *y* (and), *pero* (but) and *también* (also).

To reach Grade C, show that you can:
- Use **adjectives** such as *difícil* (difficult), *aburrida* (boring) and *fácil* (easy). Can you think of others that Jason uses?
- Use **qualifiers** with your adjectives as Jason does, e.g. *muy* (very), *bastante* (quite) and *un poco* (a bit). Remember that the endings of adjectives must agree with the noun they describe.
- Ensure your **verb tenses** are **accurate**.
- Use *porque* to give reasons and create longer sentences, e.g. *No me gusta porque es bastante incómodo.* (I don't like it because it is quite uncomfortable.)

To increase your marks:
- Jason uses the **opinion phrase** *lo malo es que* to talk about basketball. How do you say 'the good thing is that'?
- Use **another person** of the verb, such as 'we' or 'he/she'. Jason says *También estudiamos idiomas.* (We also study languages.) *Mi hermana fue al club de fútbol.* (My sister went to the football club.)

leer 1

Read the text and choose the correct title for each paragraph.

- **a** Sports and facilities
- **b** Extra-curricular activities
- **c** My teachers
- **d** A trip abroad
- **e** Transport to school

Me llamo Julio y vivo en Madrid. Normalmente voy al instituto a pie pero cuando hace mal tiempo voy en autobús. ¡Mi hermano es demasiado perezoso y siempre va en autobús!

Mi cole es público. Hay seiscientos alumnos y tenemos sesenta profesores. Creo que los profesores son muy simpáticos pero mi profesora de religión es un poco severa. Prefiero a mi profesor de informática porque es muy gracioso.

El colegio tiene unas instalaciones impresionantes. Lo bueno es que mi colegio tiene un salón de actos bastante grande. Además hay dos piscinas y ocho pistas de tenis pero no hay pista de atletismo. Me interesan los deportes y juego en el equipo de fútbol. La semana pasada hice una competición de natación y también gané un premio de fútbol.

Después del cole hago muchas actividades. Los jueves canto en el coro y la semana pasada canté unas canciones de la película *Mamma Mia*. ¡Fue fantástico! ¡La música de Abba es más guay que la música de Beethoven!

Mi asignatura preferida es el teatro porque es muy entretenido. No me gustan nada los idiomas, pero el año que viene voy a ir a Francia. Voy a pasar una semana con una familia francesa. Desafortunadamente no hablo bien el francés. ¡Qué vergüenza!

Julio

gracioso/a = *funny*
desafortunadamente = *unfortunately*

leer 2

Find the equivalent of these expressions in Spanish in the text.

1. …when the weather is bad…
2. …he always goes by bus.
3. My school is a state school.
4. I think the teachers are very nice…
5. The school has some impressive facilities.
6. The good thing is that…
7. What's more there are two swimming pools…
8. I am interested in sport…
9. My favourite subject is…
10. …next year I am going to go to France.

leer 3

Read the text again. Find three more examples of each of the following:

- Present-tense verbs (e.g. *me llamo*) or verbs expressing an opinion (e.g. *creo que…*)
- Adjectives, e.g. *perezoso*
- Preterite verbs, e.g. *hice*.

4 **Read the text again and answer the questions in English.**

1 How many teachers are there at Julio's school?
2 Name one sport Julio did last week.
3 What after-school activity does he do?
4 Why does he mention the film *Mamma Mia*?
5 What subject does Julio like? Why?
6 Where is Julio going to stay on his trip to France?
7 Why is Julio embarrassed about going to France?

5 **You might be asked to write about your school as a controlled assessment task. Use the Grade Studio to help you prepare your account.**

⭐ GradeStudio

Make sure you cover the basics.
- Use **simple structures** correctly, e.g. *vivo* (I live), *voy* (I go), *es* (it is), *hay* (there is) and *hago* (I do).
- Include a **simple negative**, e.g. *No hay pista de atletismo.*
- Include **simple opinions**, e.g. *me encanta(n)* (I love), *me gusta(n)* (I like) and *odio* (I hate).

To reach Grade C, show that you can:
- Use *porque* to extend your sentences, e.g. *Mi asignatura preferida es el teatro porque es muy entretenido.*
- Use **the present tense** to say what you usually do, e.g. *Canto en el coro.*
- Use **the preterite** to say what you did, e.g. *La semana pasada hice una competición de natación.*
- Use *fue + an adjective* to say what something was like, e.g. *¡Fue fantástico!*
- Use *voy a + infinitive* to say what you are going to do, e.g. *Voy a ir a Francia.*

To increase your marks:
- Use a **comparative**. Julio says *¡La música de Abba es más guay que la música de Beethoven!*
- Use more **complex opinions**. Julio says *Lo bueno es que mi colegio tiene un salón de actos bastante grande.*
- Use a **different form** of the verb. Julio says *Mi hermano es demasiado perezoso. El colegio tiene...*
- Add an **exclamation**. Julio uses *¡Qué vergüenza!* (How embarrassing!)

6 **Now write a full account of your school.**

- Adapt Julio's text and use language from Module 3.
- Think about what you can say in an accurate and interesting way. This is more important than being completely truthful about your school!
- Structure your text carefully. Organise what you write in paragraphs.

7 **Check carefully what you have written.**

- Does *me gusta/me encanta* need an 'n'?
- Do your adjective endings agree with the noun they describe?
- Don't forget that the near future tense is made up of three parts (present tense of verb *ir* + *a* + infinitive).

General introduction

Introduce yourself and say how you get to school

Main paragraph

What type of school is it? What are the teachers like?
What facilities are there?
Talk about activities you do or clubs you attend
Talk about an event that happened

Conclusion

Talk about the subjects and activities that you like/don't like
What are your plans for next year?

Palabras

Las asignaturas   *Subjects*

el comercio	business studies	Me encanta(n)…	I love…
el dibujo	art	Me gusta(n)…	I like…
el español	Spanish	No me gusta(n)…	I don't like…
el francés	French	Odio…	I hate…
el inglés	English	porque es…/son…	because it is/they are…
el teatro	drama	el lunes	on Monday
la educación física	PE	el martes	on Tuesday
la geografía	geography	el miércoles	on Wednesday
la historia	history	el jueves	on Thursday
la religión	RE	el viernes	on Friday
la tecnología	D&T	el sábado	on Saturday
los idiomas	languages	el domingo	on Sunday
las ciencias	science	¿Cuándo tienes…?	When do you have…?
las matemáticas	maths	Tengo (ciencias) los martes.	I have (science) on Tuesdays.

En clase   *In class*

las estaciones	the seasons	En el recreo…	During break…
la primavera	spring	A la hora de comer…	During the lunch hour…
el verano	summer	Después del instituto…	After school…
el otoño	autumn	escribo mucho	I write a lot
el invierno	winter	escucho al profe	I listen to the teacher
Normalmente…	Normally…	hablo	I talk
Por la mañana…	In the morning…	leo	I read
Por la tarde…	In the afternoon…	uso el diccionario	I use the dictionary
Siempre…	Always…	canto en el coro	I sing in the choir
A menudo…	Often…	hago natación	I go swimming
Nunca…	Never…	juego al fútbol	I play football
En verano…	In summer…	toco en la orquesta	I play in the orchestra
En invierno…	In winter…	voy al club de ajedrez	I go to the chess club
voy andando/a pie	I walk	Llevo …	I take…
voy en bici	I go by bike	un bolígrafo	a pen
No me gusta ir…	I don't like going…	un cuaderno	an exercise book
Prefiero ir…	I prefer to go…	un estuche	a pencil case
Mis clases empiezan a las…	My classes start at…	un libro	a book
En clase…	In class…	una regla	a ruler

¿Cómo es tu insti?   *What's your school like?*

Hay…	There is a…/There are some…	pizarras interactivas	interactive whiteboards
No hay…	There isn't a…/There aren't any…	Hay quinientos alumnos.	There are 500 pupils.
		Hay setenta profesores.	There are 70 teachers.
Tenemos…	We have…	La comida es…	The food is…
un campo de fútbol	a football pitch	Los profesores son…	The teachers are…
un comedor	a canteen	Lo bueno es que…	The good thing is that…
un gimnasio	a gym	Lo malo es que…	The bad thing is that…
un patio	a playground	Es un colegio…	It is a… school
un salón de actos	a drama studio, hall	antiguo/a	old, old-fashioned
una biblioteca	a library	moderno/a	modern
una piscina	a swimming pool	bueno/a	good
una pista de tenis	a tennis court	malo/a	bad
una pista de atletismo	an athletics track	grande	big
una sala de profesores	a staffroom	pequeño/a	small
unos laboratorios	science labs	femenino/masculino/mixto	girls'/boys'/mixed
unos vestuarios	cloakrooms	privado/público	private/state
unas aulas	classrooms	Está especializado en…	It specialises in…
Pero no tenemos…	But we don't have…	Las clases empiezan a las…	Classes start at… and finish
ordenadores	computers	y terminan a las…	at…

¿Qué llevas en el cole? *What do you wear to school?*

Normalmente llevo…	*I usually wear…*	blanco	*white*
un jersey	*a sweater*	gris	*grey*
un vestido	*a dress*	negro	*black*
una blusa	*a blouse*	marrón	*brown*
una camisa	*a shirt*	morado	*purple*
una camiseta	*a T-shirt*	naranja	*orange*
una chaqueta (de punto)	*a jacket (cardigan)*	rojo	*red*
una corbata	*a tie*	rosa	*pink*
unos calcetines	*socks*	verde	*green*
una falda	*a skirt*	oscuro/claro	*dark/light*
una gorra	*a cap*	(No) me gusta porque es…	*I (don't) like it because it's…*
una sudadera	*a sweatshirt*	anticuado	*old-fashioned*
unos pantalones	*trousers*	barato	*cheap*
unos vaqueros	*jeans*	cómodo	*comfortable*
unos zapatos	*shoes*	elegante	*elegant*
unas botas	*boots*	fácil	*easy*
unas medias	*tights*	feo	*ugly*
unas zapatillas de deporte	*trainers*	incómodo	*uncomfortable*
amarillo	*yellow*	práctico	*practical*
azul	*blue*	Me gustaría llevar…	*I'd like to wear…*

Las normas del insti *School rules*

Se debe…	*You must…*	llevar uniforme	*wear uniform*
No se debe…	*You mustn't…*	usar el móvil en clase	*use your mobile in class*
comer chicle	*chew gum*	En el futuro…	*In the future…*
correr en los pasillos	*run in the corridors*	El año que viene…	*Next year…*
escuchar (música) en clase	*listen (to music) in class*	voy a…	*I'm going to…*
hacer los deberes	*do your homework*	tener problemas	*have problems*
llegar a tiempo	*arrive on time*	ver ataques físicos en el patio	*see physical attacks in the playground*
llevar joyas/maquillaje/ piercings	*wear jewellery/make-up/ piercings*	tener muchos exámenes	*have a lot of exams*
llevar zapatillas de deporte	*wear trainers*		

Los profesores *Teachers*

más… que	*more… than…*	raro/a	*strange, weird*
menos… que…	*less… than…*	severo/a	*strict*
mejor que…	*better than…*	simpático/a	*nice*
peor que…	*worse than…*	tolerante	*tolerant*
tan… como…	*as… as…*	tonto/a	*stupid, crazy*
antipático/a	*unpleasant*	trabajador(a)	*hardworking*
impaciente	*impatient*	demasiado	*too*
listo/a	*clever*	muy	*very*
optimista	*optimistic*	bastante	*quite*
paciente	*patient*	un poco	*a bit*
perezoso/a	*lazy*	poco	*not very*
pesimista	*pessimistic*		

Repaso *Mi familia*

¡Perdidos! 4

 1 Lee y empareja las preguntas y las respuestas.

1 ¿Cuándo es tu cumpleaños?

2 ¿Cuántos años tienes?

3 ¿Cómo eres?

4 ¿Cómo es tu pelo?

5 ¿De qué color son tus ojos?

moreno
a Tengo el pelo rubio y rizado.
b Tengo los ojos azules.
c Mi cumpleaños es el 13 de febrero.
d Tengo quince años.
e Soy alto y delgado.

 2 Escucha. Copia y completa la tabla en inglés. (1–3)

	birthday	age	description	hair	eyes
1					

 3 Con tu compañero/a, pregunta y contesta utilizando las preguntas del ejercicio 1.

Mi cumpleaños es el… de	enero, febrero, marzo, abril, mayo, junio, julio, agosto, septiembre, octubre, noviembre, diciembre
(No) Soy	alto, bajo, delgado, gordo, guapo, feo
Tengo los ojos	azules, marrones, grises, verdes
Tengo el pelo	blanco, castaño, gris, negro, pelirrojo, rubio, moreno largo, corto, liso, rizado, ondulado

Tengo pecas   Llevo gafas

 4 Match up the pairs of words that go together. What do they mean?

Ejemplo: padre – madre (father – mother)

padre hermano abuelo tío primo hijo marido padrastro

madre prima hermana mujer madrastra abuela tía hija

⭐ Many words for family members are easy in Spanish, as the same word is used for males and females, only changing the ending:
tí**o** (uncle) – tí**a** (aunt)
hermanastr**o** (stepbrother) – hermanastr**a** (stepsister)

5 You are Pedro. Listen and write down in Spanish which member of your family is being described. (1–8)

Ejemplo: **1** mi tío Federico

> Me llamo Pedro. Nací el 16 de septiembre de 1995.

(Yo) **nací** el…
Mi hermano **nació** el…

Leandro García Machado
31 /7/1978

Viviana García Machado
17/12/1994

Pedro García Machado
16/9/1995

Rosana Gil Milá
18/4/1971

Federico Machado Pérez
28/7/1968

Juliana Machado Pérez
21/2/1955

Alejandro García Cid
15/6/1953

When you are listening to higher numbers, don't panic! Break them down into their elements.
1945   mil   novecientos   cuarenta y cinco

Luisa Pérez Cía
06/08/1935

Martín Machado Villa
11/12/1933

6 Copy out the texts about Pedro's family and correct the factual mistakes.

1 Mi abuelo se llama Martín. Tiene el pelo pelirrojo y los ojos verdes. Lleva gafas y tiene barba. Nació el once de mayo de 1922.

2 Mi hermana se llama Rosana. Tiene el pelo liso y rubio y los ojos verdes. Nació el siete de diciembre de 2001.

3 Mi tío se llama Federico. Tiene el pelo largo y los ojos azules. Nació el dieciocho de julio de 1970.

G Possessive adjectives

	singular	plural
my	mi	mis
your (singular)	tu	tus
his/her/its	su	sus

The possessive adjective changes to agree with the noun.
mi herman**a**   *my sister*
mis herman**as**   *my sisters*

7 Write descriptions of yourself and two other members of your family.

Me llamo… Nací el… Tengo los ojos… y el pelo… Soy…
Mi hermana **se llama**… **Nació** el…
Tiene los ojos… y el pelo… **Es**…

Es…
alto/a
bajo/a
delgado/a
gordo/a
guapo/a
feo/a

Es calvo.
Tiene barba.
Tiene bigote.
Tiene pecas.
Lleva gafas.

1 Los supervivientes

1 Listen and read the texts on the survivors of the plane crash. Note down each person's nationality and job.

Ejemplo: Leonora – Spanish, designer

Catástrofe aérea

Un avión de pasajeros de la aerolínea Mundial se estrelló el jueves 15 de octubre en el océano Pacífico. No se conocen las causas del accidente y no se sabe si hay supervivientes…

Leonora

Soy española. Soy una persona creativa y paciente. **Me parezco a mi padre.** Soy diseñadora gráfica. Aquí en la isla tengo una vida tranquila. Hay problemas, pero estoy feliz.

Inmaculada

Soy colombiana. Soy abogada. Soy una persona energética y honesta. **Tengo una relación problemática con mi madre. Estoy separada.**

Benedicto

Soy peruano. Soy estudiante de medicina. Tengo mucho sentido del humor. Por lo general soy tolerante y optimista. Vivo con mi mamá y mi hermana. De momento **estoy soltero**, pero espero encontrar pronto a mi chica ideal.

Eugenio

Soy estadounidense, de Los Ángeles. Soy mecánico y me encanta mi trabajo. Soy trabajador. No soy nada perezoso. **Estoy casado** con una mujer maravillosa. La quiero mucho.

Alicia

Soy peruana y soy la hermana menor de Benedicto. Estudio bachillerato y quiero ir a la universidad. Soy ambiciosa y alegre. Afortunadamente **me llevo bien con mi hermano.**

2 Read the texts again. Make notes about each person's character.

Ejemplo: Leonora – creative,…

3 Now look for these expressions about relationships in the texts (they are all in green).

1 I'm separated.
2 I'm single.
3 I'm married.
4 I have a difficult relationship with my mother.
5 I am like my father.
6 I get on well with my brother.

G *Ser y estar* ➲ **192**

Ser is used to describe a profession or an essential quality, which won't change:
Soy abogada.   *I'm a lawyer.*
Soy inteligente.   *I'm intelligent.*

Estar is used to describe a temporary situation or marital status (single, married, divorced, etc.):
Hoy estoy triste.   *Today I'm sad.*
Estoy divorciado.   *I'm divorced.*

	ser *(to be)*	estar *(to be)*
(yo)	soy	estoy
(tú)	eres	estás
(él/ella/usted)	es	está
(nosotros/as)	somos	estamos
(vosotros/as)	sois	estáis
(ellos/as/ustedes)	son	están

Con tu compañero/a, mira estos perfiles. Pregunta y contesta.

- ● ¿Cómo te llamas?
- ● ¿De dónde eres?
- ● ¿Cuántos años tienes?
- ● ¿Estás casado/a?
- ● ¿Tienes niños?
- ● ¿Cómo es tu carácter?

- ■ Me llamo…
- ■ Soy…
- ■ Tengo…
- ■ Estoy…
- ■ Tengo…
- ■ Soy…

Nombre: Rigoberta
Nacionalidad: peruana
Edad: 42
Estado civil: separada en 1996 (me casé en 1986)
Hijos: Benedicto – 23 años, Alicia – 17 años
Personalidad: honesta y trabajadora

Nombre: Diego
Nacionalidad: español
Edad: 50
Estado civil: casado
Hijos: Leonora – 30 años, Mónica – 27 años
Personalidad: creativo y paciente

Listen and complete each sentence with the correct option. (1–3)

1a Juan is Inma's **younger brother** / **uncle** / **older brother**.

1b Juan says Inma is very **intelligent and hardworking** / **intelligent and lazy** / **intelligent and honest**.

1c Juan says Inma has **no sense of humour** / **a good sense of humour** / **a good sense of style**.

2a Mónica is Leonora's **sister** / **aunt** / **grandmother**.

2b She thinks that Leonora is going to survive because she is **calm** / **strong** / **calm and strong**.

3a Silvia says that Eugenio is **honest** / **optimistic** / **patient**.

3b They met in at a party in **2003** / **1993** / **2005**.

3c They married **one** / **two** / **four** years later.

> ★ It will help if you predict the words you might hear in Spanish *before* you listen. For example, the words you may hear in connection with sentence 1a are **tío** and **hermano**. As you listen, also pay attention to whether negatives are used, as they change the meaning of what is said.

Write a description of another person who has been stranded on the island.

Soy	peruano/a, colombiano/a, mexicano/a, español(a), alemán/ana, francés/esa, inglés/esa, escocés/esa, galés/esa, irlandés/esa
Tengo	… años
Soy	abogado/a, diseñador(a), mecánico/a, estudiante
Soy También soy pero no soy	ambicioso/a, creativo/a, duro/a, enérgico/a, honesto/a, perezoso/a, tranquilo/a, trabajador(a), alegre, inteligente, paciente, tolerante, optimista
Estoy	soltero/a, casado/a, separado/a, divorciado/a

2 La vida cotidiana

 Escucha a Eugenio y lee.

a Me despierto temprano, a las cinco y media. Me levanto a las seis de la mañana.

b Me ducho. Me lavo los dientes. Me baño en el mar.

c No me peino. No me afeito nunca.

d Me visto.

e Desayuno fruta. Meriendo a las cuatro. Ceno pescado.

f Me acuesto a las nueve de la tarde.

 Contesta a las preguntas en inglés.

1 What time does Eugenio wake up?
2 What time does he get up?
3 What does he have for breakfast?
4 What time does he have tea?
5 What does he have for dinner?
6 What time does he go to bed?

 Listen to Alicia. Are the statements below true (T) or false (F)?

1a Alicia gets up at 7 o'clock.
1b First of all she eats breakfast.
1c The fruit on the island is fantastic.
2a She just eats fruit in the afternoon.
2b She showers before bed.
3a She always has fruit and coconut milk for tea.
3b She combs her hair because she doesn't want hair like Eugenio's.

G Reflexive verbs

Reflexive verbs often describe an action you do *to yourself*.

me lavo	*I wash **myself***

Present tense
Lavarse *(to wash yourself)* is a reflexive **-ar** verb:

	lavarse
(yo)	**me** lav**o**
(tú)	**te** lav**as**
(él/ella/usted)	**se** lav**a**
(nosotros/as)	**nos** lav**amos**
(vosotros/as)	**os** lav**áis**
(ellos/as/ustedes)	**se** lav**an**

Some of the reflexive verbs in this unit are also stem-changing:

despertarse *(to wake up)* → me desp**ie**rto
acostarse *(to go to bed)* → me ac**ue**sto
vestirse *(to get dressed)* → me v**i**sto

4 Estás en la isla. Con tu compañero/a, pregunta y contesta.

- ● ¿A qué hora te levantas?
- ■ Me levanto a las

- ● ¿Qué haces por la mañana?
- ■ Primero , después y <br> pero

- ● ¿Qué comes durante el día?
- ■ Desayuno . Más tarde meriendo <br> y después por la tarde ceno

- ● ¿Qué haces por la tarde?
- ■ Por la tarde  y después

- ● ¿A qué hora te acuestas?
- ■ Me acuesto a las

 5 Lee el diario de Benedicto y termina las frases en inglés.

Vivo en la isla **desde hace un año**. ¡Un año ya! Y ahora tengo una rutina. **Primero por la mañana** me despierto y me lavo los dientes. Desayuno frutos secos y bebo té. Hay una hierba especial – la verbena – que Inma cultiva. (¡Ay mi Inma! Estoy enamorado de ti **desde hace unos meses**, Inma mi amor.)

Más tarde trabajo en el jardín y **luego** meriendo a las cuatro. **Después**, por la tarde ceno a las ocho. **Normalmente** ceno pescado. Ceno pescado desde hace un año. ¡Me gustaría comer un filete de ternera **de vez en cuando**! Me acuesto **a las diez y media**.

En verano cuando hace calor me baño en el mar. Pero **en invierno** cuando llueve y hace frío prefiero ducharme. En la isla lo bueno es la fruta y también hay muchos animales interesantes. Para mí lo peor es la lluvia y la oscuridad en invierno. Pero Inma está conmigo.

oscuridad = *darkness*

 To say *how long* you've been doing something, use the phrase **desde hace** and the *present tense* of the verb. (This is different from English!)

¿Desde hace cuánto tiempo vives en la isla?
 How long have you been living on the island?
 Vivo en la isla **desde hace** un año.
 I've been living on the island **for** a year.

1 In the morning, he gets up and…
2 For breakfast, he drinks…
3 Benedicto is in love with…
4 He has dinner at…
5 On the dinner menu is…
6 At 10:30 he…
7 In summer, when it's hot,…
8 In winter he prefers to…

 6 Copy out the words in red in the text and write their meaning in English.

 7 Describe la rutina diaria de una persona perdida en una isla. Utiliza estas frases.

Vivo en la isla desde hace…	Después, por la tarde ceno…
Primero por la mañana…	En verano cuando hace calor…
Después… y… pero…	Pero en invierno cuando llueve y hace frío…
A las seis/siete/… desayuno…	En la isla lo bueno es…
Más tarde meriendo… a las…	Lo peor es…

3 Las tareas

1 Escucha. ¿Qué tareas hacen Leonora y Eugenio? Escribe las letras correctas. (1–2)

Tareas en la isla

a Lavo los platos.
b Hago la cama.
c Limpio mi dormitorio.
d Arreglo mis cosas.
e Cocino.
f Pongo la mesa.
g Quito la mesa.
h Pesco.
i Trabajo en el jardín.

Tareas en casa

j Paso la aspiradora.
k Plancho la ropa.

2 Escucha a Benedicto e Inma. ¿Qué tareas *no* hacen?
Escribe las letras del ejercicio 1. (1–2)

Listen out for negatives. They are sometimes used in the listening exam and can catch you out if you don't spot them.

For exercise 1, you need to note the activities people *do* (i.e. *not* the activities where a negative is used). For exercise 2, note the activities people *don't* do (i.e. the activities where negatives are used).

G Negatives ⮕214

Put **no** before the verb to make it negative.
No limpio.   *I don't clean.*

Here are some other negative expressions.
nunca = *never*
Nunca lavo los platos.   *I never wash the dishes.*

nadie = *no one*
Nadie pasa la aspiradora.   *No one vacuums.*

tampoco = *not either*
Tampoco pongo la mesa. *or* **No** pongo la mesa **tampoco**.
I don't lay the table either.

nada = *nothing*
No hago **nada**.
I do nothing./I don't do anything.

no… ni… = *neither… nor…*
No paso la aspiradora **ni** plancho.
I neither vacuum nor iron.

Escribe las frases en español.

Ejemplo: **1** No pesco.

   No one Never

Lee los textos y escoge el verbo correcto.

Inma

Soy muy organizada en la isla. Es importante tener una rutina. Todos los días **(1)** ⬚ mi dormitorio, **(2)** ⬚ mis cosas y luego **(3)** ⬚ en el jardín. Me gusta mucho la tranquilidad del jardín. Más tarde **(4)** ⬚ y **(5)** ⬚ la mesa y también **(6)** ⬚ los platos. ¡Nunca **(7)** ⬚ la aspiradora! Creo que Benedicto está deprimido porque no **(8)** ⬚ nada para ayudar.

Alicia

Esta rutina me da rabia. **(9)** ⬚ las camas, limpio mi dormitorio, **(10)** ⬚ a la playa. Todos los días hago lo mismo. Antes del accidente, mi rutina era mucho más interesante. Otra cosa, ¿qué pasa con Benedicto? No **(11)** ⬚ con nadie, no dice nada. No come. Tampoco bebe. Nunca **(12)** ⬚ con las tareas.

hace	habla	limpio
arreglo	trabajo	hago
ayuda	pongo	quito
lavo	paso	voy

Con tu compañero/a, imagina que eres otra persona de la isla. Pregunta y contesta.

● ¿Qué haces normalmente para ayudar en la isla?

■ Normalmente…/Todos los días…

● ¿Qué no te gusta hacer?

■ No… ni… . Nunca… . Tampoco…

Imagine you are on the island. Write a paragraph about the jobs you do on the island and the jobs you do back at home.

En la isla normalmente… También…
   todos los días.
Pero no… ni… Nunca…
En casa normalmente…

⭐ Adding a sentence using negatives is a useful way to extend what you are saying when you speak or write Spanish. This will gain you marks in speaking and writing assessments.

4 Otro accidente

1 Empareja el español con el inglés.

Ejemplo: **1** agresivo/a – **a** aggressive

❶ agresivo/a
❷ alegre
❸ amable
❹ egoísta
❺ generoso/a
❻ introvertido/a
❼ maleducado/a
❽ optimista
❾ pesimista
❿ simpático/a
⓫ sincero/a
⓬ valiente

a	aggressive
b	generous
c	cheerful
d	brave
e	introverted
f	kind
g	rude
h	friendly
i	sincere
j	selfish
k	optimistic
l	pessimistic

2 *Listen and read the sentences. Write an adjective from the box above that applies to each person. (1–6)*

Ejemplo: **1** selfish

1 Mi hermana nunca piensa en otras personas.

2 Mi mejor amigo me compra cosas todo el tiempo. Hace regalos a todo el mundo.

3 Mi amiga es una persona muy tímida y un poco nerviosa. No le gustan las fiestas o las situaciones con mucha gente.

4 Mi mujer nunca es positiva y espera lo peor en todas las situaciones.

5 Mis hijos nunca tienen miedo.

6 Mi abuela es una persona muy positiva y por lo general espera lo mejor.

> ⭐ You sometimes need to think laterally in your listening and reading exams! Can you work out what the person is like from the description in exercise 2? Be careful – you won't hear the adjectives from exercise 1 mentioned.

3 *Write a paragraph about someone you know. Change the words in brackets to apply to them.*

> Mi (hermano) se llama (Freddy). Me llevo (bien/mal) con (él/ella).
> Por lo general es (tolerante) y (simpático), pero puede ser un poco (egoísta).
> Nunca es (perezoso).
> Tiene mucho/poco sentido del humor.

> ⭐ Remember that the endings of adjectives may need to change, depending on who you are talking about.
> Mi hermano es simpátic**o**.
> *but:* Mi hermana es simpátic**a**.
>
> These adjectives stay the same when talking about a man or a woman, but do add an **s** if talking about more than one person:
> **egoísta, optimista, pesimista**
> mi padre es optimist**a**
> mi madre es optimist**a**
> mis padres son optimist**as**

escuchar 4 Escucha y lee.

El día del accidente, nos levantamos temprano porque hacía sol.

Fuimos a la playa. Eugenio fue a pescar y nosotras fuimos a buscar conchas. Benedicto estaba nervioso y se quedó en la cabaña.

Una hora después, Inma fue a buscar a Benedicto.

Normalmente Alicia no nada en el mar, pero esa mañana decidió bañarse conmigo.

En la casita, Benedicto habló con Inma. Por fin, Benedicto le declaró a Inma su amor, y le dio un gran beso.

De repente, Eugenio vio algo en el agua y empezó a gritar: '¡Tiburón, tiburón! ¡Alicia, Leonora! ¡Hay un tiburón!'

Yo salí enseguida pero Alicia se quedó en el agua. Luego el agua se llenó de sangre. Era la sangre de Alicia.

Benedicto e Inma vinieron corriendo. Alicia estaba inconsciente.

Benedicto limpió y curó la herida de su hermana. Benedicto era estudiante de medicina antes del accidente. Alicia tenía fiebre. Eugenio dijo: '¡Va a morir, va a morir!'

escuchar 5 Listen to these speakers talking about the people on the island.

- *Who do they talk about?*
- *Which adjectives do they feel apply to each person?*

hablar 6 Read the story again and decide which personal qualities each character showed. Discuss them with your partner.

- Pienso que Benedicto era introvertido.
- Estoy de acuerdo. Y en mi opinión Eugenio era…

Para mí…
En mi opinión…
Pienso que…
Estoy de acuerdo.
No estoy de acuerdo.

5 Un año después

1 Read the text below, then write a few sentences in English about the rescue.

Encuentran cinco supervivientes del avión desaparecido de la compañía 'Mundial'

El País, 9 de noviembre

Se han encontrado 5 personas en una isla desierta en el océano Pacífico. El capitán de un barco las vio en la playa con su telescopio. Contactó con el servicio de urgencias y un helicóptero vino a socorrer a las personas. …

Escucha. Copia y completa la tabla. (1–4)

	primero	luego	después
Benedicto	e		
Inma			
Eugenio			
Leonora			

⭐ As you listen to the people talking in exercise 2, listen out for negatives too. They may not be planning to do all of the things they mention!

¿Qué vas a hacer? ¿Cuál es la primera cosa que vas a hacer?

a
Voy a beber champán…

b
Voy a comer chicle y patatas fritas…

c
Voy a dormir veinte horas…

d
Voy a llamar a mi madre…

e
Voy a ducharme…

f
Voy a afeitarme…

g
Me gustaría viajar…

h
Me gustaría estudiar…

i
Quiero comprar un coche nuevo…

j
Quiero buscar un trabajo…

k
Voy a casarme…

(image b:)

G The near future tense →200

The near future is formed using the present tense of **ir** plus **a** plus the **infinitive**.
¿Qué vas a **hacer**? *What are you going to do?*
Voy a **dormir**. *I'm going to sleep.*
Voy a **casar**me. *I'm going to get married.*

These expressions can also be used with the **infinitive** to talk about the future.
Quiero… *I want to…*
Quiero **comprar** un coche. *I want to buy a car.*
Me gustaría… *I would like to…*
Me gustaría **estudiar**. *I would like to study.*

3 Con tu compañero/a, pregunta y contesta.

● ¿Qué vas a hacer?

1

2

■ Primero…

■ Luego…

■ Después…

 4 Lee el texto. Contesta a las preguntas en inglés.

A ver, **en mi opinión** soy mucho más tolerante **ahora**. **También** soy menos introvertido. Vivo con Inma y hablamos mucho. Charlamos sobre nuestros problemas y también sobre nuestras alegrías.

Después de mi experiencia en la isla, **pienso que** soy una persona más fuerte. Sé que puedo sobrevivir y **además** soy más independiente.

En el futuro me gustaría formar una familia **porque** me encantan los niños. Quiero trabajar como médico y voy a viajar con Inma.

charlar = *to chat*

1 How does Benedicto say he has changed? (2 details)
2 What does he talk about with Inma? (2 details)
3 What is he like after his experience?
4 What would he like to do in the future?
5 What job would he like to do?

⭐ You can use the phrases in red to extend what you say in Spanish and add variety.
● Use time expressions: **ahora…**, **en el futuro…**
● Highlight your opinions: **en mi opinión…**, **pienso que…**
● String ideas together: **también…**, **además…**, **porque…**

 5 Lee el texto otra vez. ¿Qué significan las palabras en rojo?

 6 Escucha. Apunta los siguientes datos en inglés.

1 What is Alicia like now?
2 What is she planning for the future?

 7 Escribe una entrevista con una persona perdida en una isla desierta.

¿Qué vas a hacer?	Primero…, luego…, después…	
¿Qué tipo de persona eres ahora?	En mi opinión/Pienso que soy una persona… Ahora soy mucho más/menos… También/Además soy…	tolerante generoso/a paciente optimista
¿Qué quieres hacer en el futuro?	En el futuro voy a… Me gustaría… Quiero…	porque…

Describing yourself

You are going to play the role of someone who is taking part in a TV reality show set on a desert island. The other contestants are all members of your family. Your teacher will play the part of the interviewer. Your teacher could ask you the following:

- What type of person are you?
- What is your routine like?
- What chores do you do?
- What did you do yesterday?
- Do you get on well with your family?
- What are you going to do in the future?

Remember that you will have to respond to an unexpected question that you have not yet prepared.

You are going to listen to Lyra, an exam candidate. Listen to Lyra's answers to the examiner's first three questions and choose the correct answers.

1 ¿Cómo es tu carácter?   **2** Describe tu rutina diaria.   **3** ¿Qué tareas haces?

a A ver, por lo general soy enérgica y generosa / optimista / alegre.
b No soy perezosa, pero soy un poco pesimista / egoísta / introvertida.
c …en la isla me despierto temprano / tarde / a las ocho.
d Primero me ducho / me lavo los dientes / me baño en el mar.
e Normalmente desayuno churros / fruta / tostadas.
f …por la tarde ceno a las nueve / ocho / diez.
g Todos los días plancho la ropa / hago la cama / lavo los platos.

Listen to part 2 of Lyra's interview and fill each gap with the correct word from the box.

generoso	nunca	cené	nadé	leí	me acosté	muy	humor	hizo	pasé

– ¿Qué hiciste ayer en la isla?
– Me levanté temprano y fui a la playa. **(1)** _____ en el mar. **(2)** _____ sol y lo **(3)** _____ genial. Me encanta la natación. Luego desayuné. Arreglé mis cosas y por la tarde **(4)** _____ un poco y limpié mi dormitorio. **(5)** _____ pescado. ¡Qué rico! **(6)** _____ a las diez.

– ¿Te llevas bien con tu familia?
– Sí, me llevo bien con mi familia. Mi hermano se llama Ben y me llevo **(7)** _____, muy bien con él. Por lo general es **(8)** _____ y amable, pero a veces puede ser un poco impaciente. **(9)** _____ es agresivo. Tiene mucho sentido del **(10)** _____. Es una persona excepcional.

Now listen to part 3 of Lyra's interview and correct the mistakes in these sentences. What is the unexpected question that Lyra is asked?

1 En el futuro, no voy a hacer muchas cosas.
2 Primero me gustaría viajar y luego quiero buscar un trabajo.
3 Quiero ir a Chile porque tengo una amiga chilena…
4 …me gustaría encontrar mi novio perfecto. Va a ser muy inteligente.
5 …me gustaría casarme y también me gustaría tener animales.
6 Quiero tener ocho niños.

hablar 4 *Now it's your turn! Prepare your answers to the task and then have a conversation with your teacher or partner.*

- Use the Grade Studio and your answers to exercises 1–3 to help you plan.
- Adapt what Lyra said to talk about yourself but add your own ideas.
- Prepare your answers to the questions and try to predict what the unexpected question could be. The examiner might base this question on something you have already said, or ask something totally new!
- Record the conversation. Ask a partner to listen to it and say how well you performed.

> *Award each other one star, two stars or three stars for each of these categories:*
> - *Pronunciation*
> - *Confidence and fluency*
> - *Range of tenses*
> - *Variety of vocabulary and expressions*
> - *Using longer sentences*
> - *Taking the initiative*
>
> *What do you need to do next time to improve your performance?*

⭐ GradeStudio

Make sure you cover the basics.

- Use **simple structures** such as *soy* (I am), *es* (he/she is), *hago* (I do/make), *desayuno* (I have… for breakfast), *ceno* (I have… for dinner), *lavo* (I wash).
- Use **no** to create a **simple negative**, e.g. Lyra says *No soy perezosa.* (I'm not lazy.)
- Use **simple connectives**. Look at how Lyra uses *y* (and), *pero* (but) and *también* (also) and include these in your conversation.

To reach Grade C, show that you can:

- Use correct endings on **adjectives**, e.g. Lyra says …*pero soy un poco introvertida*. (… but I am a bit introverted.) But about Ben, she says *Nunca es agresivo.* (He is never aggressive.)
- Use **the present tense** to talk about your routine. Lyra says …*desayuno fruta… meriendo galletas…* (I have fruit for breakfast… I have biscuits for tea…)
- Use **the preterite** to describe a day in the past. Lyra says *Arreglé mis cosas y por la tarde leí un poco…* (I tidied my things and in the afternoon I read a little…)
- Use **the near future** to talk about plans. Lyra says *Voy a hacer muchas cosas.* (I am going to do lots of things.)
- Use **sequencing words**, e.g. *primero* (first of all), *después* (after that) and *luego* (then).

To increase your marks:

- Use more **complex negatives**, e.g. *Nunca lavo los platos.* (I never wash the dishes.) *No paso la aspiradora ni plancho la ropa.* (I neither vacuum nor iron.)
- Use **me gustaría** + an infinitive to say what you would like to do. Lyra says *Un día me gustaría casarme…* (One day I would like to get married…)
- Use **quiero** + infinitive to say what you want to do, e.g. *Quiero buscar un trabajo.* (I want to look for work.)
- Give **reasons**, using **porque**, e.g. *Voy a ir a Chile porque tengo una amiga chilena.* (I'm going to go to Chile because I have a Chilean friend.)

Prueba escrita

 Read the text and choose the correct title for each paragraph.

a *My future* **c** *What I look like and who's who in my family*

b *My personality* **d** *Family relations*

1 Me llamo Lucy Beale. Tengo dieciséis años. Mi cumpleaños es el 9 de diciembre. Tengo los ojos verdes y el pelo rubio y liso. Soy alta y delgada. Mis amigas dicen que soy guapa. Soy inglesa. Vivo en Albert Square en Walford. Tengo un hermano gemelo que se llama Peter. También tengo dos hermanastros – Steven y Bobby. Mi madre murió hace diez años pero vive en mi corazón.

2 No me llevo bien con mi padre. Siempre dice 'no' y me vuelve loca. Es muy egoísta y a veces puede ser agresivo o violento. Tengo una relación problemática con mi familia en general, pero me llevo bien con mi tío Christian porque tiene mucho sentido del humor y también con mi hermanastro Bobby porque es alegre y muy amable.

3 Soy bastante enérgica. Me encanta bailar. Soy independiente y valiente pero no soy muy paciente. El verano pasado trabajé en la cafetería de mi padre – ¡qué horror! No me gustó nada. ¡Nunca jamás!

4 En el futuro me gustaría trabajar como dependienta en una tienda de ropa. Luego voy a viajar. Voy a hacer muchas cosas en mi vida pero ¡nunca me voy a casar, nunca voy a tener hijos!

murió = *died*
en mi corazón = *in my heart*

 Find the equivalent of these expressions in Spanish in the text.

1 I am tall and slim.
2 I have a twin brother who is called…
3 I don't get on well with my father.
4 …he drives me crazy.
5 …sometimes he can be aggressive…
6 I have a difficult relationship with my family…
7 Last summer I worked…
8 I didn't like it at all. Never again!
9 In the future, I would like to work as a sales assistant…
10 Then I am going to travel.

 Find five sentences in the text that have a negative in them.

leer 4 Answer the following questions in English.

1 How old is Lucy and when is her birthday?
2 What colour are her eyes?
3 How long ago did her mother die?
4 What does her father do that drives her mad?
5 Who does she get on well with in her family? (2 people)
6 How does she describe her personality? (4 details)
7 Where would she like to work in the future?
8 What does she say she will never do? (2 details)

 escribir 5 You might be asked to write about your family as a controlled assessment task. Use the Grade Studio to help you prepare your account.

★ GradeStudio

Make sure you cover the basics.

- Use **simple structures** correctly, e.g. *tengo* (I have), *soy* (I am), *vivo* (I live), *es* (he/she is) and *me encanta* + infinitive (I love to…).
- Use **connectives**. Look at how Lucy uses *y* (and), *pero* (but), *también* (also) and *o* (or).
- Include a **simple negative**, e.g. *No me llevo bien con…* (I don't get on well with…).

To reach Grade C, show that you can:

- Use **the present tense** with **adjectives**. Lucy describes herself and others: *Soy alta y delgada. Es muy egoísta.* (I am tall and slim. He is very selfish.)
- Use **the preterite**. Lucy says what work she did and gives her opinion about it: *Trabajé…, No me gustó nada.* (I worked…, I didn't like it at all.)
- Use **the near future tense** to say what you are going to do. Lucy says *Voy a viajar. Voy a hacer muchas cosas.* (I am going to travel. I am going to do lots of things.)

To increase your marks:

- Give reasons, using *porque*. Can you find two examples in the text?
- Use **an exclamation**, e.g. *¡Qué horror!* (How dreadful!)
- Use *Me gustaría* + infinitive to say what you would like to do, e.g. *Me gustaría trabajar como dependienta.* (I would like to work as a shop assistant.)
- Use **less common negatives** such as *no… nada* (not at all) and *nunca* (never), e.g. *No me gustó nada.* (I didn't like it at all.) *Nunca me voy a casar.* (I am never going to get married.)

 escribir 6 Now imagine you are a character in a soap opera and write a full account of your family.

- Adapt Lucy's text and use language from Module 4 to help you.
- Structure your text carefully. Organise what you write in paragraphs.

General summary of your family
Introduce yourself

Main paragraph
Describe members of your family
- their character
- your relationship with them
Talk about your character and a job or something else you have done in the past

Conclusion
Future plans for you and your family

 escribir 7 Check carefully what you have written.

- accents
- adjective agreement (*mi padre puede ser agresivo, mi madre es guapa*)
- verb endings for all the different people (*me llamo, se llama, vivo, vive, tengo, tiene*)

Leer y escuchar

Read this letter from Isabel, who is writing about her family. Answer the questions. (4 marks)

¡Hola!

¿Qué tal? Me llamo Isabel. Soy española y vivo con mi familia en Madrid. Somos cinco en casa. Mi padre es profesor y mi madre no trabaja. Mi hermano se llama Enrique y lleva gafas. Mi hermana Susana tiene el pelo corto. ¡Me gusta mucho mi familia! Escríbeme pronto.

Un abrazo,

Isabel

⭐ Don't be put off by the length of a text. The answers appear in the same order as the questions.

1 What question does Isabel ask at the start of her letter?

2 What is her father's job?

3 How does she describe her brother Enrique?

4 How does she describe her sister's hair?

Read Vicente's advert for penfriends in England and answer the questions. Write the correct letter. (2 marks)

Vicente (16 años)

Soy alto y delgado. Tengo el pelo castaño y los ojos azules. Soy muy simpático. Quiero escribir a amigos en Inglaterra.

⭐ Take your time to match the correct answer options to the text, especially when there are two pieces of information to get right.

1 How does Vicente describe himself physically?

   a short with blond hair   **b** tall with blue eyes   **c** thin with black hair

2 How does he describe his personality?

   a friendly   **b** funny   **c** generous

Read these teacher's comments and answer the questions. Write down the person's name each time. (4 marks)

Example: Who works hard in class? Marcos

1 Who never does homework?

2 Who always arrives late for school?

3 Who doesn't wear the right uniform?

4 Who chews gum in class?

⭐ Sometimes words and phrases appear more than once in a text, e.g. the word *deberes*. Read everything in the sentence to make sure you choose the right person, e.g. in question 1 you will be looking for the word for 'never'.

Pedro	Nunca lleva su estuche ni sus cuadernos. Come chicle en clase.
Vanesa	Hace los deberes todos los días. Es muy buena estudiante.
Emilio	Siempre llega tarde al instituto. Escucha música en clase.
Example: ~~Marcos~~	~~Es un alumno simpático. Es muy trabajador en clase.~~
Daniel	Normalmente llega a tiempo al instituto. Va al club de ajedrez.
Alicia	Es una estudiante muy perezosa. Nunca hace los deberes.
Blanca	No lleva el uniforme correcto. No escucha a sus profesores.

leer 4

Read what Daniel writes about his daily routine. Write the correct letter. (4 marks)

> It's important to understand clock times in Spanish because they help you work out a sequence of events. A longer text like this probably contains information you don't need for your answer or which could distract you.

Mi rutina

Los días de colegio me levanto a las siete. Primero me ducho y luego me visto a las siete y veinte. No me gusta el uniforme porque no es muy cómodo. Tenemos que llevar una chaqueta verde y pantalones negros, y normalmente prefiero llevar un chándal y zapatillas de deporte. Desayuno a las siete y media y voy al instituto andando porque es más divertido que ir en bicicleta. Tenemos que ir al salón de actos a las ocho y media y la primera clase empieza quince minutos más tarde.

1 Daniel gets dressed at…
- **a** 7:00
- **b** 7:20
- **c** 7:30

2 Daniel describes his uniform as…
- **a** uncomfortable
- **b** boring
- **c** unfashionable

3 Outside school hours, Daniel wears a…
- **a** baseball cap
- **b** football shirt
- **c** tracksuit

4 Daniel goes to school…
- **a** on foot
- **b** by coach
- **c** by bike

escuchar 5

Listen to Rosa talking about her school routine and answer the questions. (3 marks)

1 What time do her lessons start?

2 What does she do at break time?

3 Where does she go after school?

escuchar 6

Listen to Francisco and Yolanda talking about their favourite school subjects. Which day do you think they each prefer? Write the correct letter. (1 mark for each person)

> You may not hear the subjects below mentioned. Think about what the subjects in each group have in common. This will help you to work out the correct answer.

1 Francisco

2 Yolanda

a Monday	**b** Tuesday	**c** Wednesday	**d** Thursday
History	English	PE	Biology
Geography	French	Drama	Chemistry
RE	Italian	Art	Physics

escuchar 7

Listen to Ernesto talking about his school. What does he say are the best and worst aspects? Write the correct letter. (2 marks)

> If you are asked to identify an aspect of something, e.g. the best thing about it, you will usually hear a comment about two things and have to decide between them.

1 The best aspect is the…
- **a** library **b** classrooms **c** assembly hall

2 The worst aspect is the…
- **a** athletics track **b** laboratories **c** dining room

escuchar 8

Carmen, Javier and Lucía talk about household chores. Write down the chore each finds difficult. (1 mark for each person)

> How many negative expressions can you hear in this exercise? Pay careful attention to them because they affect the meaning.

1 Carmen **2** Javier **3** Lucía

Palabras

¿Cómo eres? *What are you like?*

Soy…	*I'm…*
No soy…	*I'm not…*
alto/a	*tall*
bajo/a	*short*
delgado/a	*slim*
gordo/a	*fat*
feo/a	*ugly*
guapo/a	*attractive*
¿Cuándo es tu cumpleaños?	*When is your birthday?*
Mi cumpleaños es el (cinco) de (enero).	*My birthday is on the (fifth) of (January).*
¿De qué color son tus ojos?	*What colour are your eyes?*
Tengo los ojos…	*I have… eyes.*
azules	*blue*
marrones	*brown*
grises	*grey*
verdes	*green*
¿Cómo es tu pelo?	*What's your hair like?*
Tengo el pelo…	*I have… hair.*
blanco	*white*
castaño	*brown*
moreno	*dark*
negro	*black*
pelirrojo	*red*
rubio	*blond*
corto	*short*
largo	*long*
liso	*straight*
ondulado	*wavy*
rizado	*curly*
Llevo gafas.	*I wear glasses.*
Tengo pecas.	*I have freckles.*

Mi familia *My family*

el abuelo/la abuela	*grandfather/grandmother*
el hermanastro/la hermanastra	*stepbrother/sister*
el hermano/la hermana	*brother/sister*
el hijo/la hija	*son/daughter*
el marido	*husband*
el padrastro	*stepfather*
el padre	*father*
el primo/la prima	*cousin*
el tío/la tía	*uncle/aunt*
la madrastra	*stepmother*
la madre	*mother*
la mujer	*wife*
Me llamo…	*My name is…*
(Yo) Nací el (seis) de (junio).	*I was born on the (sixth) of (June).*
Mi padre se llama…	*My father's name is…*
enero	*January*
febrero	*February*
marzo	*March*
abril	*April*
mayo	*May*
junio	*June*
julio	*July*
agosto	*August*
septiembre	*September*
octubre	*October*
noviembre	*November*
diciembre	*December*
Tiene el pelo…	*He/She has… hair.*
Tiene los ojos…	*He/She has… eyes.*
Es calvo.	*He's bald.*
Lleva gafas.	*He/She wears glasses.*
Tiene barba.	*He has a beard.*
Tiene bigote.	*He has a moustache.*
Tiene pecas.	*He/She has freckles.*

Los supervivientes *The survivors*

Soy…	*I'm…*
alegre	*pleasant*
ambicioso/a	*ambitious*
creativo/a	*creative*
duro/a	*hard, tough*
enérgico/a	*energetic*
honesto/a	*honest*
inteligente	*intelligent*
optimista	*optimistic*
paciente	*patient*
perezoso/a	*lazy*
tolerante	*tolerant*
tranquilo/a	*calm*
trabajador(a)	*hardworking*
alemán/ana	*German*
colombiano/a	*Colombian*
escocés/esa	*Scottish*
español(a)	*Spanish*
francés/esa	*French*
galés/esa	*Welsh*
inglés/esa	*English*
irlandés/esa	*Irish*
mexicano/a	*Mexican*
peruano/a	*Peruvian*
Soy…	*I'm a…*
abogado/a	*lawyer*
diseñador(a)	*designer*
mecánico/a	*mechanic*
estudiante	*student*
Estoy…	*I'm…*
casado/a	*married*
divorciado/a	*divorced*
soltero/a	*single*
separado/a	*separated*
feliz	*happy*
triste	*sad*

Tengo mucho sentido del humor.	*I have a good sense of humour.*	Tengo una relación problemática con…	*I have a difficult relationship with…*
Me parezco a…	*I look like/I am like…*		
Me llevo bien con…	*I get on well with…*		

La vida cotidiana *Daily life*

Me despierto temprano.	*I wake up early.*	Ceno pescado.	*I eat fish for dinner.*
Me levanto.	*I get up.*	Me acuesto a las…	*I go to bed at…*
Me baño en el mar.	*I bathe in the sea.*	No me afeito nunca.	*I never shave.*
Me ducho.	*I have a shower.*	No me peino.	*I don't comb my hair.*
Me lavo.	*I wash myself.*	más tarde	*later*
Me lavo los dientes.	*I clean my teeth.*	por la tarde	*in the afternoon/evening*
Me visto.	*I get dressed.*	desde hace un año	*for a year*
Desayuno fruta.	*I have fruit for breakfast.*	Lo peor es…	*The worst thing is…*
Meriendo a las cuatro.	*I have tea at four o'clock.*		

Las tareas *Chores*

Arreglo mis cosas.	*I tidy up my things.*	Pongo la mesa.	*I lay the table.*
Cocino.	*I cook.*	Quito la mesa.	*I clear the table.*
Hago la cama.	*I make the bed.*	Trabajo en el jardín.	*I work in the garden.*
Lavo los platos.	*I wash the dishes.*	nadie	*no one*
Limpio mi dormitorio.	*I clean my bedroom.*	no… nada	*nothing*
Paso la aspiradora.	*I do the vacuuming.*	no… ni…	*neither… nor…*
Pesco.	*I fish.*	nunca	*never*
Plancho la ropa.	*I iron the clothes.*	tampoco/no… tampoco	*neither/not… either*

Otro accidente *Another accident*

Me llevo bien con…	*I get on well with…*	optimista	*optimistic*
Por lo general es…	*He/She is generally…*	pesimista	*pessimistic*
Puede ser…	*He/She can be…*	simpático/a	*nice, friendly*
agresivo/a	*aggressive*	sincero/a	*sincere*
alegre	*cheerful*	valiente	*brave*
amable	*kind*	En mi opinión…	*In my opinion…*
egoísta	*selfish*	Para mí…	*It seems to me…*
generoso/a	*generous*	Pienso que…	*I think that…*
introvertido/a	*introverted*	X era …	*X was…*
maleducado/a	*impolite, rude*	No era…	*He/She wasn't…*

Un año después *One year later*

¿Qué vas a hacer?	*What are you going to do?*	Además soy…	*I'm also…*
Voy a…	*I'm going to…*	En el futuro voy a…	*In the future I'm going to…*
afeitarme	*shave*	Me gustaría…	*I'd like to…*
beber champán	*drink champagne*	Quiero…	*I want to…*
comer chicle y patatas fritas	*chew gum and eat crisps*	buscar un trabajo	*look for a job*
dormir veinte horas	*sleep for twenty hours*	casarme	*get married*
ducharme	*have a shower*	comprar un coche nuevo	*buy a new car*
llamar a mi madre	*call my mum*	estudiar	*study*
Ahora soy mucho más (tolerante).	*Now I'm much more (tolerant).*	viajar	*travel*

Repaso *A trabajar*

Revising jobs and places where people work
Revising masculine and feminine nouns

 leer 1 Lee y completa las frases con los lugares correctos. (1–6)

 **1** Soy jardinero y trabajo en…

 **2** Soy peluquero y trabajo en…

 **3** Soy médica y trabajo en…

 **4** Soy futbolista y trabajo en…

 **5** Soy cocinera y trabajo en…

 **6** Soy recepcionista y trabajo en…

una carnicería
una clínica
una comisaría
un estadio
un hotel
un jardín
una peluquería
un restaurante

★ In Spanish you don't use the indefinite article ('a') to explain what job you do:
Soy actriz.
I'm an actress.

 escuchar 2 Escucha e identifica el trabajo y el lugar. (1–8)

Ejemplo: **1** periodista – una oficina

¿En qué trabaja usted?

Soy…/Trabajo como/de…

abogado/a, camarero/a, carpintero/a, cocinero/a, enfermero/a, ingeniero/a, jardinero/a, mecánico/a, médico/a, peluquero/a	conductor(a) diseñador(a) profesor(a)	cantante comerciante dentista futbolista periodista recepcionista soldado	**actor/actriz dependiente/ dependienta**

un garaje
un hospital
un hotel
un instituto
un taller
un teatro
una clínica
una oficina
una tienda de ropa

G *Masculine and feminine nouns* ➲208

These patterns will help you remember how to change masculine nouns (e.g. job titles) into feminine nouns.

	masculine	feminine
Most nouns ending in **-o** become **-a**:	camarero	camarera
Most nouns ending in **-or** add an **-a**:	profesor	profesora
Most nouns ending in **-ista** or **-e** do not change:	dentista	dentista
	cantante	cantante

These are some exceptions: **actor → actriz**
dependiente → dependienta

3 Traduce al español. Usa el diccionario si lo necesitas.

Ejemplo: **1** Mi padre es bombero.

1 My father is a fireman.
2 My sister is a soldier.
3 I'm a vet.
4 My friend is a farmer.
5 My neighbour is a builder.
6 My son is a postman.
7 Miguel is an electrician.

⭐ **Dictionary skills**
When you look up words, the noun is given in the masculine form, but it is usually followed by the feminine ending, e.g.:
abogado, -a.
Make sure you use the feminine ending if you are talking about a woman.
If the word is the same for both masculine and feminine, this is shown, e.g.:
soldado *m/f*

4 Lee los textos. Copia y completa la tabla en inglés.

name	job	opinion & reason	place of work	extra information
Dario				

Mi hermano se llama Dario y es actor. Le encanta su trabajo porque es muy emocionante y nunca es aburrido. Normalmente actúa en las populares telenovelas mexicanas. Trabaja en un estudio de televisión en México. Para él, el dinero y la creatividad son importantes.

Mi prima se llama Mariana y a ella no le gusta nada su trabajo porque es bastante pesado. Es cajera y trabaja en un hipermercado cerca de Málaga. Siempre está muy ocupada.

Mi nombre es Brisa y soy azafata. Trabajo para la aerolínea española Iberia. Me gusta mucho mi trabajo. Lo bueno es que viajamos a Europa, África y Latinoamérica. Es un trabajo variado y divertido.

5 *Talk about a job that someone in your family does. Answer the questions. Then write down the information using full sentences.*

- ¿De quién quieres hablar?
- ¿Cómo se llama?
- ¿En qué trabaja?
- ¿Dónde trabaja?
- ¿Le gusta su trabajo?

- Voy a hablar de mi (hermano).
- Se llama…
- Es…
- Trabaja en un/una…
- Sí, le gusta su trabajo porque es interesante / divertido / emocionante / variado.
- No, no le gusta porque es aburrido / pesado.

❝❞ Cognates look similar to an English word and mean the same, but they are pronounced differently.

ingeniero *een – hen – yeh – ro*
oficina *o – fee – thee – na*

Pay attention to accents – stress the accented part of the word:
mecánico *meh – **kah** – nee – ko*

Listen and repeat these cognates:
secretario   actriz   clínica
médico   dentista   policía
actor

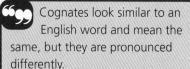

1 ¿Trabajas los sábados?

Escucha. Copia y completa la tabla. (1–5)

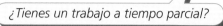
	¿Trabajo?	¿Cuándo?	¿Cuánto ganas?
1	peluquero	los fines de semana	6€ a la hora

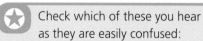
Check which of these you hear as they are easily confused:

¿Cuándo…?   When…?
¿Cuánto…?   How much…?

Lee las descripciones y escribe la letra correcta.

Reparto periódicos.

Hago de canguro.

1 Los sábados tengo que cuidar a niños pequeños.
2 Todos los días tengo que levantarme muy temprano.
3 En mi trabajo tengo que servir comida y bebida a los clientes.
4 Cuando trabajo tengo que usar agua y jabón.
5 Los fines de semana tengo que vender zapatos.
6 En mi trabajo tengo que vigilar a la gente que nada en la piscina.
7 En mi trabajo tengo que cortar la hierba y plantar flores.

Trabajo como dependienta.

Trabajo como camarero.

Lavo coches.

Trabajo como jardinera.

Trabajo como socorrista.

Read the dialogue with your partner. Then make up another dialogue, using the pictures or your own ideas.

● ¿Tienes un trabajo a tiempo parcial?
■ Sí. Reparto leche. Tengo que levantarme temprano y ser puntual.
● ¿Cuándo trabajas?
■ Trabajo por las mañanas de cinco y media a siete.
● ¿Cuánto ganas?
■ No gano mucho. Sólo gano seis euros con cincuenta a la hora.

punctual

Saturdays 8 pm–10 pm

10€

Los sábados Por las mañanas Por las tardes Todos los días Los fines de semana	tengo que	cuidar a niños vender zapatos/ropa servir comida a los clientes vigilar a la gente que nada en la piscina levantarme temprano coger el autobús ser puntual
(No) Gano mucho/Gano poco.		

leer 4 **Read Mónica's email and choose the four statements that apply.**

1 Mónica works for eight hours a day.
2 Mónica works part-time in an office.
3 Mónica's father is a watchmaker.
4 Mónica has to wear smart clothes.
5 Mónica has to answer the phone and make coffee.
6 Mónica has to get lunch for the employees.
7 Mónica works Saturdays.

G Tener que + *infinitive*

To say *have to* in Spanish, use the verb **tener** followed by **que** and the **infinitive** of the main verb.
Tengo que ser puntual.
I have to arrive on time.
Tengo que levantarme temprano.
I have to get up early.

¿Qué tal? Pues, yo estoy bien. Trabajo a tiempo parcial. Lo bueno es que gano ocho euros a la hora. Lo malo es que trabajo cada sábado de ocho de la mañana a seis y media de la tarde.

Tengo que trabajar como recepcionista en la oficina de mi padre. Mi padre es contable y tengo que ir bien vestida. No me gusta nada porque prefiero llevar vaqueros y unas zapatillas de deporte.

Por un lado el trabajo es interesante. Por otro lado es difícil. Normalmente tengo que contestar el teléfono. También a veces tengo que hacer café para los clientes. Los clientes de mi padre son muy serios y a veces son un poco antipáticos.

¿Y tú? ¿Trabajas?

Un abrazo, **Mónica** ☺☺☺

contable = *accountant*
bien vestido/a = *well dressed*

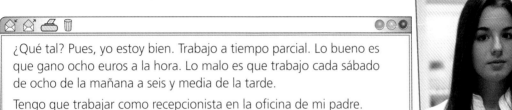

leer 5 Lee el texto otra vez. Copia y completa la tabla en inglés. (P = opinión positiva, N = opinión negativa, P+N = opinión positiva y negativa.)

	pay	working hours	clothes	duties	people
P/N/P+N	P				
details	€8/hour				

escuchar 6 Escucha. ¿Qué hacen? Escribe P, N o P+N. (1–4)

Ejemplo: **1** shop assistant – sells books, P

escribir 7 **You are working part-time in a shoe shop. Include positive and negative opinions as you write about:**

● *what you do* — Soy… Trabajo en un/una…
● *your opinion of it* — Me encanta/Odio mi trabajo porque es variado / aburrido /…
● *your working hours* — Trabajo de… a…
● *how much you earn* — Gano… a la hora.
● *what you do* — Tengo que levantarme…/coger…/ser…/vender…
● *what the clients are like* — Los clientes son interesantes / antipáticos /…

- Describing work experience
- Using the preterite and the imperfect tense

2 Prácticas laborales

 escuchar 1 Escucha y escribe el nombre correcto. (1–6)

Ejemplo: **1** Lilia

Eva
 *Hice mis prácticas laborales en una escuela.*

Jorge
 *Fui a trabajar a una tienda de ropa.*

Lilia
 *Hice mis prácticas laborales en una oficina.*

José
 *Trabajé en un polideportivo.*

Inmaculada
 *Trabajé en una empresa inglesa.*

Emilio
 *Trabajé en un restaurante.*

 leer 2 **Read the phrases and write down who may have done this activity as part of their work experience (Eva, Jorge, Lilia, José, Inmaculada or Emilio). Justify your answer.**

Ejemplo: **1** Lilia – you write letters and send emails in an office

1	Escribí cartas y mandé correos electrónicos.
2	Ayudé a los niños.
3	Hablé con los clientes en inglés.
4	Contesté llamadas telefónicas.
5	Vendí vaqueros.
6	Serví comida y refrescos.
7	Di clases de natación.

di = *I gave*

 hablar 3 Con tu compañero/a, pregunta y contesta. Utiliza los dibujos.

- ¿Dónde hiciste tus prácticas laborales?

- ■ Hice mis prácticas laborales en / /

- ¿Qué hiciste?

- ■ / /

- ¿Te gustó trabajar allí?

- ■ Lo pasé bien / Fue aburrido / Lo pasé fatal.

4 Lee e identifica los verbos en el pretérito.

Ejemplo: hice,…

Mi nombre es Ana Hernández de López. En junio hice mis prácticas en un hospital. Lo pasé muy bien pero fue un poco duro.

Trabajé con un equipo de enfermeros. El hospital era grande con quinientos pacientes. Mis pacientes eran muy simpáticos y mi jefa María era muy buena, pero un poco severa a veces.

Tuve responsabilidades diferentes. Ayudé a los pacientes, limpié la sala y serví té. El último día organicé una fiesta de cumpleaños para Teo, un niño enfermo de siete años. Sobre todo aprendí a trabajar en equipo y a hablar con los pacientes.

un equipo de enfermeros = *a team of nurses*
jefe/a = *boss*
la sala (de un hospital) = *a (hospital) ward*

 5 Lee otra vez y contesta a las preguntas.

1 Where did Ana do her work experience?
2 What did she think of it? (2 details)
3 What were the patients like?
4 What was her boss like? (2 details)
5 What were her responsibilities? (2 details)
6 What did she organise? Who was it for?
7 What did she learn during the week? (2 details)

 6 Listen to Miguel talking about his work experience and make notes under the following headings.

1 Building
2 Boss
3 Clients
4 Responsibilities and what he learnt

G Using past tenses ⟳ 196, 198

Use the **preterite** for completed actions in the past.

	-ar verbs	**-er** verbs	**-ir** verbs	**ir** *(to go)/* **ser** *(to be)*
(yo)	trabajé	comí	escribí	fui
(tú)	trabajaste	comiste	escribiste	fuiste
(él/ella/usted)	trabajó	comió	escribió	fue

El primer día **bebí** mucho café. *The first day I drank a lot of coffee.*

Use the **imperfect** to describe what something was like.
El edificio **era** muy moderno. *The building was very modern.*
Los pacientes **eran** simpáticos. *The patients were nice.*

 7 Escribe sobre tus prácticas.

Hice mis prácticas laborales en enero, febrero, … del año pasado/de este año.
Trabajé en un/una… Era moderno/a, antiguo/a, grande, pequeño/a.
Mi jefe/a era… y…
Los clientes eran agresivo/a(s), alegre(s), amable(s), callado/a(s), egoísta(s), maleducado/a(s), respetuoso/a(s), serio/a(s), simpático/a(s), tolerante(s).
Lo pasé bien/fatal. Fue divertido, aburrido, interesante.
Serví…, ayudé…, escribí…, mandé… hablé…, contesté…
Aprendí mucho. No aprendí nada.
Por ejemplo, aprendí a trabajar en equipo, ayudar a la gente, servir…, contestar…

- Describing future plans
- Using a variety of verbs to refer to the future

3 El futuro

leer 1 Lee y escribe el futuro de estos famosos.

1 *have a family*

Quiero…

2 *get a job*

Voy a…

3 *live abroad*

Me gustaría…

4 *go to university*

Quiero…

5 *do volunteer work*

Voy a…

6 *keep studying*

Me gustaría…

seguir estudiando
encontrar trabajo
ir a la universidad
trabajar como voluntario/a en…
vivir en el extranjero
formar una familia

escuchar 2 Listen and pick the correct letter. Can you note down any extra information about their future plans? (1–6)

a   b   c   d   e   f

la gente ciega = *blind people*

hablar 3 Talk about the future with your partner. Use the information in English and your own ideas.

- ¿Qué vas a hacer el año que viene?
- El año que viene voy a… *get a job*
- ¿Qué te gustaría hacer después del cole?
- Después del cole me gustaría… *do voluntary work*
- ¿Qué quieres hacer en los próximos cinco años?
- En los próximos cinco años quiero… *go to university*
- ¿Qué vas a hacer en el futuro?
- En el futuro voy a… *live abroad*

G   The future   ➲200

In Module 4 you saw these different ways to refer to your activities in the future. Use them to add variety to what you say about the future. They will help you to achieve a higher grade.

1 querer + infinitive *(to want to…)*
El año que viene **quiero ir** a la universidad.
I want to go to university next year.

2 me gustaría + infinitive *(I would like to…)*
En el verano **me gustaría ir** a Madrid.
In the summer I would like to go to Madrid.

3 the near future tense: **ir a + infinitive**
Voy a ser médico.
I'm going to be a doctor.

88   ochenta y ocho

4 **Listen and write a phrase in English for each letter below. (1–4)**

	If I...	I am going to...
1	A	be an air hostess and travel a lot
2	do more sport	B
3	C	do a vocational course
4	work a lot	D

Si (no) apruebo mis exámenes,	**voy a ir** a la universidad
Si trabajo mucho,	**voy a encontrar** trabajo
Si tengo dinero,	**voy a hacer** un curso de formación profesional
Si practico más deporte,	**voy a ser** (médico/a)
Si tengo suerte,	**voy a ganar** mucho dinero
	voy a viajar mucho
	voy a jugar al fútbol en…
	voy a ser famoso/a

5 **Read Gabriela's text and answer the questions in English.**

1 Where does Gabriela want to work and why?
2 If she passes her exams, what will she do?
3 What will happen if she doesn't? (3 details)
4 What does she say about her brother? (2 details)
5 How does Gabriela feel about foreign travel?

¡Hola! **Me llamo** Gabriela. **Tengo** dieciséis años y **vivo** en Cali, en Colombia. En el futuro, **quiero** vivir y trabajar en Cali porque mi familia **vive** allí. En Cali **hay** mucho desempleo y **es** difícil encontrar un buen trabajo. Si **apruebo** mis exámenes, **voy a ir** a la universidad para estudiar inglés. Sin embargo, si no **apruebo** mis exámenes, **voy a buscar** un trabajo como dependienta en el centro comercial cerca de mi casa. Mi hermano **trabaja** como profesor y en el futuro **va a viajar** al extranjero. A mí también **me gustaría** viajar a otros países. Escríbeme pronto.
Un abrazo, Gabriela

6 **Escribe sobre tu futuro.**

Introducción

Me llamo..., tengo... años y estudio...
Trabajo los sábados en un/una...

Tus planes

Después del cole quiero...
En los próximos cinco años me gustaría...
Si apruebo mis exámenes, voy a...
Si trabajo mucho, voy a...

Tu familia

Mi hermano quiere..., va a...

G **'If' clauses**

Use 'if' clauses to talk about possibilities in the future:
Si + **present, near future tense**

Si **trabajo** mucho, **voy a ganar** mucho dinero.
If I work a lot, I am going to earn a lot of money.

★ To aim for a C Grade or above, try to use a range of tenses. Gabriela has used the present tense, near future tense and conditional (**me gustaría** + infinitive). Can you work out which colour represents which tense?

4 Mi currículum vitae

 leer 1 Lee los textos. Busca las expresiones en español para estas frases.

a from 9 am till 11 am
b I taught in a mixed school.
c I'm interested in nature.
d I have three small children.

Me llamo **Pedro** y soy bastante tímido. Me gustaría trabajar de nueve a once de la mañana. El año pasado trabajé en una carnicería.

Me llamo **Alicia**. Hablo francés y español. El año pasado trabajé como profesora en un instituto mixto en Madrid.

Me llamo **Leandro** y busco un trabajo interesante. Soy creativo y me interesa la naturaleza.

Me llamo **Fátima** y soy ama de casa. Tengo tres hijos pequeños. Me interesa la informática y tengo un PC en casa.

 leer 2 Read the job ads (a–e) and then match each person in exercise 1 to the appropriate job. There is one ad too many.

Ejemplo: **Pedro** – d

a Se buscan profesores de idiomas. Interesados deben rellenar el siguiente formulario: http://ralimis.com/idiomas.

b Se necesita recepcionista para trabajar a tiempo parcial en una empresa internacional. Recepción de llamadas y atención al cliente. Incorporación inmediata. Tfno.: 91 462 31 18

c Se busca chico o chica joven para una floristería. Se ofrece horario flexible y no es necesario tener experiencia. Envíe una carta de presentación con currículum vitae y referencias al Apartado de Correos 1349, Oviedo.

d Se necesita carnicero y panadero para trabajar durante las mañanas en el mercado. Preferible con experiencia. Interesados deben llamar al 95 248 80 39

e ¿Eres ama de casa? ¿Tienes ordenador? Importante empresa ofrece trabajo desde tu domicilio. Experiencia no necesaria. Dominio de inglés preferible.

rellenar el siguiente formulario = *fill in the following form*
incorporación inmediata = *immediate start*

⭐ There is a lot of information in these texts. Try using these steps to help you match them up.
● Write down key words for each person, e.g. **Pedro – tímido, 9–11 las mañanas, año pasado carnicería**
● Then scan the ads to see if anything there matches your key words. In ad **d** you can see **carnicero** *(butcher)*, **con experiencia** *(experience required)* and **mañanas** *(mornings)*. These things match Pedro's information.

 escuchar 3 Listen and write down the letter of a job ad from exercise 2 for each person. (1–4)

4 Lee el currículum vitae imaginario de Shakira. Lee las frases y escribe V (verdadero), F (falso) o NM (no se menciona).

1 Nació en Colombia.
2 Habla dos idiomas.
3 Vive en Europa.
4 Le interesan los deportes.
5 Le encantan las flores y las plantas.
6 Su primera canción se llama *Servicio de lavandería*.

Currículum Vitae

Datos personales
Nombres: Shakira Isabel
Apellidos: Mebarak Ripoll
Dirección: Calle Salsa, Miami, Florida, Estados Unidos
Móvil: 07767 259011
Correo electrónico: shakira@gmail.com
Fecha de nacimiento: 2 de febrero de 1977
Lugar de nacimiento: Barranquilla, Colombia

Educación
Colegio Nuestra Señora de la Enseñanza

Experiencia laboral
- Con ocho años hice mi primera canción para mi padre: *Tus gafas oscuras*.
- En 2002 me hice famosa con el álbum *Servicio de lavandería*.
- Gané dos Premios Grammy y ocho Premios Grammy Latino.

Otros datos
Idiomas: español e inglés
Cualidades: inteligente, positiva, viva
Pasatiempos: jardinería, naturaleza
Referencias: Sony Music

5 Mira el CV de Shakira y escucha. ¿Habla Shakira? Escribe S (sí) o N (no). (1–4)

6 Escribe tu propio currículum vitae o un currículum vitae para un(a) famoso/a.

Currículum Vitae

Datos personales
Nombres:
Apellidos:
Dirección:
Móvil:
Correo electrónico:
Fecha de nacimiento:
Lugar de nacimiento:

Educación
Colegio…

Experiencia laboral
- Con… años trabajé en…

Otros datos
Idiomas:
Cualidades:
Pasatiempos:

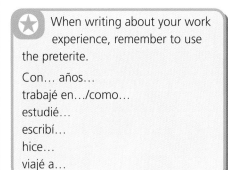
When writing about your work experience, remember to use the preterite.
Con… años…
trabajé en…/como…
estudié…
escribí…
hice…
viajé a…

- Conducting a job interview
- Forming the perfect tense

5 La entrevista

 1 Lee y empareja las frases con los dibujos. Escribe la letra correcta.

1 He trabajado en equipo.

2 He hablado idiomas extranjeros.

3 He hecho un curso de informática.

4 He mandado correos electrónicos.

5 He hablado por teléfono.

a
Bonjour, je m'appelle Sarah.

b

c

d

e

2 Escucha y lee. Escribe las palabras. (1–8)

Pregunta: ¿Qué ha estudiado usted en el instituto?
Respuesta: He estudiado asignaturas típicas como inglés, **(1)** ▢
y ciencias, pero he tenido clases de hechizos y trucos de magia.
P: ¿Por qué quiere ser **(2)** ▢ de magia?
R: Quiero ser profesor de magia porque me **(3)** ▢ la magia
y me interesa lo sobrenatural.
P: ¿Qué experiencia laboral tiene usted?
R: He enseñado magia en un colegio **(4)** ▢.
P: ¿Qué es importante para usted?
R: Los niños son muy **(5)** ▢.
P: ¿Ha trabajado en equipo antes?
R: Sí, he trabajado en equipo con mis
(6) ▢, sobre todo con mi amiga Hermione.
P: ¿Qué cualidades tiene usted?
R: Soy amable, inocente y **(7)** ▢.
P: ¿Cuál es su dirección electrónica?
R: Es… **(8)** ▢.

G *The perfect tense* ➔**198**

The perfect tense is used to say what you *have done*.
He trabajado…   *I have worked…*

Forming the perfect tense:
present tense of **haber** + past participle

(yo)	**he**	trabajado
(tú)	**has**	comido
(él/ella/usted)	**ha**	vivido

Form the past participle by taking the infinitive,
removing **-ar**, **-er** or **-ir**, and adding the ending
-ado (for **-ar** verbs) or **-ido** (for **-er** and **-ir** verbs).

Ha vivido en España. *She has lived in Spain.*

Some past participles are irregular:
hacer → hecho   escribir → escrito
ver → visto   poner → puesto

leer 3 Lee la conversación del ejercicio 2 y contesta a las preguntas.

1 What traditional school subjects has the interviewee studied?
2 Why does he want to be a teacher of magic? (2 details)
3 What experience does he have?
4 What is important to him?
5 Why does he mention his friend Hermione?
6 What is he like? (2 details)

leer 4 *Look at the conversation in exercise 2 again. Write down the four phrases in which the interviewee uses the perfect tense.*

escuchar 5 *Listen to the job interview with Yesenia and answer the questions in English.*

1 What has she studied?
2 What job is she applying for? Why?
3 What experience does she have?
4 What is important to her?
5 What is she like? (2 details)
6 What is her email address?

ZONA CULTURA

In a job interview the questions are most likely to be asked in the **usted** form, as it is a formal situation and usually the two people don't know each other. However, some interviewers may use the **tú** form. Look at the interview in exercise 2. Which form is used there? What about Yesenia's interview in exercise 5?

hablar 6 *Look at the pictures below and create a job interview using the information. Then invent your own job interview with your partner.*

¿Cómo te llamas?	Me llamo…/Mi nombre es…
¿Qué has estudiado?	He estudiado inglés, matemáticas,…
¿Por qué quieres trabajar como…?	Porque me gusta tener responsabilidades/tener un trabajo creativo/ganar un buen sueldo.
¿Qué experiencia laboral tienes?	He trabajado en…, he servido…, he hecho…
	He hablado…, he escrito…, he estudiado…
¿Has trabajado en equipo antes?	Sí, he trabajado en equipo antes.
	No, nunca he trabajado en equipo.
¿Qué es importante para ti?	La gente/El dinero/La naturaleza es importante…/
	Los niños/Los animales son importantes para mí.
¿Cómo eres?/¿Qué cualidades tienes?	Soy amable, sincero/a, trabajador(a),…
¿Cuál es tu correo electrónico?	Mi correo electrónico es…

Prueba oral

Jobs

You are going to have a conversation with your teacher about part-time jobs. Your teacher could ask you the following:

- Do you have a part-time job at the moment?
- What does your job involve?
- When do you work?
- Do you like your job?
- Did you have a part-time job last year?
- What sort of work would you like to do in the future?

Remember that you will have to respond to an unexpected question that you have not yet prepared.

 1

You are going to listen to Katie, an exam candidate, taking part in the above conversation with her teacher. Listen to part 1 and match the two halves of Katie's answers.

> ¿Tienes un trabajo a tiempo parcial?

> ¿Qué haces en el supermercado?

1 Tengo un trabajo…
2 Es un supermercado bastante…
3 Trabajo como dependienta…
4 Siempre tengo que…
5 Y a veces tengo que…
6 Lo bueno es que…

a …contestar el teléfono.
b …y tengo que hacer muchas cosas.
c …fregar el suelo del supermercado.
d …no tengo que levantarme temprano.
e …a tiempo parcial en un supermercado.
f …pequeño pero vende alimentos, bebidas y ropa.

 2

Listen to part 2 of Katie's conversation and fill each gap with the correct word from the box.

> fregar el suelo = mop the floor

media	ocho	bastante	de	seis	porque	sábado	bueno	llevar	malo

– ¿Cuándo trabajas?
– Normalmente trabajo cada **(1)** _____ de nueve de la mañana a **(2)** _____ de la tarde. A veces trabajo los domingos **(3)** _____ once de la mañana a seis y **(4)** _____ de la tarde.
– ¿Te gusta tu trabajo?
– Por lo general me gusta mi trabajo **(5)** _____ es muy fácil y la gente es **(6)** _____ simpática. Lo **(7)** _____ es el uniforme. Odio el uniforme porque es realmente feo. Tenemos que **(8)** _____ una gorra marrón. ¡Qué vergüenza! Lo **(9)** _____ es el dinero. Gano **(10)** _____ euros por hora y es mucho más que en las tiendas de ropa o en las cafeterías.

 3

Now listen to part 3 and rewrite the jumbled words in bold in each sentence.

1 Trabajé como socorrista en un **deilprotivoop**.
2 **énabimT** hice de canguro.
3 Me encantó porque es un **jorabta** fácil y divertido.
4 Me gustaría trabajar con **saileman**.
5 Este **oraven** voy a ir al campo para trabajar en una granja.
6 Me **ríasutag** aprender a **rache** equitación.

4 *What is the unexpected question that Katie is asked in part 3?*

 5 *Now it's your turn! Prepare your answers to the task and then have a conversation with your teacher or partner.*

- Use the Grade Studio and your answers to exercises 1–4 to help you plan.
- Adapt what Katie said to talk about yourself but add your own ideas.
- Prepare your answers to the questions and try to predict what the unexpected question could be. The examiner might base this question on something you have already said, or ask something totally new!
- Record the conversation. Ask a partner to listen to it and say how well you performed.

> *Award each other one star, two stars or three stars for each of these categories:*
> - *Pronunciation*
> - *Confidence and fluency*
> - *Range of tenses*
> - *Variety of vocabulary and expressions*
> - *Using longer sentences*
> - *Taking the initiative*
>
> *What do you need to do next time to improve your performance?*

⭐ GradeStudio

Make sure you cover the basics.
- Include **simple opinions**, e.g. *me gusta(n)* (I like), *odio* (I hate).
- Use **basic connectives** to make your sentences longer, such as *y* (and), *pero* (but), *o* (or) and *también* (also). Look at how Katie uses these.
- Use **simple structures** correctly, e.g. *tengo* (I have), *trabajo* (I work), *es* (it is) and *gano* (I earn).

To reach Grade C, show that you can:
- Use **time** and **frequency expressions** to add detail, such as *cada sábado* (every Saturday), *de la mañana* (a.m.), *de la tarde* (p.m.), *desde… hasta…* (from… to…).
- Don't forget to use **adjectives** and **qualifiers** to enhance what you say, e.g. *bastante pequeño* (quite small), *muy fácil* (very easy) and *muy importante* (very important).
- Your **verb tenses** must also be **accurate**. Katie uses:
  - **the present tense** to say what she does now, e.g. *Tengo un trabajo a tiempo parcial.* (I have a part-time job.)
  - **the preterite** to say what she did last year, e.g. *Trabajé como socorrista en un polideportivo.* (I worked as a lifeguard in a sports centre.)
  - **the near future tense** to talk about her plans, e.g. *Voy a ir al campo.* (I'm going to go to the country.)

To increase your marks:
- Use **verbs followed by an infinitive** such as *Tengo que contestar el teléfono.* (I have to answer the phone.)
- Express **opinions** using *Lo bueno/Lo malo. Lo bueno es el dinero.* (The good thing is the money.) *Lo malo es el uniforme.* (The bad thing is the uniform.)
- Use an **if clause** such as *si* + present tense + near future. *Si tengo un trabajo interesante, voy a ser feliz.* (If I have an interesting job, I am going to be happy.)
- Use **the imperfect** to describe people or places connected with your job last year: *Mi jefe era severo.* (My boss was strict.) *Los clientes eran simpáticos.* (The clients were nice.)

Prueba escrita

Los trabajos **5**

leer 1 Read the text and choose the correct title for each paragraph.
What words/phrases in the text support your decision?

a The tasks I did   **b** My work and study plans   **c** Getting to work   **d** The final day

❶ Me llamo Joel. Tengo quince años y estudio en el instituto St Peters, en Leeds. El mes pasado hice mis prácticas en una oficina durante quince días. Normalmente me levanto a las siete y media y voy al instituto a pie pero el primer día de las prácticas me levanté a las seis de la mañana. Cogí el tren al centro de Londres y después cogí el metro pero desafortunadamente llegué tarde.

❷ Hice muchas cosas durante mis prácticas. Durante la semana hablé con los clientes y contesté llamadas telefónicas. También mandé muchos correos, escribí cartas y a la hora de comer salí a comprar bocadillos. Nunca hice café. Mi jefe era muy simpático y bastante divertido.

❸ El último día hice muchas fotocopias. No me gusta nada hacer fotocopias porque es muy aburrido. Comí una pizza en la cantina con un amigo nuevo que se llama Sam, y luego terminé muy temprano, a las tres de la tarde. ¡Eso me gustó mucho!

Joel

❹ Sin embargo la experiencia no me gustó nada porque fue un poco pesada. En el futuro, no voy a trabajar en una oficina. Me gustaría hacer un trabajo creativo y no quiero usar un ordenador todos los días. Si apruebo mis exámenes, quiero estudiar dibujo en la universidad.

leer 2 Find the equivalent of these expressions in Spanish in the text.

1 Last month…
2 I did my work experience…
3 …for a fortnight.
4 I got up at 6 am
5 …unfortunately I arrived late.

6 I did lots of things…
7 …I went out to buy sandwiches.
8 My boss was very nice…
9 I really don't like photocopying…
10 I liked that a lot!

leer 3 Find the preterite of each of these verbs in Joel's text and translate them.

Example: hacer → hice (I did)

coger   hablar   mandar   escribir   salir

Now can you find two other verbs in the preterite that Joel uses to say what he did?

leer 4 Read the text again and answer the questions in English.

1 How long did Joel's work experience last?
2 What time does Joel normally get up?
3 How did Joel travel to work on his first day? (2 details)
4 Name four things Joel had to do as part of his work.
5 What task did Joel not enjoy?
6 What did Joel and Sam do together?
7 What did Joel think of his work experience?
8 What kind of job would Joel prefer?

escribir 5

You might be asked to write about your work experience as a controlled assessment task. Use the Grade Studio to help you prepare your account.

⭐ GradeStudio

Make sure you cover the basics.

- Use **simple structures** correctly, e.g. *me llamo* (my name is), *tengo* (I have/I am [age]) and *estudio* (I study).
- Include some words in the **preterite**, e.g. *hice* (I did), *escribí* (I wrote) and *comí* (I ate).
- Use **simple connectives** to join your sentences, e.g. Joel uses *y* (and), *pero* (but) and *también* (also).

To reach Grade C, show that you can:

- Use **the present tense**. Joel talks about himself and his normal routine, e.g. *me llamo Joel* and *me levanto a las siete y media*.
- Use **the preterite**. Joel talks about what he did on certain days, e.g. *llegué tarde* and *mandé muchos correos*.
- Use **the near future tense**. Joel talks about his future plans, e.g. *no voy a trabajar en una oficina*.
- Use **time expressions**, e.g. *normalmente* (normally), *durante la semana* (during the week), *el primer/ último día* (on the first/last day), *a la hora de comer* (at lunchtime), *de la mañana/tarde* (a.m./p.m.)
- Give **reasons** with *porque* (because). Can you find an example of where Joel does this?

To increase your marks:

- Refer to **the future** in **different ways**. As well as the near future tense, Joel uses *me gustaría* and *(no) quiero* with an infinitive. Can you find them in the text?
- Give your **opinion** in **the preterite**. Can you find where Joel gives his opinion about his work experience? Is it positive or negative?
- Include an example of **the imperfect tense**. Joel describes his boss using *era* (he was): *Mi jefe era muy simpático y bastante divertido.*

escribir 6

Now write a full account of your work experience.

- Adapt Joel's text and use language from Module 5.
- If you need to look up an adjective in a dictionary, remember that it will be given in the masculine singular form and you may need to change it to the feminine, e.g. quiet = *tranquilo* → *tranquila*; *Mi jefa era tranquila.* – My boss (female) was quiet.
- Remember to structure your text carefully. Organise what you write in paragraphs.

General summary of work experience

Introduce yourself

Main paragraph

Talk about your work experience
- *How did you get to work?*
- *Who did you work with?*
- *Describe where you worked*
- *What did you do every day?*
- *Talk about any special events*
- *Describe your boss or someone you worked with*

Conclusion

How was your work experience?
What are your plans for the future?

escribir 7

Check carefully what you have written.

- verb endings (preterite – all regular verbs take an accent in the 'I' form: *comí*, etc.)
- reflexive 'routine' verbs (have you included *me*? *me levanté*)
- grammar (check *a el* has been shortened to *al*)

Palabras

A trabajar   *Off to work*

Trabajo en…	*I work in…*
Trabaja en…	*He/She works in…*
un estadio	*a stadium*
un hotel	*a hotel*
un jardín	*a garden*
un restaurante	*a restaurant*
una carnicería	*a butcher's*
una clínica	*a clinic*
una comisaría	*a police station*
una peluquería	*a hairdresser's*
¿En qué trabaja usted?	*What is your job?*
Trabajo como/de…	*I work as a…*
Soy…	*I am a…*
Es…	*He/She is a…*
abogado/a	*lawyer*
actor/actriz	*actor/actress*
camarero/a	*waiter*
cantante	*singer*
carpintero/a	*carpenter*
cocinero/a	*cook*
comerciante	*businessman/woman*
conductor(a)	*driver*
dentista	*dentist*
dependiente/a	*shop assistant*
diseñador(a)	*designer*
enfermero/a	*nurse*
futbolista	*footballer*
ingeniero/a	*engineer*
jardinero/a	*gardener*
mecánico/a	*mechanic*
médico/a	*doctor*
peluquero/a	*hairdresser*
periodista	*journalist*
profesor(a)	*teacher*
recepcionista	*receptionist*
soldado	*soldier*
Me gusta mi trabajo…	*I like my job…*
Le gusta su trabajo…	*He/She likes his/her job…*
porque es…	*because it's…*
variado	*varied*
pesado	*tedious*

¿Trabajas los sábados?   *Do you work on Saturdays?*

¿Tienes un trabajo a tiempo parcial?	*Do you have a part-time job?*
¿Cuándo trabajas?	*When do you work?*
¿Cuánto ganas?	*How much do you earn?*
Gano mucho.	*I earn a lot.*
Gano poco.	*I don't earn much.*
Gano… a la hora.	*I earn… an hour.*
Hago de canguro.	*I'm a babysitter*
Lavo coches.	*I wash cars.*
Reparto periódicos.	*I deliver newspapers.*
Trabajo como camarero/a.	*I work as a waiter/waitress.*
Trabajo como dependiente/a.	*I work as a shop assistant.*
Trabajo como jardinero/a.	*I work as a gardener.*
Trabajo como socorrista.	*I work as a lifeguard.*
los fines de semana	*at weekends*
los sábados	*on Saturdays*
por las mañanas	*in the mornings*
por las tardes	*in the afternoons/evenings*
todos los días	*every day*
de (nueve) a (seis)	*from (nine) to (six)*
Tengo que…	*I have to…*
coger el autobús	*catch the bus*
cuidar a niños	*look after children*
levantarme temprano	*get up early*
ser puntual	*be on time*
servir comida a los clientes	*serve food to the customers*
vender zapatos	*sell shoes*
vender ropa	*sell clothes*
vigilar a la gente que nada	*supervise the swimmers*
Me encanta mi trabajo porque…	*I love my job because…*
Odio mi trabajo porque…	*I hate my job because…*
Los clientes son severos.	*The clients are difficult.*

Prácticas laborales   *Work experience*

Trabajé en…	*I worked in…*
Hice mis prácticas laborales en…	*I did my work experience in…*
un polideportivo	*a sports centre*
un restaurante	*a restaurant*
una empresa inglesa	*an English company*
una escuela	*a school*
una oficina	*an office*
una tienda de ropa	*a clothes shop*
Ayudé a los niños.	*I helped the children.*
Contesté llamadas telefónicas.	*I answered the phone.*
Di clases de natación.	*I gave swimming lessons.*
Escribí cartas y mandé correos electrónicos.	*I wrote letters and sent emails.*
Hablé con los clientes.	*I talked to the customers.*
Vendí vaqueros.	*I sold jeans.*
Mi jefe era…	*My boss was…*
Los clientes eran…	*The customers were…*
Lo pasé bien.	*I had a good time.*
Lo pasé fatal.	*I had a dreadful time.*
Fue…	*It was…*
Aprendí mucho.	*I learnt a lot.*
No aprendí nada.	*I didn't learn anything.*
Aprendí a…	*I learnt to…*

El futuro   *The future*

Quiero…	*I want to…*
Voy a…	*I'm going to…*
Me gustaría…	*I'd like to…*
encontrar trabajo	*get a job*
ir a la universidad	*go to university*
seguir estudiando	*continue studying*
formar una familia	*have a family*
trabajar como voluntario/a	*work as a volunteer*
vivir en el extranjero	*live abroad*
Si apruebo mis exámenes…	*If I pass my exams…*
Si practico más deporte…	*If I practise more sport…*
Si tengo suerte…	*If I'm lucky…*
Si trabajo mucho…	*If I work hard…*
voy a…	*I'll…*
encontrar un trabajo	*find a job*
ganar mucho dinero	*earn lots of money*
hacer un curso de formación profesional	*do a vocational training course*
ir a la universidad	*go to university*
jugar al fútbol en…	*play football in…*
ser famoso/a	*be famous*
ser (médico/a)	*be a (doctor)*
viajar mucho	*travel a lot*
el año que viene	*next year*
después del cole	*after school*
en los próximos cinco años	*in the next five years*
en el futuro	*in the future*

Mi currículum vitae   *My CV*

el anuncio	*(job) advert*
a tiempo parcial	*part-time*
dominio del inglés	*ability to speak English*
envíe una carta de presentación	*send a letter of introduction*
experiencia no necesaria	*experience not necessary*
horario flexible	*flexible hours*
incorporación inmediata	*starting immediately*
preferible con experiencia	*preferably with experience*
Interesados deben…	*If you're interested you should …*
llamar a…	*call…*
rellenar el siguiente formulario	*fill in the following form*
nombre(s)	*first name(s)*
apellido(s)	*surname(s)*
dirección	*address*
móvil	*mobile number*
correo electrónico	*email address*
fecha de nacimiento	*date of birth*
lugar de nacimiento	*place of birth*
educación	*education*
experiencia laboral	*work experience*
otros datos	*other information*
idiomas	*languages*
cualidades	*qualities*
pasatiempos	*hobbies*
referencias	*references*
Con (16) años trabajé en…	*At the age of (16) I worked in…*
estudié inglés	*I studied English*
viajé a…	*I travelled to…*

La entrevista   *The interview*

¿Qué has estudiado?	*What have you studied?*
He estudiado…	*I've studied…*
He hecho un curso de (informática).	*I've done an (IT) course.*
¿Por qué quieres trabajar como…?	*Why do you want to work as a…?*
Porque me gusta…	*Because I like…*
tener responsabilidades	*having responsibilities*
tener un trabajo creativo	*having a creative job*
ganar un buen sueldo	*earning a good salary*
¿Qué experiencia laboral tienes?	*What work experience do you have?*
He trabajado en…	*I've worked in…*
He escrito…	*I've written…*
He hablado idiomas extranjeros.	*I've spoken foreign languages.*
He hablado por teléfono.	*I've talked on the phone.*
He hecho…	*I've done…*
He mandado correos electrónicos.	*I've sent emails.*
He servido…	*I've served…*
¿Has trabajado en equipo antes?	*Have you worked in a team before?*
Sí, he trabajado en equipo antes.	*Yes, I've worked in a team before.*
No, nunca he trabajado en equipo.	*No, I've never worked in a team.*
¿Qué es importante para ti?	*What is important to you?*
La gente es importante para mí.	*People are important to me.*
El dinero es importante.	*Money is important.*
Los animales son importantes.	*Animals are important.*
¿Qué cualidades tienes?	*What qualities do you have?*
Soy sincero/a, trabajador(a),…	*I'm sincere, hardworking…*
¿Cuál es tu dirección electrónica?	*What is your email address?*

Repaso 1 La tele

Mi tiempo libre 6

1 Escucha y escribe la letra correcta. (1–5)

Ejemplo: **1** b

 **a** el telediario/ las noticias

 **b** los programas de deportes

 **c** los documentales

 **d** los concursos

 **e** las series de policías

 **f** los programas de tele-realidad

 **g** las telenovelas

¿Qué ponen en la tele hoy/esta tarde/mañana?
¿Quieres venir a mi casa a ver (una telenovela)?
¿Quieres ver (el telediario) conmigo?

Before you start exercise 2, refresh your memory on telling the time in Spanish:
a la una… …y cuarto
a las dos/tres/cuatro… …y veinte
…y media
…menos cuarto

2 Escucha otra vez. ¿A qué hora ponen el programa? (1–5)

3 Lee los textos. Copia y completa la tabla en inglés.

	type of programme	opinion (P/N/P+N)	reason
1			

1 Me encantan las comedias porque son muy entretenidas. La comedia que más me gusta se llama *Gavin y Stacey*. Los actores son excelentes y por eso cada episodio es muy gracioso. ¡Es fenomenal! Siempre me hace reír. **Isabel**

2 A mí no me gustan nada los programas de tele-realidad porque son muy aburridos. El peor es un programa inglés que se llama *I'm a celebrity, get me out of here!* ¡La mayoría de la gente famosa que participa es tonta o antipática! **Javier**

3 A veces veo programas de música porque me encanta escuchar música rock y música pop. El problema es que muchos de los programas de música son muy lentos y sólo hay uno o dos que son buenos. Mi favorito es *El Factor X*. **Andrés**

gracioso = *funny*

4 *Read the texts again and try to note at least two extra details in each text.*

Ejemplo: **1** likes 'Gavin and Stacey' best, actors are excellent, every episode funny, makes her laugh

5 Escucha. Contesta a las preguntas en inglés. (1–4)

a What is the name of the programme?
b What type of programme is it?
c How is it described? (Give two details.)

Hospital Central　**Amistades Peligrosas**

La Vuelta al Mundo　　**El Factor X**

Todo el mundo quiere a Raymond　　**Antivicio**

El programa es…	La telenovela es…	Los concursos son…	Las telenovelas son…
entretenido	entretenida	entretenidos	entretenidas
educativo	educativa	educativos	educativas
curioso	curiosa	curiosos	curiosas
lento	lenta	lentos	lentas
largo	larga	largos	largas
malo	mala	malos	malas
tonto	tonta	tontos	tontas
emocionante, genial, guay		emocionantes, geniales, guays	

 6 Con tu compañero/a, haz diálogos, cambiando los datos subrayados.

● ¿Cuál es tu programa favorito?
■ Mi programa favorito es una telenovela. Se llama *Hollyoaks*.
● ¿Por qué te gusta?
■ Me encanta este programa porque es guay y nunca es aburrido.

G **The definite and indefinite articles** ➲208

Use the definite article after opinion verbs and when talking generally about a subject.
Odio **los** concursos.　*I hate game shows.*
Los documentales son informativos.　*Documentaries are informative.*

Use the indefinite article (**un/una**) when you want to refer to a particular programme.
Ponen **una** telenovela muy buena este fin de semana.
There's a very good soap on this weekend.

 7 Write about a programme that you like and one that you don't like.

Me gusta mucho *(Hollyoaks)*.
Es una telenovela/un concurso/…
Me gusta porque es muy/un poco/bastante…
No me gusta nada *(El Factor X)*.
Es un/una…
No me gusta porque es…

⭐ As you write, add in extra details. Use the texts in exercise 3 for ideas. For example:
Siempre me hace reír.
It always makes me laugh.
Los actores son excelentes.
The actors are excellent.
Cada episodio es muy gracioso.
Every episode is very funny.

Repaso 2   El cine

- Revising types of films
- Using a range of opinions

escuchar 1

Escucha y escribe la letra correcta. (Sobra un dibujo.) (1–8)

Ejemplo: **1** d

a
son las mejores

b
me gustan los caballos

c
me interesa la historia

d
me hacen feliz

e
me dan miedo

f
son muy emocionantes

g
son muy guays

h
me hacen reír

i
son muy graciosos

las películas…
de acción
de artes marciales
de ciencia-ficción
de guerra
del Oeste
románticas
de terror
las comedias
los dibujos animados

leer 2

Lee la conversación y luego escoge la(s) palabra(s) correcta(s).

Juan: Hola, Charo. ¿Qué tal?
Charo: Pues… Bien, gracias.
Juan: ¿Quieres ir al cine esta noche?
Charo: De acuerdo. ¿Qué ponen?
Juan: Ponen *El increíble Hulk*. ¿La conoces? Es una película de acción.
Charo: Claro que sí, tío. Me gustan mucho las películas de acción porque son emocionantes y divertidas.
Juan: Empieza a las ocho y diez.
Charo: Vale. ¿A qué hora termina?
Juan: Creo que termina a las diez y media.

1 Charo está **fatal** / **bien**.
2 **A Charo le gustaría** / **Charo no quiere** ir al cine.
3 Ponen una película **de amor** / **acción**.
4 A Charo le gusta mucho este tipo de película porque es **divertido** / **educativo**.
5 La película empieza antes de las **nueve** / **siete**.
6 La película dura más de **una hora** / **dos horas**.

3 Escucha. Copia y completa la tabla. (1–4)

	tipo de película	opinión ♥ / 💔	¿Por qué?
1	terror	💔	malas, me dan miedo

Me gustan más | las películas de…
Prefiero | porque (no) son
Me encantan | guays/aburridas/…
Me gustan
Me interesan
No me gustan
Odio

4 Have a conversation about films. First practise the dialogue with a partner. Then change the underlined words to match the picture prompts. Finally, make up your own conversation.

- ¿Te gustan las películas de acción?
- Sí, me gustan porque son emocionantes y algunas son muy guays.
- ¿Te interesan los dibujos animados?
- No, no me interesan los dibujos animados. Son tontos, pero me encantan las comedias.
- ¿Cuál es tu película favorita?
- Mi película favorita se llama Narnia. Es una película emocionante y genial.

 ? ✓ entertaining and exciting
 ? ✗ long, stupid and boring
 Juno – brilliant and entertaining

5 Escribe un párrafo sobre tus películas preferidas.

Me gustan mucho las películas de… porque son…
Mi película favorita es…
También me interesan las pelis de… Son… y…
Pero odio las pelis de… Para mí son…

6 Escucha. Copia y completa la tabla. (1–4)

	película	número de entradas	sesión	precio de entradas en total	comida/bebida
1	Juno	2	8:00	12€	palomitas de maíz

Quiero dos entradas para…/
¿Me da dos entradas para…?
Lo siento, pero no quedan entradas.
¿Para qué sesión?
Para la sesión de las cuatro y media.
¿Cuánto cuestan las entradas?
¿Quiere palomitas de maíz/caramelos/refrescos?

Aquí tiene.

Narnia
La Brújula Dorada
Kung Fu Panda
El Caballero Oscuro
27 Vestidos
Juno
Superman

1 La paga

1 Escucha y escribe las letras correctas. (1–5)

Ejemplo: **1** g, j

Verbs + infinitive	Conjugated verbs
Me gusta…	
hacer esquí	**hago** esquí
jugar al billar	**juego** al billar
jugar al fútbol	**juego** al fútbol
jugar al tenis de mesa	**juego** al tenis de mesa
nadar	**nado**
patinar	**patino**
salir con amigos	**salgo** con amigos
escuchar música	**escucho** música
leer libros/revistas	**leo** libros/revistas
ver la tele	**veo** la tele

G Infinitives v. conjugated verbs ⮕206

Infinitives
Some verbs are followed by an **infinitive**:
Me gusta
Me encanta
Me interesa } **jugar** al fútbol
Prefiero
Odio
Suelo *(I usually…)*

Conjugated verbs
You can also use conjugated verbs in the present tense to talk about your hobbies:
Juego al rugby.   *I play rugby.*

2 Con tu compañero/a, pregunta y contesta.

- ● ¿Qué haces en tu tiempo libre?
- ■ Me gusta **hacer/jugar/salir**…
- ● ¿Qué deportes haces en el colegio?
- ■ Suelo **hacer/jugar**…
- ● ¿Prefieres jugar al fútbol o al tenis de mesa?
- ■ Prefiero **jugar**…
- ● ¿Con qué frecuencia nadas?
- ■ Nado…

 Add in some adverbs of frequency as you speak.

todos los días *(every day)*
dos veces al mes *(twice a month)*
una vez a la semana *(once a week)*
los miércoles *(on Wednesdays)*
nunca *(never)*

leer **3** Lee el blog de Esther. ¿Verdadero (V), falso (F) o no se menciona (NM)?

1 Esther hace poco en su tiempo libre.
2 En su tiempo libre, a Esther le gusta ir al cine.
3 Esther chatea por Internet y descarga música.
4 A Esther le gusta leer.
5 Esther toca un instrumento.

En mi tiempo libre me encanta hacer muchas cosas distintas. En casa me gusta jugar con mi ordenador. Suelo chatear por Internet con mi novio y también descargo música. A veces mando correos electrónicos a mi hermana que vive en Estados Unidos. Me interesa leer, sobre todo libros de misterio. Además toco la guitarra en un grupo de música rock pero no canto.
Esther

 escuchar **4** Escucha y lee las frases. Escribe las letras correctas.

1 A veces me gusta comprar algo caro como ropa.
2 Mis padres me dan diez euros a la semana y siempre lo gasto en maquillaje.
3 Mis abuelos me dan dos euros al día. Gasto mi dinero en caramelos o chocolate.
4 No gasto la paga. Ahorro mi dinero porque quiero comprarme una moto.
5 Mi padrastro me da diez euros al mes y lo gasto en crédito para mi móvil.

 escuchar **5** Escucha. Copia y completa la tabla en inglés. (1–5)

	How much?	How often?	Buys/Saves for…?
1	€30	monthly	fashion magazines

> **G** *Direct object pronoun* lo
>
> The pronoun **lo** *(it)* is used instead of repeating the word **dinero**.
> Me dan **dinero**. **Lo** gasto en caramelos.
> *They give me **money**. I spend **it** on sweets.*

 escribir **6** *Write a paragraph about your hobbies and your pocket money.*

En mi tiempo libre hago/juego/nado/
    salgo/escucho/veo…
También me gusta (+ **infinitivo**), pero
    odio (+ **infinitivo**)
Mis padres me dan… Lo gasto en…
Además ahorro para comprar…

¿Cuánto dinero te dan tus padres?
¿Tus padres te dan paga?

Mis padres me dan	…euros …libras	al día a la semana al mes

¿Cómo lo gastas?
¿Qué haces con tu dinero?

Lo gasto en Compro Ahorro para comprar	revistas videojuegos un ordenador/un iPod/…

2 El campeonato

1 Escucha. Copia y completa la tabla en inglés. (1–4)

¿Practicas algún deporte?

	sports they do regularly	sports done recently
1	goes jogging	Basque pelota

a hacer atletismo

b hacer alpinismo

c hacer footing

d hacer gimnasia

e hacer vela

f montar a caballo

g practicar baloncesto

h jugar a la pelota vasca

i ir de pesca

G Present and past verbs

Verbs will help you spot whether someone is talking about the present or the past.

present: 'I' form	preterite: 'I' form
hago	hice
practico	practiqué
juego	jugué
voy	fui

Time expressions will also give you a clue:

present	past
generalmente	ayer
normalmente	la semana pasada
los miércoles	el lunes pasado
todos los días	hace dos semanas

2 Read the email and work out what the words in red mean. Use the Vocabulario *section to check. Then answer the questions.*

1 What sport does Sara play at school?
2 Who is her favourite player and why does she like him (one reason)?
3 What sport did she play recently? What happened?

⊕ ZONA CULTURA

La Pelota Vasca

This is a sport which originated in the Basque country. It is similar to handball and is played in a *frontón* (a court with walls) by two teams of one or two players. Players use their hand, a racket or a basket to hit the ball.

¡Hola amiga! Me encanta el deporte. Ahora el tenis es mi deporte favorito. Juego bien y soy miembro del **equipo titular** del cole. **Entrenamos** dos veces a la semana y tenemos por lo menos tres partidos cada sábado. Soy fan de Rafael Nadal. Para mí, es el mejor jugador porque **golpea** bien **la pelota** y marca puntos sin problemas.
El miércoles pasado mis amigos y yo jugamos al **hockey sobre hielo** por primera vez. Me pareció muy difícil. Aunque suelo jugar al **hockey sobre hierba**, es mucho más difícil sobre hielo. ¡Patiné fatal y no marqué ningún gol! ¿Y tú? ¡Escríbeme pronto! **Sara**

por lo menos = *at least*
sin problemas = *without problems*

3 *Prepare a spoken presentation on sports. Answer the following questions.*

- ¿Te gusta hacer deporte?
- ¿Practicas deporte en tu colegio?
- ¿Practicas algún deporte en tu tiempo libre?
- ¿Qué deportes hiciste la semana pasada/el mes pasado?
  (Use the preterite.)

Me encanta	jugar al fútbol, voleibol, …	porque es divertido/…
En el colegio Los sábados En mi tiempo libre	hago/practico… juego al… juego en el equipo de…	una vez a la semana dos veces a la semana
Entrenamos en	un parque, una piscina, el polideportivo, el estadio, una pista de tenis, una pista de atletismo	
La semana pasada El mes pasado	jugué al…, marqué…goles, practiqué…, hice…	

4 Escribe un blog sobre deportes.

5 *Read about Fernando Torres. Work out the English for the words and phrases in red. Then decide if the statements are true (T) or false (F).*

Fernando Torres "El Niño" – Una biografía

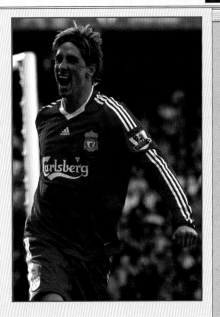

Soy fan del futbolista Fernando Torres. Es español y juega en la posición de **delantero**. Es también uno de los mejores jugadores del mundo.

Nació en Madrid y es el **menor** de tres hermanos. Es un apasionado del fútbol desde que era muy pequeño. Comenzó su carrera profesional en 2001 en el famoso club de fútbol español Atlético de Madrid. Aquí marcó **una media de** quince goles por temporada. En 2007 Fernando fue a jugar al club inglés Liverpool FC. 'El niño' también juega en la Selección Nacional Española. En 2006 participó en **la Copa Mundial** de Fútbol y también participó en **la Copa de Europa** 2008 donde marcó el gol que dio la victoria al equipo español.

'El niño' es un ídolo para millones de personas debido a su inmenso talento. Torres es un verdadero campeón. ¡Es un crack!

por temporada = *per season*
la Selección Nacional Española = *the Spanish national team*
que dio la victoria = *winning*
debido a = *because of, due to*
es un crack (slang) = *he's a genius*

1 He is a goalkeeper.
2 He has no brothers or sisters.
3 He started playing professionally in 2001.
4 He did not play in the 2006 World Cup.
5 He scored the winning goal for Spain in the European Cup in 2008.
6 He is admired by so many people because he is a great player.

3 ¿Quedamos?

1 Escucha y lee. Completa el diálogo con palabras del cuadro.

Abuela: ¿Dígame?
María: (1) _____. ¿Está Martín?
Abuela: ¿De parte de (2) _____?
María: Soy María del Carmen.
Abuela: Un momento. ¡Martín…, Martín…! Lo siento, no (3) _____. Está jugando al fútbol en el parque con su (4) _____. ¿Quieres dejarle algún mensaje?
María: ¿Puede decirle que voy a ir al (5) _____ esta tarde?
Abuela: ¿Al polideportivo? De (6) _____.
María: Gracias. ¡Hasta luego!
Abuela: ¡Hasta luego!

polideportivo	está	hermano	quién	amiga	cine	hola	acuerdo

2 Lee la conversación del ejercicio 1 y contesta a las preguntas.

1 Where is Martín?
2 Who is he with?
3 What message does María leave for him?

Lo siento pero (Miguel) no está en casa porque…	
está	trabajando jugando al fútbol/tenis/rugby haciendo sus deberes en casa de (Juan)
¿Puede decirle que voy a ir/ no puedo ir	al cine/al parque/ al polideportivo/a la bolera?

3 Escucha. Copia y completa la tabla. (1–3)

	What is the person doing?	Message left?
1	homework at grandmother's house	going to cinema tomorrow

G The present continuous

The present continuous tense is used to say what you *are doing* (e.g. 'I am playing football'). Use **estoy** *(I am)* + the present participle.

To form the present participle, you remove the **-ar**, **-er** or **-ir** from the infinitive and add:
jug**ar** → jug**ando**
com**er** → com**iendo**
escrib**ir** → escrib**iendo**

Estoy viendo la televisión.   *I am watching television.*
No **estoy haciendo** nada.   *I am not doing anything.*

4 Read the text messages and match them to the correct picture. (There is one picture too many.) Then write out what each text says in correct Spanish.

1 ola. stoy tomando un café en el centro comercial. t kiero. a2. Sofía XXX

2 stoy viendo una peli. nos vemos mñna en la bolera. a2. Javier –x

3 stoy en la ciudad tb. kedamos en el parque? salu2. Helena. –)

4 ola. stoy descansando. quieres venir a una fiesta? besos. Oscar. –))

5 Listen. Where do they suggest meeting? What excuse is given for saying no? Write the correct letter. (1–5)

Ejemplo: **1** beach – f

¿Quieres ir al/a la…?

No puedo ir porque…

… no tengo dinero.

Tengo que…

 hacer de canguro

 limpiar mi dormitorio

 hacer los deberes

 salir con mis padres

 lavarme el pelo

 trabajar

6 Read the conversation below aloud in pairs. Then change the underlined words to make a new conversation, using the information on the right.

● Hola, Leonardo. ¿Qué haces?
■ Nada, estoy jugando con el ordenador.
● ¿Quieres ir al cine esta tarde?
■ Lo siento, pero no puedo.
● ¿Por qué?
■ Tengo que salir con mis padres.
● Pues… ¿Quieres ir al polideportivo mañana?
■ Sí, sí. ¿A qué hora quedamos?
● ¿A las seis y media?
■ Vale. ¿Dónde quedamos?
● En el parque.
■ De acuerdo. ¡Hasta luego!

this afternoon?

?

10:30?

While you're having your conversation, use these phrases to give yourself thinking time:
Pues… *Well…* A ver… *Let's see…*
Bueno… *Well…* Vale… *OK…*

7 Listen and take notes in English. Where and when will they meet? (1–2)

4 Una crítica

 1 Look at this image from the film **Pan's Labyrinth**. Which adjectives would you use to describe the scene? Look up any you don't know in the Vocabulario section and then write a few sentences in Spanish.

Ejemplo: Esta escena de la película es sorprendente…
También es… pero no es…

Es…

misteriosa
bonita
original
emocionante
extraña
fea
mágica
terrorífica
sorprendente
impresionante
triste
feliz

 2 Listen and read the text about **El laberinto del fauno**. Look for these phrases in Spanish in the text. (They are all in bold type.)

1 the characters
2 the sound effects
3 it tells the story of
4 the special effects
5 what I like best
6 I would recommend it because
7 directed by
8 it is about
9 plays the role of
10 takes place
11 I have just seen
12 the end

G Acabar de

When you want to say that you *have just done* something, use **acabar de** + **infinitive**

The verb **acabar** works like a normal **-ar** verb and is used in the *present* tense to say what you have just done.
Acabo de leer un libro muy interesante.
I have just read a very interesting book.

laberinto = *labyrinth (a complicated maze)*
fauno = *faun (a mythical creature, half man, half beast)*

Acabo de ver una película increíble que se llama *El laberinto del fauno*. **Trata de** una niña de trece años que se llama Ofelia. La película **tiene lugar** cinco años después de la Guerra Civil en España.

La película **cuenta la historia de** Ofelia. Vive con su madre y su cruel padrastro en un pequeño pueblo. Una noche Ofelia descubre un laberinto donde vive un fauno mágico. El fauno dice que Ofelia es la princesa de un mundo mágico.

Lo que más me gusta de la película son **los personajes** fantásticos del mundo mágico. Ivana Baquero **actúa en el papel de** Ofelia y es una actriz excelente. **Los efectos sonoros** y **los efectos especiales** son excelentes y la fotografía es espectacular. **El final** de la película es muy triste pero también es alegre.

La película fue **dirigida por** Guillermo Del Toro, el famoso director de *Blade 2* y *Hellboy*. No es una película de aventuras tipo *Narnia*. Es una historia muy seria. **La recomendaría porque** es emocionante y bonita.

Lee el texto y escoge las tres frases correctas.

1 The thirteen-year-old girl discovers a labyrinth.
2 The monster is a type of dinosaur.
3 Ofelia's stepfather is a horrible man.
4 The ending of the film is very funny.
5 There are no special effects in the film.
6 The action takes place in Spain.
7 The reviewer did not like the film.

G *Emphatic adjectives*

Add **-ísimo** to the end of a Spanish adjective to emphasise it. (If the adjective ends in a vowel, remove it before adding this ending.)
difícil *difficult* → dificil**ísimo** *incredibly difficult*
hermoso *beautiful* → hermos**ísimo** *really beautiful*

The ending changes as for normal adjectives ending in **-o**.

Lee las frases. ¿A quién admiran?

1 Me llamo Javier. Admiro a este autor porque escribe libros buenísimos sobre magia.

2 Me llamo Laura. Admiro a este actor porque es guapísimo. Actúa en el papel de James Bond.

3 Me llamo Joan. Admiro a esta artista. Es famosísima pero no es joven.

4 Me llamo Margarita. Admiro a esta actriz española porque también diseña ropa bellísima.

este/a = *this*   **Penélope Cruz**

Madonna   **J.K. Rowling**   **Daniel Craig**

Habla de artistas, autores, actores o músicos.

● ¿A quién admiras? ¿Por qué?
■ Admiro a <u>J.K. Rowling</u> porque <u>sus libros son interesantísimos</u>.
● ¿A quién odias? ¿Por qué?
■ Odio a <u>Britney Spears</u> porque <u>su música es aburridísima</u>.

Admiro a…	porque sus películas son	interesantísimo/a(s).
Adoro a…	porque sus libros son	divertidísimo/a(s).
Odio a…	porque su música es	feísimo/a(s).
		bellísimo/a(s).
		buenísimo/a(s).
		aburridísimo/a(s).

Escucha. Copia y completa la tabla en inglés. (1–6)

	What is discussed?	opinion (✓/✗) + detail (really…)
1	film	✓ sound effects are really good

Escribe sobre una película que te interese.

Adoro a… porque sus películas son…

Voy a escribir sobre una película que se llama… Trata de…

Los personajes principales son…

… actúa en el papel de…

Cuenta la historia de… Tiene un final…

Lo que más me gusta de la película es la historia/la fotografía.

Los efectos especiales/Los personajes son buenísimos/…

- Talking about new technology
- Revising comparatives

5 La tecnología

escuchar 1 Listen and choose the correct letters. Write in English how often they do each activity. (1–4)

Ejemplo: **1** b – twice a week, e – every day

a descargo música

b navego por Internet

c hago compras por Internet

d mando correos electrónicos

e uso Facebook

f veo vídeos

g chateo

h juego con videojuegos del PC

siempre
de vez en cuando/a veces
todos los días
una vez a la semana
dos veces a la semana
los fines de semana
por las noches

hablar 2 Con tu compañero/a, mira los dibujos y haz los diálogos.

● ¿Qué haces con tu ordenador?
■ Siempre mando correos electrónicos y uso Facebook dos veces a la semana.

a sometimes, weekends

b twice a week, every day

leer 3 Lee los textos. Copia y completa la tabla en inglés.

	comparing...	with...	opinion
1	shopping online	shopping in city	online is cheaper

1 Me llamo Margarita y siempre hago compras por Internet porque creo que es más barato que ir de compras en una ciudad.

2 Me llamo David y creo que los correos electrónicos son más fáciles que las cartas tradicionales. Además los correos electrónicos son más rápidos.

3 Me llamo Victoria y en mi opinión chatear por Internet es más peligroso que hacer una llamada telefónica porque hay muchos hombres malos que usan los chats.

4 Mi nombre es Benito y me encantan los videojuegos. Son buenísimos. Para mí los videojuegos son mejores que el ajedrez porque hay más variedad.

4 Escucha. Copia y completa la tabla del ejercicio 3 en inglés. (1–3)

descargar música	es más... que...
comprar discos	son más... que...
las compras en el centro comercial	barato/a(s), caro/a(s),
las compras por Internet	fácil(es), difícil(es),
los correos electrónicos	peligroso/a(s), seguro/a(s),
las cartas tradicionales	rápido/a(s), lento/a(s)

5 Lee los textos y escribe M (María) o J (Juan).

Who...

1 uses the internet to do homework?
2 downloads music and chats online?
3 won't give out key information about him/herself online?
4 mentions activities with friends away from the computer?
5 has parents who think there are dangers?
6 thinks that libraries are less entertaining than surfing the net?

G Comparing things ➜212

más + adjective + **que**...	*more... than...*
menos + adjective + **que**...	*less... than...*
mejor que...	*better than...*
peor que...	*worse than...*
tan + adjective + **como**...	*as... as...*

Remember to make your adjectives agree with the nouns you are describing:
Tu **ordenador** portátil es más **caro** que mi PC.
Your laptop is more expensive than my computer.

María

Uso mucho el ordenador en mi tiempo libre. Por las tardes descargo música y hablo con mis amigas en los chats. Mis padres piensan que los chats son peligrosos. Sin embargo nunca doy información personal a las personas con quien hablo.
También suelo hacer compras por Internet. Pienso que en el futuro la gente no va a ir a los centros comerciales.

Juan

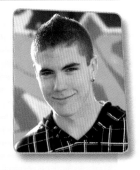

Hola, ¿qué tal? En mi opinión Internet es esencial. Personalmente, uso Internet para hacer mis deberes todos los días. Es más fácil, más rápido y más entretenido que ir a la biblioteca. En el futuro creo que mucha gente va a leer libros electrónicos. Por supuesto me gusta hacer otras cosas como jugar al fútbol o charlar con mis amigos. No paso todo mi tiempo en el ordenador.

6 *Write about using the internet. Try to include the points below.*

● *How often you use the internet and what for:*
  Uso Internet todos los días/cada semana/...
  Chateo..., mando..., veo..., descargo...
● *Your opinion about online activities (use comparatives):*
  Creo que (los correos electrónicos) son más... que...
● *What else you do in your free time:*
  También tengo otros pasatiempos. Por ejemplo, me gusta jugar al.../leer...
● *Your opinion about what people will do with technology in the future:*
  En el futuro pienso que la gente va a...

En el futuro creo que la gente (no) va a...
leer libros electrónicos
ir a los centros comerciales
hacer muchas compras por Internet
mandar cartas tradicionales

Mi tiempo libre
b

> **Leisure**
> You are going to play the role of a young actor or actress and your teacher will play the role of the interviewer. Your teacher could ask you the following:
>
> - Tell me a bit about yourself.
> - What films do you prefer?
> - Which actor or actress do you admire and why?
> - What did you do in your spare time last weekend?
> - Do you use a computer much?
> - What are you going to do this evening?
>
> Remember that you will have to respond to an unexpected question that you have not yet prepared.

1 *You are going to listen to Cheryl, an exam candidate, taking part in the above interview with her teacher. Listen to part 1 and choose the correct word or phrase.*

> *Háblame un poco de ti.*

> *¿A qué actor o actriz admiras?*

> *¿Qué tipo de películas prefieres ver?*

a Vivo con mi novio y tengo **treinta y dos** / **veintidós** / **veinte** años.

b Prefiero las películas románticas porque son muy **emocionantes** / **entretenidas** / **interesantes**.

c También me interesan **los concursos** / **las noticias** / **los dibujos animados** porque son divertidos.

d Mi actor **favorito** / **preferido** / **peor** es Kiefer Sutherland.

e En mi opinión es un actor **bueno** / **excelente** / **guapo**.

f Es una actriz buenísima y habla inglés y **español** / **francés** / **italiano**.

2 *Listen to part 2 of Cheryl's interview and fill each gap with the correct word(s) from the box.*

| al | encantan | mañana | además | fui | fuimos |
| pero | de vez en cuando | jugué | emocionantes |

- ¿Qué hiciste el fin de semana pasado?
- Bueno… el sábado por la **(1)** _____ jugué al tenis con mi amiga y luego **(2)** _____ al parque. Por la tarde **(3)** _____ con videojuegos en casa. Me **(4)** _____ los videojuegos porque son muy **(5)** _____. El domingo fui **(6)** _____ cine y vi una película de acción **(7)** _____ no me gustó. Trata de un niño misterioso y extraño pero los efectos especiales son malos. Por la tarde **(8)** _____ a la playa y nadé en el mar. ¡Fue muy divertido!
- ¿Usas Internet mucho en casa?
- **(9)** _____ hago compras por Internet porque es bastante barato. **(10)** _____ me gustan los videojuegos de PC.

3 Now listen to part 3 of Cheryl's interview. In which order does she use these phrases? What is the final question that she is asked?

a ...pero también me encanta leer libros sobre Hannah Montana.
b Primero vi la serie y me gustó mucho...
c Por eso voy a lavarme el pelo y planchar mi ropa...
d ...pero no puedo porque quiero prepararme para mañana.
e Pues, normalmente leo revistas de moda...
f Esta tarde me gustaría leer mi libro y comer una pizza...

¿Qué vas a hacer esta tarde?

quiero prepararme = I want to get myself ready

4 Now it's your turn! Prepare your answers to the task and then do the interview with your teacher or partner.

- Use the Grade Studio and your answers to exercises 1–3 to help you plan.
- Adapt what Cheryl said to talk about yourself but add your own ideas.
- Prepare your answers to the questions and try to predict what the unexpected question could be. The examiner might base this question on something you have already said, or ask something totally new!
- Record the conversation. Ask a partner to listen to it and say how well you performed.

Award each other one star, two stars or three stars for each of these categories:
- Pronunciation
- Confidence and fluency
- Range of tenses
- Variety of vocabulary and expressions
- Using longer sentences
- Taking the initiative

What do you need to do next time to improve your performance?

⭐ GradeStudio

Make sure you cover the basics.
- Use **basic connectives** to make your sentences longer, such as *y* (and), *pero* (but) and *también* (also).
- Use **simple structures** correctly, e.g. *soy* (I am), *tengo* (I have), *vivo* (I live), *hago* (I do), *leo* (I read).
- Include **simple opinions**, e.g. *me encanta(n)* (I love), *me gusta(n)* (I like) and *prefiero* (I prefer).

To reach Grade C, show that you can:
- Use **the present tense** to describe yourself or a film, e.g. *Tengo veintidós años.* (I am 22.) *Los efectos especiales son malos.* (The special effects are bad.)
- Use **the preterite** to say what you did last weekend, e.g. *Jugué al tenis... fui al cine... vi una película.* (I played tennis... I went to the cinema... I saw a film.)
- Use **fue** to give your opinion of what it was like. Cheryl uses *¡Fue muy divertido!* (It was really fun!). What other adjectives could you use with *fue*?
- Use **the near future tense** to say what you are going to do, e.g. *Voy a lavarme el pelo.* (I am going to wash my hair.)
- Include **adjectives** and ensure they agree with the noun they describe, e.g. *Prefiero los libros porque son más informativos.* (I prefer books as they are more informative.)

To increase your marks:
- Use more **complex opinions**. Cheryl uses *También me interesan los dibujos animados* (I am also interested in cartoons); *La actriz que más me gusta...* (The actress that I like most...)
- Include a wider **range of connectives**, e.g. *Además* (In addition); *Por eso* (Because of this).
- Use an **emphatic adjective**. Cheryl uses *buenísima* to describe her favourite actress.

leer

1 Read the text and choose the correct title for each paragraph. Which words/phrases in the text support your decisions?

a Description of a film   **b** Future purchases   **c** A passion for films   **d** A trip to the cinema

1 Me encantan las películas buenas. Voy mucho al cine y normalmente veo dos o tres películas en la tele cada semana. Las películas que más me gustan son las películas de terror porque son muy emocionantes y algunas son un poco graciosas. Sin embargo, mi película preferida del momento no es una película de terror. Se llama *El ultimátum de Bourne* y es una película de espías y de acción.

Eva

2 La película cuenta la historia de Jason Bourne y los problemas que tiene por su trabajo con la CIA. La película está dirigida por Paul Greengrass, y Matt Damon actúa en el papel de Bourne. En mi opinión, Matt Damon es bastante guapo y además es un actor excepcional.

3 Fui a ver esta película con una amiga del cole que se llama Fátima. Fuimos al cine en el centro comercial. Me gusta mucho porque siempre venden palomitas de maíz que están riquísimas. Después fuimos de compras y compré unos vaqueros grises.

4 Esta semana no voy a ir al cine porque estoy ahorrando para comprar unos DVDs nuevos. Quiero comprar la película española de terror *El orfanato* y también me gustaría comprar la película de terror clásica *El exorcista*.

gracioso/a = *funny*

leer

2 Find the equivalent of these expressions in Spanish in the text.

1 I go to the cinema a lot…
2 The films I like best are…
3 …some are a bit funny.
4 However, my favourite film at the moment…
5 The film tells the story of…
6 The film is directed by…
7 Matt Damon plays the part of…
8 We went to the cinema…
9 …they sell delicious popcorn.
10 I'm saving up to buy…

leer

3 Which phrase from exercise 2 uses the preterite? Now find three more phrases in the text which use a verb in the preterite.

leer

4 Read the text again and answer the questions in English.

1 What type of films does Eva usually prefer?
2 Why does she like them?
3 What type of film is Eva's current favourite? What's it called in Spanish?
4 What does she think of Matt Damon?
5 Where is the cinema she went to?
6 Why does she like this cinema?
7 What did they do after seeing the film?
8 Why is Eva not going to the cinema this week?

5 You might be asked to write about films as a controlled assessment task. Use the Grade Studio to help you prepare your account.

⭐ GradeStudio

Make sure you cover the basics.

- Use **simple structures** correctly, e.g. *voy* (I go), *veo* (I watch), *es* (it is), *se llama* (it is called) and *fui* (I went).
- Use **simple opinions** to describe what type of films you like or dislike, e.g. *me encantan…* (I love…), *me gustan…* (I like…) and *odio…* (I hate…). Which of these opinion verbs does Eva use?
- Use **qualifiers** to add detail. Eva uses *muy* (very), *un poco* (a bit) and *bastante* (quite). Use at least two of these in your text.

To reach Grade C, show that you can:

- Use **the present tense**. Eva talks about her film preferences, e.g. *voy mucho al cine.*
- Use **the preterite**. Eva talks about her recent trip to the cinema, e.g. *fui a ver esta película con una amiga del cole.*
- Use **the near future tense**. Eva uses it to talk about her plans, e.g. *esta semana no voy a ir al cine.*
- Use **adjectives** and make sure they agree with the noun they are describing. Referring to films, Eva says *…son muy emocionantes.* Which other adjectives does she use to describe films?
- Use **connectives** to make your sentences longer. Eva uses *además* (what's more) and *sin embargo* (nevertheless).

To increase your marks:

- Use the **'we' form** of the verb. Eva uses *fuimos* to describe what she and Fátima did. Can you find any other examples in the text?
- Use **more complex opinion phrases**, e.g *Las películas que más me gustan son… Mi película preferida del momento es…*

6 Now write about films and going to the cinema.

- Adapt Eva's text and use language from Module 6.
- When describing the plot or theme of a film, keep it simple. When you look up words in a dictionary, make sure you choose the right one by looking carefully at any examples given.
- Structure your text carefully. Organise what you write in paragraphs.

7 Check carefully what you have written.

- accents (correct on nouns: *película* and regular verbs in the 1st person preterite: *comí*?)
- adjective agreement (correct when talking about masculine, feminine, plural?)
- verb endings (correct when talking about films: *me gustan/me encantan*?)

General introduction

Introduce yourself
What sort of films do you like? Why?
What is your favourite film?

Main paragraph

Give some details about a film you have seen:
- What is it called and what type of film is it?
- When did you see the film?
- Who did you go with?
- What is the story about?
- Which actors/actresses are in it? What are they like?
- Who is the director?
- What are the best aspects of the film?

Conclusion

When are you going to go to the cinema next?
What DVDs would you like to buy?
What are you going to watch on TV and when?

5–6

leer 1 Look at this extract from a Spanish TV guide. Write down the letter of the programme each person will watch. (1 mark for each person)

		Cadena 1 (viernes, tarde)
a	17:45	Dibujos animados
b	18:00	Serie de policías
c	18.50	Telediario
d	19:10	Telenovela
e	19:40	Concurso
f	20:30	Película de aventuras
g	21:55	Documental – animales

⭐ In this type of exercise, there will always be more options than you need. Remember not to use an option more than once.

1 **Diego**: I'd like to watch a film.
2 **Javi**: I love cartoons.
3 **Patricia**: I like game shows.
4 **Santiago**: I would like to watch the news.
5 **Catalina**: I don't want to miss my favourite soap.

leer 2 Read Alfonso's and Bárbara's CVs and answer the questions. Write A (Alfonso), B (Bárbara) or A+B (Alfonso + Bárbara). (6 marks)

Currículum Vitae
Nombre: Alfonso Duarte
Edad: 18
Educación: He hecho un curso de informática.
Idiomas: inglés, alemán
Experiencia laboral:
Hice mis prácticas laborales en una empresa inglesa; he trabajado como cajero en un supermercado y como recepcionista en un hotel.
Pasatiempos: tocar la guitarra, leer libros y revistas
Planes para el futuro: visitar América Latina, ser músico profesional

Currículum Vitae
Nombre: Bárbara Sánchez
Edad: 19
Educación: He estudiado comercio.
Idiomas: francés, italiano
Experiencia laboral:
He trabajado como camarera en un restaurante y como secretaria en una oficina; hice mis prácticas laborales en una escuela primaria.
Pasatiempos: hacer atletismo, montar a caballo
Planes para el futuro: ser azafata, viajar por toda Europa

1 Who speaks two foreign languages?
2 Who has worked as a cashier?
3 Who did work experience in a school?
4 Who plays a lot of sport?
5 Who wants to go abroad in the future?
6 Who has done computer studies?

⭐ Always read both texts before deciding on the answers, in order to spot when the answer should be 'A + B'. Look at the question and then use the headings in the CV to help you to locate the relevant information.

3 Read the report on Miguel's work experience written by his boss. What does his boss think of his performance in each of the following categories? Write A (good), B (average) or C (poor). (5 marks)

1 punctuality
2 attitude
3 dress sense
4 ability to learn
5 people skills

Informe sobre las prácticas laborales del estudiante Miguel Santero

Miguel lleva tres días trabajando en esta oficina. Llega a tiempo todos los días y nunca sale del trabajo antes de la hora correcta.

Es una persona bastante positiva con el entusiasmo normal de un joven de quince años. No es perezoso pero su trabajo es regular.

No lleva ropa sucia o inapropiada – su ropa es muy elegante. Siempre lleva pantalones negros, una camisa blanca con corbata y zapatos.

En tres días ha aprendido muy poco. El curso de informática ha sido demasiado difícil para él y no hace preguntas si tiene problemas.

Ha hablado poco con los clientes. Ha preferido estar en una oficina tranquila y no ha trabajado en equipo.

> ★ Be aware of qualifiers, e.g. *demasiado* (too), *muy* (very), *bastante* (quite) and *un poco* (a bit), as they can change the opinion expressed. In order to answer each question, you need to find the relevant paragraph and decide how you would summarise Miguel's performance (good, average or poor?).

 4 Listen to this telephone conversation between Jorge and Marisol arranging to go out and answer the questions. (5 marks)

1 When on Saturday does Jorge want to play tennis?
2 Why can Marisol not accept his invitation?
3 What do they arrange to do instead?
4 Where do they agree to meet?
5 How much will they each have to pay?

> ★ When listening to people making arrangements you may hear quite long sections of conversation. Wait until you've heard the whole dialogue before finalising your answers.

 5 During a job interview, Daniel is asked about his previous job as a waiter. Write the letters of the topics discussed. (3 marks)

Example: **b**

a	colleagues	d	duties
b	~~place of work~~	e	uniform
c	hours of work	f	salary

 6 When does Silvia most enjoy doing these activities? Write the correct letter for each one. (4 marks)

Activity
1 going to parties
2 listening to music
3 shopping
4 watching sport

Enjoyed...
a at the weekend
b when the weather is nice
c on holiday
d at home
e on a special occasion

> ★ If you are asked to identify what someone 'most enjoys', be prepared to spot what they don't enjoy. They may mention those things as well. To answer correctly you need to tell the difference between positive and negative opinions.

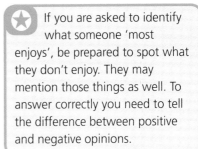

Palabras

La tele *Television*

el telediario/las noticias	*the news*	emocionante(s)	*exciting*
las series de policías	*detective series*	entretenido/a(s)	*entertaining*
las telenovelas	*soaps*	genial(es)	*brilliant*
los concursos	*gameshows*	guay(s)	*great*
los documentales	*documentaries*	largo/a(s)	*long*
los programas de deportes	*sports programmes*	lento/a(s)	*slow*
los programas de tele-realidad	*reality TV programmes*	malo/a(s)	*bad*
El programa es…	*The programme is…*	tonto/a(s)	*stupid*
Los concursos son…	*Gameshows are…*	Mi programa favorito es (una telenovela).	*My favourite programme is (a soap).*
curioso/a(s)	*curious, odd*	Se llama…	*It's called…*
educativo/a(s)	*educational*	(No) me gusta porque es…	*I (don't) like it because it's…*

El cine *Cinema*

Me gustan más…	*I like… best…*	me interesa la historia	*I'm interested in history*
Prefiero…	*I prefer…*	me dan miedo	*they scare me*
Me interesan…	*I'm interested in…*	me hacen feliz	*they make me happy*
las películas de acción	*action films*	me hacen reír	*they make me laugh*
las películas de artes marciales	*martial arts films*	son las mejores	*they're the best*
las películas de ciencia-ficción	*sci-fi films*	son muy emocionantes/graciosos/as	*they're very exciting/funny*
las películas de guerra	*war films*	Quiero (dos) entradas para…	*I'd like (two) tickets for…*
las películas románticas	*romantic films*	Lo siento, pero no quedan entradas.	*I'm sorry, but there are no tickets left.*
las películas de terror	*horror films*	Para la sesión de las…	*For the… showing.*
las películas del Oeste	*Westerns*	¿Cuánto cuestan las entradas?	*How much are the tickets?*
las comedias	*comedies*		
los dibujos animados	*cartoons*	¿Quiere palomitas de maíz?	*Do you want popcorn?*
porque…	*because…*	¿Quiere refrescos?	*Do you want soft drinks?*
me gustan los caballos	*I like horses*		

La paga *Pocket money*

Me gusta…	*I like to…*	veo la tele	*I watch TV*
Suelo…	*I usually…*	Mis padres me dan…	*My parents give me…*
escuchar música	*listen to music*	Mi padre/Mi madre me da…	*My dad/My mum gives me…*
hacer esquí	*go skiing*		
jugar al billar	*play billiards*	al día	*per day*
jugar al tenis de mesa	*play table tennis*	a la semana	*per week*
leer libros y revistas	*read books and magazines*	al mes	*per month*
nadar	*swim*	Lo gasto en…	*I spend it on…*
patinar	*skate*	Ahorro para comprar…	*I'm saving up to buy…*
salir con amigos	*go out with friends*	caramelos	*sweets*
ver la tele	*watch TV*	crédito para mi móvil	*top-ups for my mobile*
escucho música	*I listen to music*	maquillaje	*make-up*
hago esquí	*I go skiing*	revistas	*magazines*
juego al…	*I play…*	ropa	*clothes*
leo…	*I read…*	videojuegos	*video games*
nado	*I swim*	una moto	*a motorbike/scooter*
patino	*I skate*	un iPod	*an iPod*
salgo con amigos	*I go out with friends*		

El campeonato *The championship*

Me encanta…	*I love…*	montar a caballo	*horse-riding*
hacer alpinismo	*going climbing*	hacer vela	*sailing*
hacer atletismo	*doing athletics*	ir de pesca	*going fishing*
hacer gimnasia	*doing gymnastics*	jugar a la pelota vasca	*playing Basque pelota*

practicar baloncesto	*playing basketball*	La semana pasada…	*Last week…*
En el colegio…	*At school…*	El mes pasado…	*Last month…*
Los sábados…	*On Saturdays…*	hice/practiqué/jugué al…	*I did/played…*
juego en el equipo de…	*I play for the… team*	marqué (tres) goles	*I scored (three) goals*

¿Quedamos?   *Shall we meet?*

¿Está Martín?	*Is Martin there?*	¿Dónde quedamos?	*Where shall we meet?*
Está…	*He's…*	Lo siento. No puedo ir	*I'm sorry, I can't come*
Estoy…	*I'm…*	porque…	*because…*
comiendo	*eating*	No tengo dinero.	*I haven't got any money.*
descansando	*resting*	Tengo que…	*I have to…*
escribiendo	*writing*	hacer de canguro	*babysit*
jugando…	*playing…*	hacer los deberes	*do my homework*
viendo la televisión	*watching TV*	lavarme el pelo	*wash my hair*
No estoy haciendo nada.	*I'm not doing anything.*	limpiar mi dormitorio	*clean my room*
¿Quieres ir al/a la…?	*Do you want to go to the…?*	salir con mis padres	*go out with my parents*
Vale.	*OK.*	trabajar	*work*
¿A qué hora quedamos?	*What time shall we meet?*		

Una crítica   *A review*

La película es…	*The film is…*	divertidísimo/a(s)	*really fun*
bonita	*lovely*	famosísimo/a(s)	*really famous*
emocionante	*exciting, moving*	feísimo/a(s)	*really ugly*
extraña	*strange*	guapísimo/a(s)	*really good-looking*
fea	*ugly*	hermosísimo/a(s)	*really beautiful*
feliz	*happy*	interesantísimo/a(s)	*really interesting*
impresionante	*impressive*	el artista	*artist*
mágica	*magical*	el autor	*author*
misteriosa	*mysterious*	el actor/la actriz	*actor/actress*
original	*original, unusual*	los efectos especiales	*special effects*
sorprendente	*surprising*	los efectos sonoros	*sound effects*
terrorífica	*terrifying*	la fotografía	*photography, cinematography*
triste	*sad*	la historia	*story*
Acabo de ver/leer…	*I have just seen/read…*	los personajes (principales)	*(main) characters*
Admiro/Adoro/Odio a X…	*I admire/adore/hate X…*	Cuenta la historia de…	*It tells the story of…*
porque sus películas son…	*because his/her films are…*	Trata de…	*It's about…*
aburridísimo/a(s)	*really boring*	Tiene un final…	*It has a… ending.*
bellísimo/a(s)	*really beautiful*	X actúa en el papel de…	*X plays the role of…*
buenísimo/a(s)	*really good*		

La tecnología   *Technology*

¿Qué haces con tu ordenador?	*What do you do with your computer?*	veo vídeos	*I watch videos*
Siempre…	*Always…*	descargar música	*downloading music*
De vez en cuando/A veces…	*Sometimes…*	comprar discos	*buying CDs*
Todos los días…	*Every day…*	las compras en el centro comercial	*shopping at the shopping centre*
Una vez/Dos veces a la semana…	*Once/Twice a week…*	las compras por Internet	*shopping online*
Los fines de semana…	*At weekends…*	los correos electrónicos	*emails*
Por las noches…	*In the evenings…*	las cartas tradicionales	*traditional letters*
chateo	*I chat online*	barato/a(s)	*cheap*
descargo música	*I download music*	caro/a(s)	*expensive*
hago compras por Internet	*I shop online*	fácil(es)	*easy*
juego con videojuegos del PC	*I play PC games*	difícil(es)	*difficult*
mando correos electrónicos	*I send emails*	peligroso/a(s)	*dangerous*
navego por Internet	*I surf the net*	seguro/a(s)	*safe, secure*
uso Facebook	*I use Facebook*	rápido/a(s)	*fast*
		lento/a(s)	*slow*

Repaso *Mi casa*

¡Viva mi barrio!
7

1 Escucha la descripción y escribe la letra de la casa correcta.

a

arriba (primera planta)

fuera

abajo (planta baja)

b

arriba (primera planta)

abajo (planta baja)

fuera

2 Con tu compañero/a, describe la otra casa del ejercicio 1.

Vivo en		un piso / una casa / un apartamento / un chalé		
abajo	hay	un aseo	un dormitorio	un jardín
arriba		una cocina	un estudio/despacho	un salón
fuera		un comedor	un garaje	una terraza
		un cuarto de baño		

3 Lee las frases y escribe el nombre de la habitación en inglés.

1 Esta es la habitación donde escucho música y hago mis deberes, y por supuesto duermo.

2 Esta es la habitación donde mi madre prepara la comida y donde, a veces, mi padre lava los platos.

3 Esta es la habitación donde me ducho y me lavo los dientes. Hay un aseo.

4 Esta es la habitación donde vemos la televisión y charlamos un rato.

5 Esta es la habitación donde cenamos, pero normalmente comemos en la cocina.

6 Este es el lugar donde tenemos la mesa de ping-pong en vez del coche.

⭐ Questions often begin with a question word.
¿Dónde está mi toalla? *Where is my towel?*
These words can also be used in the middle of a sentence, in a relative clause. They then lose their accent.
Esta es la habitación **donde** veo la televisión.
*This is the room **where** I watch TV.*

4 *Listen. Which item is missing from each description? (1–3)*

1 un armario · un ordenador · un equipo de música · una cama

2 una estantería · una lámpara · un sofá · un televisor

3 una ventana · una lavadora · una puerta · una nevera

 5 **Look at the picture. Choose the correct preposition in the sentences below.**

G Prepositions

Prepositions show the relationship of one thing to another.

delante de	*in front of*
detrás de	*behind*
encima de	*on*
debajo de	*under*
al lado de	*next to*
a la derecha de	*on the right of*
a la izquierda de	*on the left of*
entre	*between*

de + el → del
de + la → de la

La mesa está **al lado del** armario.
The table is next to the wardrobe.

1 Hay un equipo de música **encima de** / **debajo de** la mesa.
2 Hay una silla **al lado de** / **delante de** la mesa.
3 Hay un armario **a la derecha de** / **a la izquierda de** la mesa.
4 Hay un sombrero **detrás del** / **encima del** armario.
5 Hay zapatos **debajo del** / **al lado del** armario.
6 Las revistas están **detrás de** / **debajo de** la cama.
7 La cama está **debajo de** / **a la derecha de** la ventana.
8 La pizza está **encima de** / **delante de** la cama.

 6 **Listen and look at the picture of the bedroom. Which object is being described? Write the correct word in Spanish. (1–6)**

 7 **Describe tu dormitorio.**

● *Say what there is:* En mi dormitorio hay… En las paredes hay…
● *Say where things are:* …está(n) al lado de…
● *Say what you do there:* En mi dormitorio normalmente mando mensajes…

1 ¿Cómo es tu casa?

1 Escucha y escribe la letra de la foto correcta. (1–5)

Ejemplo: **1** e

Vivo en…	adosado/a	Está…
un apartamento	antiguo/a	en un pueblo
un chalé	bonito/a	en la ciudad
una casa	cómodo/a	en las afueras
un piso	feo/a	en el campo
una granja	moderno/a	en la costa
un bloque de pisos	nuevo/a	en la montaña
un edificio	pequeño/a	
	viejo/a	
	grande	

⭐ Make sure you understand all the adjectives, as they are often tested in listening and reading exams. Including them in your speaking and writing will also help you to gain a C Grade, but make sure you use the correct endings!

2 *Listen again and write down the adjectives you hear in Spanish. Then translate them into English. (1–5)*

Ejemplo: **1** pequeña – small,…

3 Con tu compañero/a, haz tres diálogos.

- ● ¿En qué tipo de casa vives?
- ■ Vivo en…
- ● ¿Dónde está?
- ■ Está…
- ● ¿Cómo es?
- ■ Es… pero también es…
  Me gusta mucho./No me gusta nada.

4 Listen. Are the people's opinions of their houses positive (P), negative (N) or both (P+N)? Listen again and write down what facilities each person has or doesn't have. (1–4)

Lo bueno es que	hay	(un) aparcamiento	(un) sótano
Lo malo es que	no hay	(un) ático	(una) terraza
Lo que más me gusta es que	tenemos	(un) garaje	calefacción
Lo que menos me gusta es que	no tenemos	(un) jardín (con césped)	habitaciones grandes

5 Mira la casa de Shakira y la casa de Rosa. Lee los textos. Copia y completa la tabla. (1–6)

	Whose house?	opinion	reason
1	Shakira's	beautiful house	likes the swimming pool

1 ¡Qué casa tan bonita! Lo que más me gusta es la piscina. **Javi**

2 Me encanta esta casa porque es modesta y muy cómoda si quieres vivir en el centro de una ciudad. Es un lugar ideal si tienes mascotas. **José**

3 Me encanta esta casa porque es elegante y clásica. Además tiene unas vistas a la piscina y al río maravillosas. **Claudia**

4 Yo pienso que esta casa es perfecta para esta cantante porque es una buena persona. **David**

5 Prefiero la casa pequeña. Creo que el dinero no da la felicidad. **Isa**

6 No me gustan nada las casas de la gente rica. En mi opinión es importante tener una casa pequeña si te preocupa el medio ambiente. **Inés**

La casa de Shakira

La casa de Rosa

mascotas = *pets*

 6 Write about your house. Answer the questions in Spanish below.

- ¿Dónde vives? **Vivo en…**
- ¿En qué tipo de casa vives? **Vivo en…**
- ¿Dónde está? **Está…**
- ¿Cómo es? **Mi casa es… También es…**
- ¿Cuántas habitaciones hay? **Hay…**
- ¿Qué hay fuera de tu casa? **Fuera hay…**
- ¿Qué opinas de tu casa? **En mi opinión, mi casa es… porque…**
  Lo bueno es que tenemos… Lo malo es que…

 To aim for a C Grade in speaking and writing, use a variety of phrases to express your opinions:

Pienso que…
Creo que…
En mi opinión…

And try to give reasons for your opinions:
…porque…

2 Mi barrio

 leer 1 Empareja los dibujos con las frases.

 **a**

 **b**

 **c**

 **d**

 **e**

 **f**

 g

h

 **i**

j

En mi barrio…
1 hay muchos turistas.
2 hay mucho tráfico.
3 hay muchos habitantes.
4 hay muchas tiendas.
5 hay una zona peatonal.
6 hay muchos museos y muchas galerías de arte.
7 no hay muchos árboles.
8 no hay muchos espacios verdes.
9 no hay muchas áreas de ocio.
10 no hay red de transporte público.

 escuchar 2 Escucha. ¿Positivo (P), negativo (N) o positivo y negativo (P+N)? (1–4)

> ⭐ Listen for clues to positive and negative opinions. Sometimes you may hear both, in which case it's probably a mixed opinion.
>
> | positive phrases ✓ | positive adjectives ✓ | negative phrases ✗ | negative adjectives ✗ |
> |---|---|---|---|
> | Lo bueno es que… | bueno | Lo malo es que… | malo |
> | Lo mejor es que… | bonito | Lo peor es que… | feo |
> | Me gusta… | interesante | No me gusta… | aburrido |
> | Me encanta… | barato | Odio… | caro |
> | | | Por desgracia… | |

 escribir 3 Write some positive and negative opinions about where you live. Use as many of the expressions above as possible.

Vivo en…	
✓	✗
Me gusta mi barrio/ciudad/pueblo.	No me gusta mi barrio/ciudad/pueblo.
Lo mejor es que tenemos…	Lo peor es que (no) tenemos…

 escuchar 4 Escucha la entrevista. Escribe los datos siguientes en inglés.

1 where exactly Diego lives
2 what it's like
3 what there is in town
4 positive and negative aspects of his town
5 where he would like to live and why

hablar 5 *With your partner, talk about the two places shown below. Use your imagination.*

- ● ¿Dónde vives?
- ■ Vivo en un pueblo / una ciudad histórico/a, moderno/a, pequeño/a, turístico/a, grande, industrial…
- ● ¿Dónde está?
- ■ Está en el norte / sur / este / oeste de…
- ● ¿Cómo es tu barrio?
- ■ Mi barrio es bonito, feo, ruidoso, tranquilo…
- ● ¿Qué hay allí?
- ■ Hay un centro comercial, un polideportivo, un cine, parques, una biblioteca, una pista de tenis, salas de juegos, bares, discotecas, restaurantes…
- ● ¿Qué opinas de tu barrio?
- ■ Lo bueno es que hay… /Lo malo es que hay…
- ● ¿Dónde te gustaría vivir?
- ■ Me gustaría vivir…

> ★ When you are writing or speaking, you can gain marks by referring to future plans or hopes. Use phrases like these, with the **infinitive**:
>
> Me gustaría **vivir**…   *I would like to live…*
> Quiero **vivir**…   *I want to live…*
> Voy a **vivir**…   *I'm going to live…*

leer 6 **Lee y contesta a las preguntas.**

Vivo en una ciudad turística muy grande. Está en el norte de España. En mi ciudad hay bares, discotecas, restaurantes y un centro comercial. Tenemos muchos museos y muchas galerías de arte. También hay muchísimas áreas de ocio: hay un polideportivo y parques bonitos, pero no me gusta vivir aquí. Opino que mi barrio es feo y lo malo es que hay mucho ruido. Para mí, lo peor de mi ciudad es que hay demasiada gente. Hay muchos habitantes y también muchísimos turistas.

A mí me encantan los árboles y los espacios verdes. Me gustaría vivir en una granja tranquila en el campo cerca de un pueblo pequeño.

Raúl

1 What is Raúl's town like? (Give two details.)
2 Where is it?
3 Name six things you can find there.
4 What two things doesn't he like about his neighbourhood?
5 What does he say is the worst thing about his town? (Give two details.)
6 Where exactly would he like to live? (Give three details.)

escribir 7 *Write about where you live and where you would like to live.*
Use the questions in exercise 5 to help you structure your text.

3 El centro comercial

1 Escucha y escribe la letra correcta. (1–4)

1 ¿Prefieres comprar…
a en los centros comerciales?

b por Internet?

2 ¿Prefieres
a las tiendas pequeñas?

b los grandes almacenes?

3 ¿Prefieres
a pagar más y recibir las cosas inmediatamente?

b pagar menos y esperar?

4 ¿Prefieres
a comprar cosas nuevas?

b comprar cosas de segunda mano?

2 Con tu compañero/a, haz el sondeo del ejercicio 1.

> ★ When answering the questions in the survey, remember to change the verb form **¿Prefieres…?** *(Do you prefer…?)* to **Prefiero…** *(I prefer…).* You can also make your answers more varied by using **me gusta más** instead of **prefiero**.

3 *Read the messages. Then copy the English summaries, correcting the four errors in each.*

Simón: Me gusta mucho ir de compras. Generalmente voy de compras una vez a la semana con mi hermana. ¡Lo pasamos bomba! Prefiero comprar cosas nuevas en tiendas pequeñas porque son tranquilas. No me gusta nada comprar por Internet – ¡qué aburrido!

Julia: Me gusta ir de compras y generalmente voy con mi madre una vez a la semana. Me gustan los grandes almacenes porque son baratos. No me gustan las tiendas pequeñas. En mi opinión son demasiado caras.

a Simón goes shopping once a week with his mother. He likes buying new things in department stores because they are interesting. He loves internet shopping.

b Julia goes shopping with her mother twice a week. She likes department stores because they are exclusive. She likes small shops because they are cheap.

4 Write a paragraph about your shopping preferences. Answer these questions:

- *Do you like to shop?*
- *How often do you go shopping?*
- *Do you prefer to buy things new or second hand?*
- *Where do you prefer to shop? Why?*

(No) Me gusta mucho ir de compras.	
Voy de compras	una vez a la semana una vez al mes dos veces al mes
Voy con	mis amigos mi hermana mis padres
Prefiero comprar Me gusta más comprar	en los centros comerciales/por Internet cosas de segunda mano/cosas nuevas
(No) Me gustan	los grandes almacenes las tiendas pequeñas
porque son	baratos/as, caros/as, interesantes, aburridos/as, tranquilos/as, ruidosos/as

5 Escucha y lee.

Dependiente: Buenas tardes. ¿En qué puedo servirle?

Mónica: Me gusta <u>este abrigo</u>. ¿Me <u>lo</u> puedo probar?

…

Dependiente: ¿Qué tal le queda?

Mónica: ¿<u>Lo</u> tiene en <u>rojo</u>?

Dependiente: Aquí <u>lo</u> tiene.

Mónica: Perfecto. <u>Lo</u> voy a comprar.

G *Saying 'this', 'these', 'it' and 'them'*

	this/these	it/them
el abrigo:	¿Tiene **este abrigo** en blanco?	Sí, **lo** tengo en blanco.
la corbata:	¿Tiene **esta corbata** en rojo?	Sí, **la** tengo en rojo.
los guantes:	¿Tiene **estos guantes** en verde?	Sí, **los** tengo en verde.
las gafas:	¿Tiene **estas gafas de sol** en amarillo?	Sí, **las** tengo en amarillo.

6 Escucha. Copia y completa la tabla en inglés. (1–2)

	item	problem	Bought? ✓/✗
1			

el abrigo

el sombrero

la corbata

la gorra

las gafas de sol

de cuero / seda / algodón / lana

7 Practise the dialogue in exercise 5 with your partner, changing the underlined words. Use the clothes vocabulary in exercise 6 to help you.

4 Compras y quejas

leer 1

In which department would you buy the items shown in the pictures?

Ejemplo: **a** Hogar – electrodomésticos

¡Rebajas hasta 50%, mejores que nunca!

Grandes ofertas y descuentos en todos los departamentos.

Electrónica
DVD y fotografía
Telefonía

Hogar
Electrodomésticos
Textil
Muebles

Ocio y cultura
Librería y papelería
Música

Moda
Ropa y zapatería
Joyería y relojería

Salud y belleza
Peluquería
Perfumería
Maquillaje

Deportes
Ropa deportiva
Calzado deportivo

Regalos
Flores
Cestas de fruta

escuchar 2

Escucha y contesta a las preguntas en inglés. (1–2)

a When did they go shopping?
b Where did they shop?
c What did they buy?
d How much did they spend?

leer 3

Lee y termina las frases en inglés.

Me gusta mucho ir de compras y generalmente voy con mis amigos. Tengo mucha suerte porque vivo en una ciudad bastante grande. Lo que más me gusta es que hay un centro comercial muy bueno y también muchas tiendas pequeñas interesantes. El fin de semana pasado fui de compras con una amiga, Anita. Lo pasamos genial. Vimos unas cosas muy bonitas. Anita compró unas gafas de sol Gucci de segunda mano y yo compré un sombrero. Lo mejor es que no gasté mucho dinero – solamente 5 euros.
Rodrigo

Ayer…
El fin de semana pasado…
La semana pasada…
  fui de compras con…
  fuimos a…
  vi…
  vimos…
  compré…
  gasté…
  lo pasamos…

1 Generally Rodrigo goes shopping with…
2 He is very lucky because…
3 What he likes best about his town is that…
4 Last weekend he went shopping with…
5 Anita bought…
6 Rodrigo bought…

tengo mucha suerte = *I'm very lucky*

leer 4 Busca estas palabras en español en el texto del ejercicio 3.

I went

we saw

she bought

I didn't spend

⊃196

G *Preterite verb endings*

As you read or listen to Spanish, you will probably see a variety of verbs in the preterite. Knowing the verb endings will help you to understand them.

	comprar	beber	ver	ir
(yo)	compré	bebí	vi	fui
(él/ella)	compró	bebió	vio	fue
(nosotros/as)	compramos	bebimos	vimos	fuimos

escribir 5 Write a paragraph about shopping. Answer the following questions:

- Do you like shopping? **(No) Me gusta ir…**
- What type of shops do you prefer? Why? **Prefiero (las tiendas pequeñas) porque…**
- Where did you go on a recent shopping trip? **La semana pasada fui de compras en…**
- Who with? **Fui con…**
- What did you buy? **Vi…, compré… / Vimos…, compramos…**
- How much money did you spend? **Gasté… libras.**

escuchar 6 Escucha los diálogos y escribe la letra correcta.
Listen again and note what happens: exchange, refund or nothing? (1–4)

 **a**  **b**  **c**  **d**

Quisiera un reembolso.
Quisiera cambiar…
   esta camiseta / esta maleta
   esta sudadera / este reloj.
Es demasiado grande / pequeño/a.
Está roto/a.
No funciona.
Quiero hablar con el director.

¿Tiene el recibo?
Le voy a dar otro/a…
Lo siento. No puedo cambiar…

hablar 7 Con tu compañero/a, haz diálogos, cambiando los datos subrayados.

- Buenos días. ¿Qué quería?
- ■ Compré <u>esta gorra la semana pasada</u>. <u>Es demasiado grande</u>. Quisiera un reembolso.
- ¿Tiene el recibo?
- ■ Sí, aquí lo tiene.
- Muy bien. Aquí tiene su reembolso.

a Too big! **b** Broken!

c  Too small! **d** Doesn't work!

Home and local area

You are going to have a conversation with your teacher about your home and local area. Your teacher could ask you the following:

- Where do you live? Where is it?
- What is your town like?
- What is there in your town?
- What do you think of your town? Why?
- What did you do in town last weekend?

Remember that you will have to respond to an unexpected question that you have not yet prepared.

1 *You are going to listen to Robbie, an exam candidate. Listen to Robbie's answers to the examiner's first three questions and choose the correct answers.*

¿Dónde vives? ¿Dónde está?

¿Cómo es tu ciudad?

¿Qué hay en tu ciudad?

a Vivo en un bloque de pisos **antiguo** / **cómodo** / **moderno**.
b Bristol está en el **suroeste** / **sureste** / **oeste** de Inglaterra.
c Es histórica y bastante **importante** / **industrial** / **turística**.
d Hay muchos cines y **discotecas** / **restaurantes** / **tiendas**.
e Lo mejor es que hay muchos **turistas** / **parques** / **museos**.
f Hay **una biblioteca** / **una sala de juegos** / **una galería de arte** muy cerca de mi casa.

2 *Listen to part 2 of Robbie's interview and fill each gap with the correct word from the box.*

juego	hay	porque	o	peor	también	además	malo	vivir	verano

– ¿Qué opinas de tu ciudad?
– Me gusta mucho **(1)** _____ en Bristol. Lo bueno es que **(2)** _____ muchos espacios verdes. Me gusta mucho jugar al fútbol **(3)** _____ dar una vuelta en bicicleta en los parques. **(4)** _____ al fútbol tres veces a la semana por lo menos. **(5)** _____ hay un polideportivo con piscina cerca de mi piso. En **(6)** _____, voy a hacer natación todos los días. **(7)** _____ en mi ciudad hay museos y galerías de arte interesantes. Me encantan las galerías **(8)** _____ me gusta mucho el dibujo. Lo **(9)** _____ en Bristol es que hay mucho tráfico y lo **(10)** _____ es que hay mucha basura. ¡Qué lástima!

3 *Now listen to part 3 of Robbie's interview and correct the mistakes in these sentences.*

1 A ver, el sábado por la mañana fui al cine.
2 …y luego visité un monumento.
3 Después cené en un restaurante con mi familia.
4 Comimos tortilla de patatas. Lo pasé fatal.
5 …me gustaría vivir en una casa antigua en la ciudad.
6 Me encantaría hacer natación todos los días.

4 Listen to part 3 again. What is the final unexpected question that Robbie is asked? What does it mean?

5 Now it's your turn! Prepare your answers to the task and then have a conversation with your teacher or partner.

- Use the Grade Studio and your answers to exercises 1–4 to help you plan.
- Adapt what Robbie said to talk about yourself but add your own ideas.
- Prepare your answers to the questions and try to predict what the unexpected question could be. The examiner might base this question on something you have already said, or ask something totally new!
- Record the conversation. Ask a partner to listen to it and say how well you performed.

> Award each other one star, two stars or three stars for each of these categories:
> - *Pronunciation*
> - *Confidence and fluency*
> - *Range of tenses*
> - *Variety of vocabulary and expressions*
> - *Using longer sentences*
> - *Taking the initiative*
>
> What do you need to do next time to improve your performance?

GradeStudio

Make sure you cover the basics.
- Use **simple structures** such as *vivo* (I live), *está* (it is – to refer to location), *es* (it is – to say what it's like), *hay* (there is/are), *juego* (I play) and *fui* (I went).
- Use **simple opinions**. Look at how Robbie uses *Me gusta mucho…* (I like… a lot) and *Me gusta bastante…* (I quite like…)
- Use **simple connectives**. Find examples of *y* (and), *pero* (but), *o* (or) and *también* (also) in Robbie's conversation.

To reach Grade C, show that you can:
- Use the correct endings on **adjectives**, e.g. *Es una ciudad muy grande. Es histórica y bastante turística.* Find as many other adjectives as you can in Robbie's conversation.
- Use **intensifiers** correctly. Robbie uses *muy* (very), *bastante* (quite) and *un poco* (a bit). Try to use them in your conversation.
- Use **different tenses** correctly. Robbie uses:
  - **the present tense** to say what Bristol is like, e.g. *Es una ciudad muy grande.*
  - **the preterite** to describe what he did last weekend. *Compré una camiseta y luego visité una galería de arte.*
  - **the near future tense** to say what he is going to do, e.g. *Voy a hacer natación todos los días.*

To increase your marks:
- Use *porque* to give reasons, e.g. *Me encantan las galerías porque me gusta mucho el dibujo.* (I love galleries because I like art a lot.)
- Use **more complex opinion-giving phrases**, e.g. *Lo bueno/Lo malo es que…, Creo que…, Pienso que…*
- Use *Me gustaría* and *Me encantaría* to say what you would like/love to do, e.g. *Me gustaría vivir en una casa antigua en el campo.* (I would like to live in an old house in the country.)
- Use **fillers** to make yourself sound more Spanish. Robbie uses *Bueno…* (Well…) and *A ver…* (Let's see…).
- Borrow this expression from Robbie: *¡Qué lástima!* (What a pity!)

Prueba escrita

1 **Read the text and put these topics in the order of the text.**

- **a** What's good about my town
- **b** The bad points about my town
- **c** Town or country living?
- **d** My home
- **e** A day in the park

Isabel

Vivo en una ciudad histórica: Sevilla. Está en Andalucía, en el sur de España. Me gusta mucho vivir aquí. Vivo en un piso moderno y me gusta bastante porque es muy cómodo. Tenemos una cocina, dos cuartos de baño, un salón, un comedor y tres dormitorios. Lo bueno es que hay mucho espacio y las habitaciones son bastante grandes pero lo malo es que no tenemos jardín.

En Sevilla hay mucho que hacer. Hay muchas tiendas y museos interesantes. También hay restaurantes, discotecas y bares. Lo mejor es que tiene muchos espacios verdes muy bonitos. Ayer, por ejemplo, pasé el día entero en el parque de María Luisa. Primero di una vuelta en bicicleta y luego visité la Isleta de los Pájaros. Leí, mandé mensajes, disfruté de la tranquilidad… ¡Lo pasé genial!

En Sevilla lo peor es que, a veces, puede ser ruidosa porque hay mucho tráfico.

Sin embargo, me encanta vivir en la ciudad. No me gustaría nada vivir en el campo. ¡Qué aburrido! En el futuro voy a viajar pero después voy a volver a Sevilla porque es la mejor ciudad del mundo.

2 **Find the equivalent of these expressions in Spanish in the text.**

- **1** I like living here a lot.
- **2** The good thing is that…
- **3** …but the bad thing is that…
- **4** …there is a lot to do.
- **5** The best thing is that…
- **6** Yesterday, for example,…
- **7** I spent the whole day…
- **8** Nevertheless, I love living in the city.
- **9** I would not like to live in the country at all.
- **10** It's the best city in the world.

3 **Look at the text again. Make a list of nine words and phrases used to give opinions.**

4 **Read the text and answer the questions in English.**

- **1** How does Isabel describe Seville in the first paragraph?
- **2** Where exactly is Andalucia?
- **3** What is the good thing about Isabel's flat? (1 detail)
- **4** What is the bad thing?
- **5** What does Isabel like most about Seville?
- **6** Name three things Isabel did in the park.
- **7** What does Isabel not like about Seville? (2 details)
- **8** Why would Isabel not like to live in the countryside?

5 *You might be asked to write about your local area as a controlled assessment task. Use the Grade Studio to help you prepare your account.*

⭐ GradeStudio

Make sure you cover the basics.

- Use **simple structures** correctly, e.g. *vivo* (I live), *está* (it is – location), *es* (it is), *hay* (there is) and *tiene* (it has).
- Give a **simple opinion**. Isabel does this by using *me gusta bastante* (I quite like) and *me encanta* (I love).
- Use **connectives** to make longer sentences. Look at how Isabel uses *y* (and), *pero* (but) and *también* (also).

To reach Grade C, show that you can:

- Use **adjectives** correctly and ensure they agree with the noun they refer to, e.g. *un piso moderno, una ciudad histórica, muchos espacios verdes muy bonitos*.
- Use **the present tense** correctly to describe your local area.
- Show that you can use **the preterite**, as Isabel does: *pasé el día entero* (I spent the whole day), *di una vuelta en bicicleta* (I went on a bike ride), *visité…* (I visited), *leí…* (I read), *mandé…* (I sent).
- Use **the near future tense** (*voy a* + infinitive). Isabel uses this twice. Can you find the two examples in the text?
- Use *porque* to give reasons and make your sentences longer, e.g. *me gusta bastante porque es muy cómodo*. (I quite like it because it's very comfortable.)
- Use **sequencing words**, e.g. *primero* (first), *luego* (then) and *después* (afterwards). Find where Isabel uses sequencing words in her text.

To increase your marks:

- Give your opinion using **more complex phrases** like *lo bueno es que…, lo malo es que…, lo peor es que…, lo mejor es que…*
- Use *(no) me gustaría* + infinitive to say what you would (or wouldn't) like to do.
- Use **simple exclamations**, e.g. *¡Qué aburrido! ¡Lo pasé genial!*

6 *Now write a full account of your local area.*

- Adapt Isabel's text and use language from Module 7.
- Structure your text carefully. Organise what you write in paragraphs.

General summary of area
Where do you live? Whereabouts is that? What is your house like?

Main paragraph
What is your area like?
What are the good things?
What are the bad things?
What have you done recently in your area?

Conclusion
Where are you going to live in the future?
Where would you like (or not like) to live?

7 *Check carefully what you have written.*

- adjectives (agree with the nouns that they describe?)
- spelling (check words that are similar to the English, but spelt differently, e.g. *tráfico, restaurantes, bares*)
- accents on the ends of verbs in the preterite

Palabras

Mi casa   *My home*

Vivo en…	*I live in…*	un armario	*a wardrobe*
un apartamento	*an apartment*	un equipo de música	*a stereo*
un chalé	*a chalet*	un ordenador	*a computer*
un piso	*a flat*	un sofá	*a sofa*
una casa	*a house*	un televisor	*a TV set*
abajo	*downstairs*	una cama	*a bed*
arriba	*upstairs*	una estantería	*a bookcase*
fuera	*outside*	una lámpara	*a lamp*
hay…	*there is…*	una lavadora	*a washing machine*
un aseo	*a toilet*	una nevera	*a fridge*
un comedor	*a dining room*	una puerta	*a door*
un cuarto de baño	*a bathroom*	una silla	*a chair*
un dormitorio	*a bedroom*	una ventana	*a window*
un estudio/un despacho	*a study*	a la derecha de	*on the right of*
un garaje	*a garage*	a la izquierda de	*on the left of*
un jardín	*a garden*	al lado de	*next to*
un salón	*a lounge*	debajo de	*under*
una cocina	*a kitchen*	delante de	*in front of*
una habitación	*a room*	detrás de	*behind*
una terraza	*a terrace*	encima de	*on*
Esta es la habitación donde me ducho, …	*This is the room where I shower, …*	entre	*between*
		En mi dormitorio hay…	*In my bedroom, there is/are…*
Hay…	*There is…*	En las paredes hay…	*On the walls, there is/are…*

¿Cómo es tu casa?   *What's your house like?*

¿En qué tipo de casa vives?	*What sort of house do you live in?*	la costa	*the coast*
		la montaña	*the mountains*
¿Dónde está?	*Where is it?*	las afueras	*the suburbs*
Vivo en…	*I live in…*	un pueblo	*a village/small town*
un bloque de pisos	*a block of flats*	Lo bueno es que…	*The good thing is that…*
un rascacielos	*a tower block*	Lo malo es que…	*The bad thing is that…*
una granja	*a farm*	Lo que más me gusta es que…	*What I like most is that…*
adosado/a	*semi-detached*		
antiguo/a	*old*	Lo que menos me gusta es que…	*What I like least is that…*
bonito/a	*nice*		
cómodo/a	*comfortable*	Hay…	*There is…*
feo/a	*ugly*	Tenemos…	*We have…*
grande	*large*	calefacción	*heating*
moderno/a	*modern*	habitaciones grandes	*large rooms*
nuevo/a	*new*	un aparcamiento	*a parking space*
pequeño/a	*small*	un ático	*an attic*
viejo/a	*old*	un garaje	*a garage*
Está en…	*It's in…*	un jardín (con césped)	*a garden (with lawn)*
el campo	*the countryside*	un sótano	*a cellar*
la ciudad	*the city*	una terraza	*a terrace*

Mi barrio   *My neighbourhood*

En mi barrio…	*In my neighbourhood…*	no hay muchos espacios verdes	*there aren't many green spaces*
hay mucho tráfico	*there's a lot of traffic*		
hay muchos habitantes	*there are lots of residents*	no hay muchas áreas de ocio	*there aren't many recreational areas*
hay muchos museos	*there are lots of museums*		
hay muchas galerías de arte	*there are lots of galleries*	no hay red de transporte público	*there's no public transport network*
hay muchos turistas	*there are lots of tourists*		
hay muchas tiendas	*there are lots of shops*	Lo mejor es que…	*The best thing is that…*
hay una zona peatonal	*there's a pedestrian zone*	Lo peor es que…	*The worst thing is that…*
no hay muchos árboles	*there aren't many trees*	Por desgracia…	*Unfortunately…*

Vivo en un barrio…	I live in a… neighbourhood	Hay…	There is/are…
grande	large	bares	bars
histórico/a	historic	discotecas	discos
industrial	industrial	parques	parks
moderno/a	modern	restaurantes	restaurants
pequeño/a	small	salas de juegos	amusement arcades
turístico/a	tourist	un centro comercial	a shopping centre
Mi barrio es…	My neighbourhood is…	un cine	a cinema
bonito/a	attractive	un polideportivo	a sports centre
feo/a	ugly	una biblioteca	a library
ruidoso/a	noisy	una pista de tenis	a tennis court
tranquilo/a	quiet	Me gustaría vivir en…	I'd like to live in…

El centro comercial *The shopping centre*

(No) me gusta mucho ir de compras.	I (don't) like going shopping very much.	aburridos/as	boring
Generalmente voy de compras…	I usually go shopping…	baratos/as	cheap
		caros/as	expensive
una vez por semana	once a week	interesantes	interesting
una vez por mes	once a month	ruidosos/as	noisy
dos veces por mes	twice a month	tranquilos/as	quiet
Voy con…	I go with…	Me gusta(n)…	I like…
Prefiero…	I prefer…	este abrigo	this coat
Me gusta más…	I prefer…	este bolso	this bag
comprar cosas de segunda mano	to buy things second hand	este sombrero	this hat
		esta gorra	this cap
comprar cosas nuevas	to buy new things	estas gafas de sol	these sunglasses
comprar en los centros comerciales	to shop in shopping centres	de algodón	made of cotton
		de cuero	made of leather
comprar por Internet	to shop online	de lana	made of wool
pagar más y recibir las cosas inmediatamente	to pay more and get things straight away	de seda	made of silk
		¿Me lo/la/los/las puedo probar?	Can I try it/them on?
pagar menos y esperar	to pay less and wait	¿Lo/La/Los/Las tiene en (azul)?	Have you got it/them in (blue)?
(No) Me gustan…	I (don't) like…		
los grandes almacenes	big stores	Lo/La/Los/Las voy a comprar.	I'll take it/them.
las tiendas pequeñas	little shops		
porque son…	because they are…		

Compras y quejas *Purchases and complaints*

Ayer…	Yesterday…	Es demasiado grande / pequeño/a.	It's too big/small.
El fin de semana pasado…	Last weekend…		
La semana pasada…	Last week…	Está roto/a.	It's broken.
fui de compras con…	I went shopping with…	No funciona.	It doesn't work.
fuimos a…	we went to…	Quiero hablar con el director.	I want to talk to the manager.
vi…	I saw…		
compré…	I bought…	¿Tiene el recibo?	Have you got the receipt?
gasté…	I spent…	Sí, aquí lo tiene.	Yes, here it is.
lo pasamos…	we had a… time	Le voy a dar otro (reloj).	I'll give you another (watch).
Quisiera un reembolso.	I'd like a refund.	Lo siento. No puedo cambiar el (reloj).	I'm sorry, I can't exchange the (watch).
Quisiera cambiar…	I'd like to exchange…		
esta camiseta/maleta/sudadera	this T-shirt/suitcase/sweatshirt	Muy bien. Aquí tiene su reembolso.	Fine. Here's your refund.
este reloj	this watch		

- Talking about the body and illnesses
- Using **doler** to say what hurts

Repaso 1 *Pasándolo mal*

chapter

La salud
8

escuchar 1 Escucha y escribe la(s) letra(s) correcta(s). (1–7)

- **a** los ojos
- **b** la nariz
- **c** las muelas/los dientes
- **d** la mano
- **e** el brazo
- **f** el estómago
- **g** el pie
- **h** la pierna
- **i** la espalda
- **j** la garganta
- **k** la boca
- **l** los oídos
- **m** la cabeza

Me duele	**el** brazo **la** cabeza
Me duele**n**	**los** ojos **las** muelas
Tengo dolor de Tiene dolor de	espalda oídos

escuchar 2 Listen and write down what hurts and how long it has been hurting. (1–6)

Ejemplo: **1** eyes, 2 weeks

> ☹ No me encuentro bien.
> Me siento mal.
>
> | ¿Desde hace cuánto tiempo? | Desde hace…
una hora
un día
una semana
quince días
un mes
dos horas / días / semanas / meses |
> |---|---|

G Doler

Doler *(to hurt)* works in the same way as **gustar**.
Me duele **el** pie.   *My foot hurts.*
Te duele **la** cabeza.   *Your head hurts.*

Use **duelen** for plural nouns (feet, eyes, etc.) or more than one part of the body.
Me duele**n los** brazos.   *My arms hurt.*

Remember to use the definite article (**el**, **la**, **los**, **las**) to talk about parts of the body with **doler**.

escribir 3 Escribe los mensajes.

Ejemplo:

> No puedo salir porque no me encuentro bien.
> Me duelen los pies desde hace tres días.

1  3 weeks

2  5 hours

3 1 month

138 ciento treinta y ocho

leer 4 Lee y escribe la letra correcta.

1 Tienes que beber mucha agua.
2 Tienes que ponerte esta crema.
3 Tienes que descansar en casa.
4 Tienes que tomar este jarabe.
5 Tienes que tomar una aspirina.
6 Tienes que ir al hospital inmediatamente.

escuchar 5 Escucha y completa la tabla en inglés. (1–3)

	problems	suggested treatment
1	tired,...	

> ⭐ Remember that words like **cansado** and **enfermo** will change depending on whether the speaker is male or female:
>
> estoy cansad**o**,
> estoy enferm**o**
>
> estoy cansad**a**,
> estoy enferm**a**

SERVICIO DE URGENCIAS

Estoy enfermo/a.

Estoy cansado/a.
Tengo sueño.

Tengo un resfriado.

Tengo gripe.

Tengo una insolación.

Tengo tos.

Tengo fiebre. Tengo frío/calor.

hablar 6 Con tu compañero/a, haz diálogos, cambiando los datos subrayados.

● ¿Qué te pasa?
■ No me encuentro bien. <u>Estoy cansado</u> y <u>tengo un resfriado</u>.
● ¡Vaya! ¿Desde hace cuánto tiempo?
■ Desde hace <u>dos días</u>.
● Ay, ¡qué mal! Tienes que <u>descansar</u> y <u>beber mucha agua</u>.
■ Vale, muchas gracias.

a 1 week

b 4 hours

Repaso 2   ¿Cuánto es?

escuchar 1

Escucha. Escribe la(s) letra(s) correcta(s). (1–10)

Ejemplo: **1** m

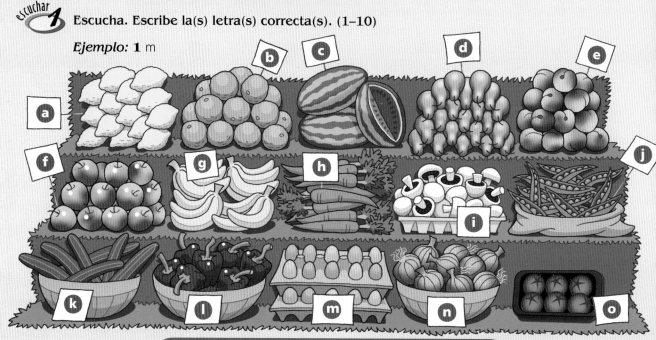

los melocotones	los tomates	las cebollas
los huevos	los melones	las zanahorias
los guisantes	los champiñones	las naranjas
los limones	los pepinos	las peras
los plátanos	los pimientos rojos	las manzanas

leer 2

Match each picture to an item on the shopping list. Then look up any words on the list that you still don't understand. Finally, copy the phrases into the correct column of the grid.

frutas	verduras y legumbres	bebidas	otros alimentos

a quinientos gramos de queso
b medio kilo de melocotones
c un kilo de tomates
d una bolsa de patatas
e una barra de pan
f un paquete de mantequilla
g un paquete de azúcar
h un paquete de arroz
i una botella de aceite
j una lata de atún
k un cartón de leche
l una docena de huevos
m una caja de pasteles

⭐ Sorting groups of vocabulary into categories will help you learn them. Look at each column in the exercise 2 grid for a minute and then cover it up. Can you remember all the phrases? Next, close your book and try to remember the whole list.

3 Lee los precios y escribe los números correctos.

Ejemplo: **1** – 9,50€

1 Nueve euros con cincuenta =
2 Ocho euros con veinticinco céntimos =
3 Diez euros con setenta y cinco =
4 Once euros con sesenta =
5 Catorce euros con cuarenta =
6 Quince euros con ochenta y cinco céntimos =

> ⭐ It's very important to learn numbers carefully, as they crop up in almost every topic area. Prices sometimes include the word **con**, which separates euros and cents. Cents tend to be in multiples of five, but not always.

 4 Escucha. ¿Qué compran? Copia y completa la tabla. (1–6)

	comida y bebida	cantidad	precio
1	pan	3 barras	1,20€

> ¿En qué puedo servirle?
> Deme…, por favor.
> Lo siento, no queda(n)…
> Aquí tiene. ¿Algo más?
> No, nada más.
> ¿Cuánto es?
> Son… euros con… en total.
>
> 100 cien
> 200 doscientos
> 300 trescientos ⎫ gramos de…
> 400 cuatrocientos
> 500 quinientos ⎭
> Medio kilo / Un kilo / Dos kilos de…
> Media/Una docena de huevos.

 5 Lee la conversación. Escribe la letra correcta.

● Buenas tardes. ¿En qué puedo servirle?
■ Hola, buenas tardes. Deme <u>dos barras de pan</u>, por favor.
● ¿Algo más?
■ Sí, necesito <u>un paquete de mantequilla</u> y <u>tres latas de tomates</u>.
● Aquí tiene <u>la mantequilla</u>. Pero lo siento, <u>no me quedan latas de tomates</u>.
■ Vale.
● ¿Algo más?
■ Sí, deme también <u>dos cartones de leche</u>, por favor. ¿Cuánto es?
● A ver… son <u>seis euros con setenta y cinco</u>.
■ Muy bien. Aquí tiene. ¡Gracias!
● Muchas gracias, ¡adiós!

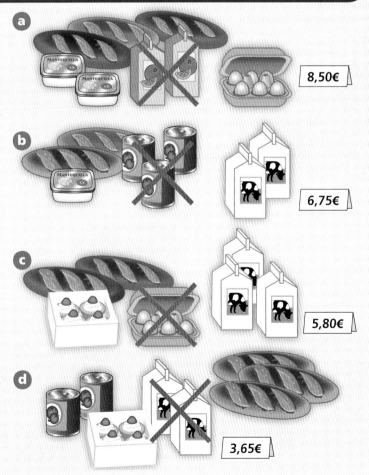

a 8,50€

b 6,75€

c 5,80€

d 3,65€

 6 With your partner, practise the conversation from exercise 5. Then create new conversations in a grocery shop, using the pictures in exercise 5 and changing the underlined phrases.

1 Estar en forma

escribir 1

Are these food items healthy (✓) or unhealthy (X)? How often do you eat them? Write a sentence about each one.

Ejemplo: **1** ✓ De vez en cuando como ensalada.

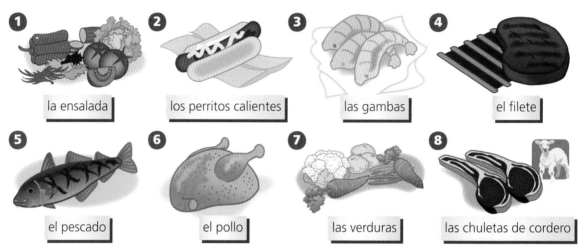

| 1 la ensalada | 2 los perritos calientes | 3 las gambas | 4 el filete |

| 5 el pescado | 6 el pollo | 7 las verduras | 8 las chuletas de cordero |

escribir 2

Look at the shopping baskets and write a sentence about each. Use the fruit and veg on page 140 as well as the vocabulary on this page.

Ejemplo: **1** Bebo agua y como plátanos,…

a   b
c   d

Para estar en forma…		
siempre	como	agua, Coca-Cola,
a menudo	bebo	limonada, zumo,
normalmente	desayuno	leche, café, té,
frecuentemente	ceno	lechuga,
de vez en cuando		filete/bistec,
rara vez		chuletas de cordero,
nunca		carne de cerdo,
no		huevos, yogur,
		queso, pan,
		patatas fritas,
		hamburguesas,
		pasteles, galletas

escuchar 3

Escucha a los famosos. Escribe la letra correcta del ejercicio 2. (1–3)

Sara Baras

Gael García Bernal

Salma Hayek

Contiene(n)…
muchas vitaminas
muchas proteínas
mucha grasa

bailadora de flamenco = *flamenco dancer*

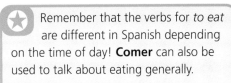

4 Habla de tu estilo de vida. Contesta a las preguntas.

- ¿Qué comes normalmente?
- ■ En general desayuno…/Como…/Meriendo…/Ceno… Nunca como…
- ¿Qué bebes?
- ■ Bebo mucho/a… porque quiero estar en forma./ porque contiene…

> ★ Remember that the verbs for *to eat* are different in Spanish depending on the time of day! **Comer** can also be used to talk about eating generally.
>
> **Desayunar:** **Desayuno** cereales.
> *I eat cereal for breakfast.*
> **Comer:** **Como** pescado.
> *I eat fish (for lunch).*
> **Merendar:** **Meriendo** fruta.
> *I eat fruit for tea.*
> **Cenar:** **Ceno** ensalada.
> *I eat salad for dinner.*

5 Lee los textos. Copia y completa la tabla en inglés.

name	in the past	in the future
Nico	ate meat, …	drink water, …

Nico

Benjamín

Nerea

> *La semana pasada comí mucha carne y bebí mucha limonada y naranjada. Esta semana quiero llevar una vida más sana y por eso voy a beber mucha agua y voy a dormir ocho horas. También voy a jugar al baloncesto con mis amigos.*

> *El fin de semana pasado bebí mucha Coca-Cola y comí dos pasteles y un paquete de galletas. Este fin de semana voy a comer más comida buena. Quiero comer pollo frito y voy a beber zumo de manzana.*

> *Hoy voy a comer muchas hamburguesas o patatas fritas porque la comida basura me gusta mucho. También voy a ver la tele. Ayer comí pescado y verduras y bebí mucha agua pero me sentí mal.*

6 ¿Qué haces para estar en forma? ¿Qué comes normalmente? Escribe un párrafo.

- *What you eat and drink every day:* **Cada día desayuno…, como…, meriendo… y ceno… Bebo…**
- *Why:* **porque contiene(n) muchas vitaminas/ muchas proteínas.**
- *What you try to avoid:* **Nunca como/bebo…**
- *What you ate last week:* **La semana pasada comí… y bebí…**
- *What you plan to do next week:* **La semana que viene voy a beber…, voy a comer…, voy a jugar al…, voy a ir al insti en…**

> ★ There are lots of clues to tell you whether someone is talking about the past or the future.
>
> Look out for verbs:
>
> | preterite – past | near future | |
> |---|---|---|
> | comí | voy a | } + infinitive |
> | bebí | quiero | |
>
> Look out for time expressions:
>
> | past | near future |
> |---|---|
> | Ayer | Hoy |
> | La semana pasada | Esta semana |
> | El fin de semana pasado | Este fin de semana |

- Giving advice on lifestyle
- Using the conditional of **deber**

2 ¿Llevas una vida sana?

leer

1 Read the problems and match each one with a piece of advice. Write the correct letter.

Ejemplo: **1** c

Tus problemas

PROBLEMAS

1 Estoy un poco gordo y estoy cansado todo el tiempo.

2 Fumo mucho y no estoy en forma. Las chicas no quieren salir conmigo.

3 Como demasiada comida basura, que contiene mucha grasa, y no me siento bien.

4 Bebo demasiada Coca-Cola y tengo muchos problemas con los dientes. ¡Qué lástima!

5 Odio todo tipo de deporte y siempre tengo mucho sueño aunque no puedo dormir.

CONSEJOS

a ¡Qué sorpresa! Los refrescos son malísimos para la salud. **Deberías beber más agua, leche o zumo.**

b **Deberías ir al instituto en bicicleta.** Así puedes hacer ejercicio de otra manera.

c **Deberías comer bien** y hacer más ejercicio. Así vas a perder peso.

d **No deberías comer todos esos perritos calientes y hamburguesas.** Son muy malos para tu cuerpo. **Deberías comer fruta y verduras cada día.**

e **No deberías comprar cigarrillos.** Sin los cigarrillos vas a ponerte guapo para las chicas.

escribir

2 Escribe las frases **en negrita** del ejercicio 1 en inglés.

Ejemplo: Deberías beber más agua, leche o zumo. → You should drink more water, milk or juice.

escuchar

3 Identify who is speaking and write down the advice they are given in English. (1–3)

G   The verb deber   ➲204

The verb **deber** generally means *must* when used in the present tense. When used in the conditional, it means *should*.

(yo)	deber**ía**	*I should*
(tú)	deber**ías**	*you should*
(él/ella)	deber**ía**	*he/she should*

Deber is followed by an **infinitive**.

Yo debería comer menos pizza.   *I should eat less pizza.*

Deberías beber más agua.   *You should drink more water.*

Nadia

Alejandro

Jorge

hablar 4 Con tu compañero/a, haz diálogos.

¿Qué debería hacer?

Deberías beber agua, zumo o leche.

 **1**

 **2**

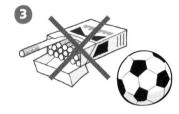 **3**

escribir 5 Write out the pieces of advice you gave in exercise 4.

Deberías…
No deberías…

leer 6 Busca estas frases en español en el texto.

1 I'm very worried because I'm a bit overweight.
2 I'd like to lose weight.
3 They are really thin.
4 I avoid fast food but I can't lose weight.

5 What can I do not to get fat?
6 Being ultra slim is not good.
7 You shouldn't spend so much time at home.

Querida Tía Tita:

Estoy muy preocupado porque estoy un poco gordo. Me gustaría perder peso porque las chicas del cole no quieren salir conmigo. Ellas están delgadísimas. Evito la comida rápida pero no puedo perder peso. ¡No sé por qué! No hago ejercicio porque odio los deportes. Prefiero jugar al ajedrez o navegar por Internet. ¿Qué debería hacer para no engordar?

José, Cádiz

Querido José:

¡No te preocupes! Estar delgadísimo no es bueno. Muchas chicas quieren ser como las modelos de las revistas de moda, pero muchas modelos son anoréxicas. Para perder peso no deberías pasar tanto tiempo en casa. Si no te gusta hacer deporte, deberías ir al colegio a pie o en bicicleta.

Tía Tita

perder peso = to lose weight
evito = I avoid
engordar = to get fat

leer 7 Lee otra vez las cartas del ejercicio 6. Contesta a las preguntas en inglés.

1 Why is José unhappy?
2 Why does he want to lose weight?
3 Why doesn't he exercise?
4 Name two activities he enjoys.
5 What does Tía Tita advise him to do? Mention two things.

⭐ The layout of a text is important too. Identifying different sections will help you to look in the right place for each answer. In exercise 6 there are two letters. Which question in exercise 7 refers to the second letter?

3 Los jóvenes

1 Lee las frases y escribe el nombre y la letra correcta.

> No fumo. Creo que **fumar** es peligroso.

David

> A veces **tomo drogas blandas**. No es una cosa muy seria.

Ignacio

> Pienso que **tomar drogas duras** es muy peligroso.

Marisa

> De vez en cuando **bebo alcohol** pero es perjudicial para la salud.

Natalia

> No **llevo navajas** nunca. Es una tontería.

Pablo

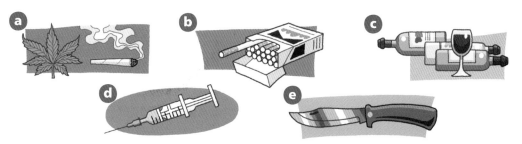

2 Busca estas frases en español en los textos.

1 I think that taking hard drugs is very dangerous.
2 I know smoking is stupid.
3 Tobacco kills a lot of people.
4 The problem is that cigarettes are very expensive.
5 …on the other hand, alcohol is bad for your health.
6 Knives are banned.
7 …because it's a waste of time.

> ★ Remember that there are several ways of expressing a point of view. Learn the following key phrases to express your own views successfully.
>
> **Creo que (no)…**
> **Pienso que (no)…**
> **Sé que…**
> **En mi opinión…**
> **El problema es que…**
> **Por un lado… por otro lado…**

Los vicios – tu opinión

a Pienso que tomar drogas duras es muy peligroso. Los jóvenes tienen problemas muy serios con estas drogas. Es una tontería.

b Fumo mucho. Sé que fumar es tonto y el tabaco mata a mucha gente pero me encanta el tabaco. El problema es que los cigarrillos son muy caros.

c De vez en cuando bebo alcohol. Por un lado me gusta beber cerveza con mis amigos pero por otro lado el alcohol es perjudicial para la salud.

d Nunca llevo navajas porque es una tontería. No me gusta nada la violencia, y las navajas están prohibidas.

e En mi opinión todas las drogas son malas. Yo nunca tomo drogas blandas como la marihuana porque es una pérdida de tiempo.

 3 *Read the website in exercise 2 again and write P (positive), N (negative) or P+N (positive and negative) for each opinion. Justify your answer.*

Ejemplo: **a** N – it's dangerous/stupid, young people have serious problems with hard drugs

 4 Escucha. Copia y completa la tabla en inglés. (1–4)

	things they do	things they don't do
1	smoke	take drugs

 5 Escribe tu opinión sobre cada dibujo del ejercicio 1.

| No…
A veces…
Nunca… | fumo cigarrillos
tomo drogas blandas
tomo drogas duras
bebo alcohol
llevo navajas | porque es | ☹
una pérdida de tiempo
una tontería
peligroso
perjudicial para la salud
caro

☺
divertido
fácil
relajante |

 6 Escucha y lee el poema. Rellena los espacios en blanco con palabras del cuadro.

> estoy   hacer   duele   cigarrillo
> mañanas   futuro   gusta   beber

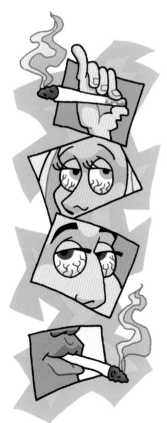

Fumo, porque me **(1)** _____.
Cuando estoy con mis amigos
Con **(2)** _____ *y copa en mano*
Me siento bien y **(3)** _____ *contento.*
Pero en casa después de fumar
O después de **(4)** _____,
No me gusto a mí mismo.
Me **(5)** _____ *el cuerpo,*
Odio estas adicciones.

En el **(6)** _____ *no voy a fumar más.*
Voy a respirar aire limpio,
Voy a **(7)** _____ *deporte,*
Voy a levantarme por las **(8)** _____
Sin pensar en cigarrillos.
Voy a ser libre.

Interview with a celebrity

You are going to play the role of a celebrity. Your teacher will play the part of the interviewer. Your teacher could ask you the following:

- Do you have a healthy lifestyle?
- What do you normally eat and drink?
- What did you eat and drink last week?
- Do you smoke or take drugs? Why or why not?
- What are you going to do to live more healthily?
- What advice can you give a young person about staying healthy?

Remember that you will have to respond to an unexpected question that you have not yet prepared.

1 You are going to listen to Jamie, an exam candidate, taking part in the above interview with his teacher. Listen to part 1 of the interview and match the beginnings and ends of these sentences.

> ¿Llevas una vida sana?

> ¿Qué comes y bebes normalmente?

1 Creo que llevo…
2 Hago natación…
3 También me gusta viajar en…
4 Desayuno pan, huevos y queso y siempre…
5 Pero a menudo como…
6 Sé que las patatas fritas contienen…

a …bebo zumo de naranja.
b …mucha grasa, pero están muy ricas.
c …una vida bastante sana.
d …hamburguesas y patatas fritas.
e …dos veces a la semana.
f …bicicleta o ir a pie, porque es más sano.

2 Listen to part 2 of Jamie's interview and fill each gap with the correct word from the box.

demasiado	porque	comí	mucha	comer	blandas	fui	desde	tomo	ni

- ¿Qué comiste y bebiste la semana pasada?
- La semana pasada **(1)** ▓▓▓ a Londres para hacer un concierto de rock. Por eso **(2)** ▓▓▓ mucha pizza y bebí **(3)** ▓▓▓ cerveza. También comí **(4)** ▓▓▓ chocolate. Durante la semana entera no comí fruta **(5)** ▓▓▓ pescado. Siempre es difícil **(6)** ▓▓▓ bien cuando no estoy en casa.

- ¿Fumas o tomas drogas?
- No **(7)** ▓▓▓ drogas duras ni tomo drogas **(8)** ▓▓▓. Creo que es una tontería **(9)** ▓▓▓ las drogas son muy malas. Desafortunadamente fumo **(10)** ▓▓▓ hace dos años pero no me gusta.

3 Now listen to part 3 of Jamie's interview and rewrite the jumbled words in bold.

> ¿Qué vas a hacer para llevar una vida más sana?

> ¿Qué consejos tienes para los jóvenes?

1 Siempre estoy cansado y no puedo **rodirm** bien.
2 Voy a comer menos **domica** basura.
3 También voy a beber más **ugaa**.
4 Deberías **oecmr** bien.
5 Nunca deberías **rumaf** ni tomar drogas.
6 **saVom** a comer una ensalada.

4 *In part 3 what is the final question that Jamie is asked?*

 5 *Now it's your turn! Prepare your answers to the task and then have a conversation with your teacher or partner.*

- Use the Grade Studio and your answers to exercises 1–4 to help you plan.
- Adapt what Jamie said to talk about yourself but add your own ideas.
- Prepare your answers to the questions and try to predict what the unexpected question could be. The examiner might base this question on something you have already said, or ask something totally new!
- Record the conversation. Ask a partner to listen to it and say how well you performed.

> *Award each other one star, two stars or three stars for each of these categories:*
> - *Pronunciation*
> - *Confidence and fluency*
> - *Range of tenses*
> - *Variety of vocabulary and expressions*
> - *Using longer sentences*
> - *Taking the initiative*
>
> *What do you need to do next time to improve your performance?*

★ GradeStudio

Make sure you cover the basics.

- Use **connectives** to extend your sentences, such as *y* (and), *pero* (but), *o* (or) and *también* (also). Look at how Jamie uses these.
- Use **simple structures** correctly, e.g. *llevo* (I lead), *hago* (I do), *como* (I eat), *bebo* (I drink), *desayuno* (I have… for breakfast), *fumo* (I smoke).
- Use **no** to make **simple negative** statements about your lifestyle, e.g. *No como verduras.* (I don't eat vegetables.)

To reach Grade C, show that you can:

- Use **different tenses**. Jamie uses:
  - **the present tense** to describe his current lifestyle: *Hago natación dos veces a la semana.* (I go swimming twice a week.)
  - **the preterite** to say what he ate and drank last week: *Comí mucha pizza y bebí mucha cerveza.* (I ate a lot of pizza and drank lots of beer.)
  - **the near future tense** to explain how he is going to be healthier *Voy a comer menos comida basura.* (I am going to eat less junk food.)
- Use **expressions of frequency** and **qualifiers**. Look at how Jamie uses *bastante* (quite), *muy* (very), *mucho* (a lot of) and *demasiado* (too much).

To increase your marks:

- Give **reasons**, e.g. *Creo que es una tontería porque las drogas son muy malas.* (I think it's stupid, because drugs are very bad.)
- Use different **verb phrases with an infinitive**, e.g. Jamie uses *no puedo dormir* (I can't sleep) and *deberías comer* (you should eat).
- Add **variety to your opinions**, by using *Sé que…* (I know that…) and *desafortunadamente* (unfortunately).
- Include more **complex negatives**, e.g. *No comí fruta ni pescado, Nunca deberías fumar.*
- Try using **desde hace** – *fumo desde hace dos años…* (I have been smoking for two years…).

leer
1
Read the text and choose the correct title for each paragraph.
What words/phrases support your decisions?

a A recent unhealthy meal **c** James's fitness programme
b What he will do to stay healthy **d** What James likes for his meals

1 Me llamo James y tengo quince años. Creo que llevo una vida bastante sana. Siempre como mucha fruta y normalmente bebo mucha agua porque es muy buena para la salud. Además desde hace seis meses voy al gimnasio dos veces a la semana. Para mantenerme en forma también me gusta practicar deporte y nunca tomo drogas porque es muy peligroso.

James

2 Generalmente me gusta desayunar cereales pero a veces como tostadas. Para el almuerzo o la cena como carne o pescado con ensalada y me encanta el yogur. El problema es que también me gusta la comida basura (¡me encantan las hamburguesas!) y a veces no quiero comer ni pescado ni verduras.

3 Por ejemplo, el sábado pasado fui a un restaurante con mi familia y comí muy mal. Primero pedí una pizza grande (y generalmente la pizza tiene mucha grasa) y también bebí dos Coca-Colas. Lo peor es que de postre comí un pastel de chocolate con helado y nata. ¡Qué vergüenza!

4 El año que viene voy a hacer más deporte porque quiero mantenerme en forma. Me gustaría hacer equitación o jugar al golf. No voy a comer comida basura ni a beber alcohol porque es perjudicial para la salud.

el almuerzo = *lunch*

leer
2
Find these expressions in Spanish in the text.

1 I always eat a lot of fruit…
2 …because it is very good for your health.
3 To keep myself fit…
4 …I like to do sport…
5 For lunch or dinner I eat…
6 The problem is that I also like…

7 …sometimes I don't want to eat either fish or vegetables.
8 The worst thing is that…
9 I'm not going to eat junk food…
10 …it damages your health.

leer
3
Which paragraphs of the text are not completely in the present tense? Give three examples from each of these paragraphs of verbs which do not refer to the present.

leer
4
Read the text again and answer the questions in English.

1 How healthy does James think his lifestyle is?
2 What does he drink a lot of?
3 What does he do to keep fit? (2 details)
4 Name something he never does.
5 What does he usually eat for breakfast?

6 What does he eat for lunch or dinner?
7 Name two unhealthy things James ate last Saturday.
8 Name two things James wants to do in the future.

escribir 5 *You might be asked to write about healthy lifestyles as a controlled assessment task. Use the Grade Studio to help you prepare your account.*

⭐ GradeStudio

Make sure you cover the basics.

- Use **simple structures** correctly, e.g. *me llamo* (I am called), *como* (I eat), *bebo* (I drink), *voy* (I go), *es* (it is).
- Use **connectives** to make your sentences longer and more interesting, e.g. *y* (and), *o* (or) and *también* (also).
- Use **simple opinions** to describe your food preferences, e.g. *me gusta…* (I like), *no me gusta…* (I don't like). How does James say 'I love yoghurt' and 'I love hamburgers'? Why is there an *n* on the verb in 'I love hamburgers'?

To reach Grade C, show that you can:

- Use **the present tense** correctly. James uses it to talk about his lifestyle now.
- Use **the preterite**. James talks about a recent meal he had.
- Use **the near future tense**. James uses this to talk about his lifestyle hopes.
- Use **time** and **frequency words**. Which of these does James use in his text: *siempre* (always), *normalmente* (normally), *generalmente* (generally), *de vez en cuando/a veces* (sometimes), *a menudo* (often), *frecuentemente* (frequently)?

To increase your marks:

- Use **negatives** such as *nunca* (never) and *ni… ni…* (neither… nor…) to talk about your lifestyle, as James does. Invent your own phrases using these.
- Use *me gusta* + infinitive to say what you like eating. James says *me gusta desayunar cereales*. Think of another infinitive you could use with *me gusta*.
- Use *(no) quiero* + infinitive, e.g. *quiero mantenerme en forma*. (I want to stay fit.)
- Use *desde hace* + present tense to say how long you have been doing something. James says *desde hace seis meses voy al gimnasio*. (I have been going to the gym for six months.)

escribir 6 *Now write a full account of your lifestyle.*

- Adapt James's text and use language from Module 8. Write at least 200 words.
- If you need to write something which is not in the book, keep it simple. When you look up a word in a dictionary, make sure that you choose the right one. Look carefully at any examples given. Cross-check by looking up the Spanish word in the Spanish-English part of the dictionary.
- Structure your text carefully. Organise what you write in paragraphs.

General summary

Introduce yourself
Do you think you have a healthy lifestyle?
What sport or other keep-fit activities do you do?

Main paragraph

Talk about your lifestyle
- What do you eat and drink?
- What are your opinions on smoking, alcohol, drugs, etc?
Talk about a recent meal out
- Who did you go with?
- Where did you go?
- What did you eat/drink?

Conclusion

What are you going to do in the future to be more healthy?

escribir 7 *Check carefully what you have written.*

- spelling (a lot of food words are near-cognates, e.g. *cereales*, *yogur*)
- endings on *me gusta(n)* and *me encanta(n)* (When do you need to use the *n*?)
- accents on verbs (preterite: *bebí, comí,* etc.)

 leer 1 **Read Carmen's supermarket receipt and answer the questions. (4 marks)**

Supermercado Supervalor	
arroz (medio kilo)	0,90€
naranjas (un kilo)	1,50€
leche (dos litros)	1,10€
huevos (una docena)	2,30€
patatas (bolsa)	0,80€
galletas (paquete grande)	1,40€
Total	8,00€

Gracias por su compra

1 What fruit did Carmen buy?
2 What vegetables did she buy?
3 What exactly did she pay €2.30 for?
4 What quantity of biscuits did she buy?

⭐ Any question with the word 'exactly' in it means you need to give a full answer (e.g. item and quantity in this one) in order to get the mark.

 leer 2 **Read Antonio's description of his house and answer the questions. (2 marks)**

Mi casa tiene dos plantas. Arriba hay tres dormitorios, un despacho y el cuarto de baño. Mi dormitorio está al lado del despacho. Abajo hay una cocina, un comedor y un salón. El aseo está detrás del comedor.

⭐ It's very important to know phrases of position in Spanish (above, next to, etc.) in order to answer questions that ask where exactly things are.

1 Where upstairs is Antonio's bedroom?
2 Where downstairs is the toilet?

 leer 3 **Read what Elena writes about her home town and choose the word that summarises each section of her description. Write the correct letter. (5 marks)**

1 Mi pueblo tiene más de cincuenta mil habitantes. El centro es muy popular pero muchas familias viven en las afueras. Mucha gente visita el pueblo porque es histórico y bonito.

2 No tenemos estación pero es muy fácil llegar aquí en autocar. El tráfico no puede entrar en la zona peatonal pero hay varios aparcamientos cerca del centro. Es muy fácil ir a todos los sitios a pie.

3 Hay un centro comercial bastante moderno cerca de la calle principal. Allí hay tiendas de todo tipo donde se puede buscar ropa, recuerdos o comida típica por ejemplo. Normalmente los precios son buenos.

4 Si te interesa la cultura hay una galería de arte estupenda. Si prefieres la vida nocturna puedes visitar los bares y clubs. Si quieres mantenerte en forma hay dos polideportivos fenomenales.

5 A veces el centro es un poco ruidoso, especialmente los fines de semana. Todos los días hay demasiada basura en las calles. También hay muy pocos espacios verdes en las partes industriales.

a housing
b shopping
c people
d jobs
e leisure
f problems
g transport

⭐ In longer texts there are often several clues to help you answer the question. If you don't know some of the words, use others that you do know to help you work out the answer.

escuchar 4

Listen to Ernesto talking to his mum. Answer the questions in English. (4 marks)

1 Where is Ernesto's mum?
2 What is she doing?
3 What's the matter with Ernesto's trainers?
4 When will he get new ones?

> ★ You are listening to Spanish, but the questions are in English, so make sure you answer them in English, too.

escuchar 5

Listen to Marisol talking about the area she lives in and identify the three places she likes. Write the three correct letters. (3 marks)

> ★ Make sure you answer the question. Listen out for places that the speaker likes and reject the places she doesn't like.

escuchar 6

Listen to these customers buying clothes and answer the questions in English. (4 marks)

1 What colour coat does the customer want?
2 What size of hat does the customer want?
3 What kind of socks does the customer want?
4 How much is the bag the customer buys?

calcetines = socks

> ★ Be careful of details that are in each dialogue to distract you. For example, if you are being asked for a colour, two may be mentioned and you will need to decide which one the customer chooses.

escuchar 7

Listen to these four young people, Ramón, Teresa, Nacho and Gloria, talking about their lifestyle and how healthy it is. Write H (healthy), U (unhealthy) or H+U (healthy and unhealthy). (4 marks)

> ★ In this kind of question each speaker will say at least two things to help you make your decision. Listen out for qualifiers (e.g. *mucho*) and phrases of frequency (e.g. *siempre, a menudo, nunca*) which provide useful information.

Ramón   **Teresa**   **Nacho**   **Gloria**

Palabras

Pasándolo mal   *Feeling ill*

el brazo	arm	una semana	a week
el estómago	stomach	quince días	a fortnight
el pie	foot	un mes	a month
la boca	mouth	dos horas/días/semanas/	two hours/days/weeks/months
la cabeza	head	meses	
la espalda	back	Estoy cansado/a.	I'm tired.
la garganta	throat	Tengo sueño.	I'm tired.
la mano	hand	Estoy enfermo/a.	I'm ill.
la nariz	nose	Tengo fiebre.	I've got a temperature.
la pierna	leg	Tengo frío.	I'm cold.
las muelas/los dientes	teeth	Tengo calor.	I'm hot.
los oídos	ears	Tengo gripe.	I've got flu.
los ojos	eyes	Tengo tos.	I've got a cough.
Me duele(n)…	My… hurts	Tengo un resfriado.	I've got a cold.
Tengo dolor de (estómago).	I have (stomach) ache.	Tengo una insolación.	I've got sunstroke.
¿Qué te pasa?	What's the matter?	Tienes que…	You have to…
No me encuentro bien.	I don't feel well.	beber mucha agua	drink a lot of water
Me siento mal.	I feel ill.	descansar en casa	rest at home
¿Desde hace cuánto	For how long?	ir al hospital	go to hospital immediately
tiempo?		inmediatamente	
Desde hace…	For…	ponerte esta crema	put this cream on
una hora	an hour	tomar este jarabe	take this syrup
un día	a day	tomar una aspirina	take an aspirin

¿Cuánto es?   *How much is it?*

las cebollas	onions	Aquí tiene. ¿Algo más?	Here you are. Anything else?
las manzanas	apples	No, nada más.	No, nothing else.
las naranjas	oranges	¿Cuánto es?	How much is it?
las peras	pears	Son… euros con… en total.	That's… euros and…cents in all.
las zanahorias	carrots	quinientos gramos de…	500 grams of…
los champiñones	mushrooms	medio kilo/un kilo/dos	half a kilo/one kilo/two
los guisantes	peas	kilos de…	kilos of…
los huevos	eggs	un cartón de leche	a carton of milk
los limones	lemons	un paquete de azúcar	a packet of sugar
los melocotones	peaches	un paquete de arroz	a packet of rice
los melones	melons	un paquete de mantequilla	a packet of butter
los pepinos	cucumbers	una barra de pan	a stick of bread
los pimientos rojos	red peppers	una botella de aceite	a bottle of oil
los plátanos	bananas	una caja de pasteles	a box of cakes
los tomates	tomatoes	una docena de huevos	a dozen eggs
¿En qué puedo servirle?	How can I help you?	media docena de huevos	half a dozen eggs
Deme…, por favor.	Give me…, please.	una lata de atún	a tin of tuna
Lo siento, no queda(n)…	I'm sorry, there's no… left.		

Estar en forma   *Being in shape*

Para estar en forma…	To be in shape…	el té	tea
siempre	always	el yogur	yogurt
a menudo	usually, often	el zumo	juice
frecuentemente	frequently	la carne de cerdo	pork
de vez en cuando	sometimes	la chuleta	chop
raramente	rarely	la comida basura/rápida	junk/fast food
raras veces	occasionally	la ensalada	salad
nunca	never	la fruta	fruit
(no) como/bebo	I (don't) eat/drink	la leche	milk
desayuno	I have breakfast	la lechuga	lettuce
meriendo	I have tea	la limonada	lemonade
ceno	I have dinner	las galletas	biscuits
La semana pasada comí…	Last week I ate…	las gambas	prawns
Ayer bebí…	Yesterday I drank…	las hamburguesas	hamburgers
La semana que viene voy a comer/beber…	Next week I am going to eat/drink…	las patatas fritas	crisps
		las verduras	vegetables
el agua (f)	water	los huevos	eggs
el bistec/filete	steak	las legumbres	vegetables
el café	coffee	los pasteles	cakes
el cordero	lamb	los perritos calientes	hot dogs
el pan	bread	Contiene(n)…	It contains (They contain)…
el pescado	fish	mucha grasa	a lot of fat
el pollo	chicken	muchas proteínas	a lot of proteins
el queso	cheese	muchas vitaminas	a lot of vitamins

¿Llevas una vida sana?   *Do you lead a healthy life?*

Estoy (un poco) gordo/a.	I'm (a bit) overweight.	comer bien	eat well
Siempre estoy cansado/a.	I'm always tired.	ir al instituto en bicicleta	go to school by bike
Para perder peso…	In order to lose weight…	no deberías…	you shouldn't…
Para no engordar…	In order not to get fat…	comer hamburguesas	eat hamburgers
deberías…	you should…	comprar cigarrillos	buy cigarettes
beber más agua	drink more water	pasar tanto tiempo en casa	spend so much time at home

Los jóvenes   *Young people*

En mi opinión…	In my opinion…	divertido	fun
Creo que…	I think…	fácil	easy
Pienso que…	I think…	peligroso	dangerous
Sé que…	I know…	perjudicial para la salud	bad for your health
Por un lado…, por otro lado…	On one hand…, on the other hand…	relajante	relaxing
		una pérdida de tiempo	a waste of time
El problema es que…	the problem is that…	una tontería	stupid
Me da igual…	I'm not bothered…	no es una cosa muy seria	isn't very serious
beber alcohol	drinking alcohol	No/A veces/Nunca…	I don't/occasionally/never…
fumar	smoking	bebo alcohol	drink alcohol
llevar navajas	carrying knives	fumo cigarrillos	smoke cigarettes
tomar drogas blandas	taking soft drugs	llevo navajas	carry knives
tomar drogas duras	taking hard drugs	tomo drogas blandas/duras	take soft/hard drugs
es…	is…		

Repaso Cambios medioambientales

leer 1

Empareja las frases con la foto correcta.

1 Mucha gente va en coche o en moto todos los días.
2 Hay demasiado tráfico y muchos atascos.
3 Hay mucha contaminación del agua.
4 No hay espacios verdes.
5 Hay muchas fábricas.
6 No llueve mucho y por eso la sequía es un problema.
7 En nuestra ciudad hay mucha basura.

la sequía = *drought*

leer 2

Busca estas frases en español en el ejercicio 1.

a too much traffic
b a lot of traffic jams
c a lot of pollution
d green spaces
e factories
f a lot of rubbish

escuchar 3

Escucha y escribe la(s) letra(s) correcta(s). (1–6)

Se debe…
Es necesario…

a comprar productos ecológicos
b consumir menos energía
c proteger la naturaleza
d reciclar papel y vidrio
e reducir la contaminación
f usar el transporte público
g plantar árboles

No se debe…

h malgastar agua
i tirar basura al suelo

Gastar can mean *to spend* money, or *to use* energy.
Malgastar means *to waste* (literally, *to use badly*).

4 Escucha. Copia y completa la tabla en inglés. (1–3)

	area lived in	environmental problems	solutions
1	industrial area	pollution	use public transport,...

Vivo en	un barrio industrial el centro de… una ciudad turística una ciudad histórica

G **Se debe/Es necesario** → 204

Use **se debe** *(must)* followed by an **infinitive**.
To express the same thing, you can also use
es necesario + **infinitive**.
Se debe proteger la naturaleza.
We must protect nature.
Es necesario proteger la naturaleza.
It is necessary to protect nature.

 5 Con tu compañero/a, pregunta y contesta, cambiando los datos subrayados.

● ¿Dónde vives?
■ Vivo en <u>un barrio industrial</u>.
● ¿Qué problemas hay en tu región?
■ El mayor problema es que <u>hay mucha contaminación</u>.
● ¿Qué se debe hacer para proteger el medio ambiente?
■ Creo que se debe <u>usar el transporte público</u>.

⭐ Use a model to help you answer the questions, but add your own information. Vary what you say by using phrases you have seen before to give your point of view:

Opino que…
Para mí…
Creo que…

 6 *Everything in its place. Where would you put each object? Write the correct number.*

1 el contenedor azul – papel y cartón

2 el contenedor verde – vidrio

3 el contenedor amarillo – envases de plástico, tetrabrik

4 la caja de compostaje

5 la basura

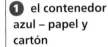

a  una manzana

b una botella de plástico vacía

c una bolsa de plástico

d  un periódico

e 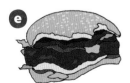 los restos de una hamburguesa

f un tetrabrik de leche vacío

g una botella de cristal vacía

h un bote de champú vacío

 7 Escribe un artículo sobre el medio ambiente. Contesta a las preguntas del ejercicio 5.

7 Piensa globalmente

leer 1 Empareja las frases con las fotos. ¿Qué significan?

a   la destrucción del ecosistema
b   la contaminación del aire
c   el calentamiento global
d   las especies amenazadas
e   la sequía

escuchar 2 *Listen. Which issue is each speaker **most** concerned about? Write a letter from exercise 1. (1–5)*

Ejemplo: **1** a

> ★ In exercise 2 you may hear two things mentioned. You need to listen for the one that the person is *most* worried about. Understanding these phrases will help you.
> Me preocupa(n) más…   *I'm most worried about…*
> El mayor problema es…   *The biggest problem is…*
> El peor problema es…   *The worst problem is…*

hablar 3 Con tu compañero/a, haz este cuestionario.

● Para ahorrar agua, es mejor ducharse.
■ Estoy de acuerdo./No estoy de acuerdo. Es mejor bañarse.

en vez de + infinitivo = *instead of + ing*

1 Para ahorrar agua, es mejor…
a   ducharse.
b   bañarse.

2 Para reducir la contaminación del aire, es mejor…
a   andar o ir en bici, en vez de usar el coche.
b   usar más el coche.

3 Para consumir menos energía, es mejor…
a   encender las luces.
b   apagar las luces.

> ★ Use the following expressions to play for time when you are speaking:
> **A ver…**   **Un momento…**
> **Pues… no lo sé.**   **Espera…**

4 Para usar menos gasolina, es mejor…
a   comprar productos locales.
b   comprar productos de países lejanos.

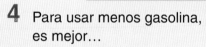
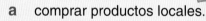

5 Para evitar la basura, es mejor…
a   llevar una bolsa a la compra.
b   pedir muchas bolsas de plástico.

6 Para luchar contra el calentamiento global, es mejor…
a   ver la televisión.
b   hacerse miembro de un grupo ecologista.

4 Escucha y escribe las letras correctas del cuestionario (ejercicio 3). (1–6)

Ejemplo: **1** a

 5 Lee el texto y rellena los espacios en blanco con las palabras del cuadro.

Para **(1)** _____ el medio ambiente, es importante pensar globalmente y actuar localmente. Por ejemplo, para **(2)** _____ menos energía, es necesario apagar las luces en casa.

Para **(3)** _____ agua, es importante ducharse en vez de bañarse. Para **(4)** _____ la contaminación se debe usar más el transporte público.

Para proteger la naturaleza se debe reciclar y reutilizar cosas. Para **(5)** _____ la destrucción del ecosistema, por favor piensa globalmente, actúa localmente.

ahorrar   consumir   evitar
proteger   reducir

G *Para*

Para + **infinitive** = *in order to…*
Para **proteger** la naturaleza…
In order to protect nature…
Para **usar** menos gasolina…
In order to use less oil…

 6 Lee el texto. Contesta a las preguntas en inglés.

En mi opinión el calentamiento global es el mayor problema. Si no hacemos algo, las plantas y los animales van a morir. Para ayudar, se debe consumir menos energía. Yo siempre intento apagar la luz cuando salgo de una habitación. También voy al colegio en bici o andando.
Otro problema es el precio de la gasolina. Para usar menos gasolina, es mejor comprar productos locales. Un tomate de España necesita menos gasolina para su transporte que un tomate de otro país.
Mustafá

1 What is the biggest problem facing the planet according to Mustafá?
2 What does he say will happen if we don't do anything?
3 What does he personally do to reduce his energy consumption? (Give three details.)
4 What is the other problem that he mentions?
5 Why are Spanish tomatoes better than others for him?

 7 *Write a paragraph giving your opinions on global issues.*

En mi opinión **el calentamiento global** es el mayor problema.
Para ayudar, **se debe ir a pie o en bicicleta**.
Otro problema es **la contaminación**. Para **reducir la contaminación** es mejor **usar productos ecológicos**.

2 Voluntarios

1 Lee las frases. ¿Qué significan?

Ejemplo: **1** If I become a volunteer,…

1 *Si me hago voluntaria,…*

Silvana

2 *Si doy dinero a Oxfam,…*

Hasan

3 *Si apadrino a un niño,…*

Gabriel

4 *Si reciclo y reutilizo,…*

Sabrina

5 *Si compro productos de comercio justo,…*

Juan Pablo

2 Listen to the phrases from exercise 1, which are now finished off by the speakers. Write the letter of the phrase below that they use. What does it mean? (1–5)

Ejemplo: **1** a – I will improve society.

a mejoraré la sociedad.
b daré al niño la posibilidad de sobrevivir.
c cuidaré el medio ambiente.
d ayudaré a otras personas.
e ayudaré a los trabajadores.

> mejorar = *to improve*
> sobrevivir = *to survive*

3 Con tu compañero/a, haz estos diálogos.

- ¿Cómo te llamas?
- Me llamo…
- ¿Cuántos años tienes?
- Tengo…
- ¿Por qué quieres trabajar como voluntario/a?
- Si…

Name: Pablo
Age: 16
If: buy Fairtrade products
Will: help the workers

Name: Esther
Age: 15
If: recycle and reuse
Will: care for the environment

G **The future tense** ⟳**202**

The future tense is used to say that you *will* do something. To form it, you normally take the **infinitive** of the verb and add these endings:

ayudar *(to help)*

(yo)	**ayudaré**	*I will help*
(tú)	**ayudarás**	*you will help*
(él/ella)	**ayudará**	*he/she will help*

Sometimes you don't use the infinitive, but an irregular stem:

hacer	→	**har**é	*I will do/make*
tener	→	**tendr**é	*I will have*
poner	→	**pondr**é	*I will put*
salir	→	**saldr**é	*I will go out*

Can you spot examples of the future tense in the phrases in exercise 2?

G **Si… (If…)**

Si + **present tense**, **future tense**
Use this construction to talk about things that are likely to happen.
Si trabajo como voluntario, **mejoraré** la sociedad.
If I work as a volunteer, I will improve society.

4 Lee y empareja las frases con las fotos.

1 los sin techo **3** la discriminación y el racismo
2 la pobreza y el hambre **4** el terrorismo

 5 Escucha. Copia y completa la tabla en inglés. (1–4)

	problem	action
1	famine in Africa	

 6 Read the texts and answer the questions below. Write K (Karim), S (Silvia) or K+S (Karim and Silvia).

¿Quieres ser voluntario?

Me llamo **Karim**. Soy voluntario de Cruz Roja en España. Ayudo a personas mayores.
Si te haces voluntario, conocerás a gente nueva y tendrás experiencias muy positivas. Doy mi tiempo, pero hago amigos nuevos, lo que es una cosa preciosa.

Me llamo **Silvia** y soy voluntaria de un grupo ecologista. A los diecisiete años fui de vacaciones a África. Vi la sequía y la pobreza de este continente, y me hice voluntaria.
Ser voluntario es una experiencia muy buena que recomiendo a todo el mundo. Es una experiencia muy positiva y conoces a mucha gente.

Who…
1 has joined an environmental group?
2 helps the elderly?
3 gets to know people through their work?
4 became a volunteer after a journey?
5 gives their time but makes new friends in return?
6 recommends volunteering to everyone?

 7 You are Luis. Write a paragraph about your ambitions. You can also add your own ideas. Try to include sentences with 'si + present + future'.

Name: Luis
Age: 17
Hobbies: writing in blog, playing football
If: become a volunteer
Will: help other people, improve society

3 Sin techo, sin derecho

1 Read the text on homeless people and complete the sentences below.

Tres millones de personas viven en la calle en Europa. En España **30 000** no tienen casa. Los hombres son el **82,7** por ciento de las personas sin techo. Las mujeres llegan al **17,3** por ciento.

El **29,9** por ciento de las personas que viven en España sin casa tienen entre 18 y 30 años. El **40** por ciento tienen entre 31 y 44. **Casi la mitad** de todas ellas son extranjeras.

1 _____ people live on the street in Europe.

2 In Spain _____ are homeless.

3 _____ % of homeless people in Spain are male.

4 _____ are aged between 18 and 30.

5 Almost _____ % of the homeless are foreign.

2 Listen and read. Match each numbered section of the text with one of the pictures.
Ejemplo: **1** a

1 Reportero: ¿Cómo te llamas?
Arantxa: Me llamo Arantxa.
R: ¿Cuántos años tienes, Arantxa?
A: Tengo veinticuatro años.

2 R: Y Arantxa, te quedaste sin techo hace unos años, ¿verdad?
A: Sí, hace cuatro años.
R: ¿Qué te pasó exactamente?
A: Pues, primero **perdí** a mi papá y luego a mi mamá. No tenía dinero ni familia.

3 R: ¿Qué tal lo pasaste?
A: Lo **pasé** muy mal. En la calle hay problemas muy graves como el consumo de alcohol y de drogas y la violencia…

4 R: ¿Cómo **saliste** de esta situación?
A: Un día **conocí** a un voluntario y este hombre me ayudó mucho. Ahora **trabajo** para su organización humanitaria. La organización se llama 'Café y bollos para los sin hogar'. **Vivo** en un piso en el centro.

5 R: ¿Cómo es un día típico para una persona sin techo?
A: Difícil y triste. Por lo general, estás solo. Andas mucho. Buscas comida o dinero. Un día una señora me dio diez euros. Pasé el día entero en una cafetería. **Bebí** chocolate y **leí** el periódico. ¡Qué lujo!

6 R: ¿Qué planes de futuro tienes?
A: A ver, en el futuro **voy a viajar**. Me encantaría conocer otros países. Me preocupa mucho el medio ambiente, sobre todo el calentamiento global. Si **puedo** ayudar, **seré** feliz…

> sin hogar = *homeless*
> andas (andar) = *you walk (to walk)*
> sobre todo = *above all*

3 Lee el diálogo otra vez y contesta a las preguntas en inglés.

1 How many years ago was Arantxa homeless?
2 How much money did she have?
3 What problems did she see on the street? (Mention three things.)
4 Who helped her?
5 Where does she work now?
6 How does she describe a typical day for a homeless person? (Mention three things.)
7 What enabled her to spend a whole day in a café drinking hot chocolate?
8 What is she most concerned about?

- If the questions are in English, remember to answer in English.
- Make sure you are answering the question and not giving unnecessary information.
- Pay attention to instructions like 'mention three things'. You will need to mention three things to gain all three marks allocated to the question.

 4 *Match up the Spanish and English infinitives.*

1 perder
2 salir
3 conocer
4 trabajar
5 vivir
6 leer
7 beber
8 viajar
9 poder
10 ser

to get to know
to work
can/to be able to
to drink
to lose
to travel
to get out
to read
to be
to live

 5 *Copy and complete the grid with the colour-coded verbs from the exercise 2 text which refer to the past, present and future. Add the English.*

past	present	future	English
perdí			I lost

 6 *Invent an interview with a homeless person. Use the* Vocabulario *section to help you.*

- ¿Cómo te llamas?
- ¿Cuántos años tienes?
- Te quedaste sin casa hace unos años, ¿verdad?
- ¿Cómo saliste de esta situación?

- ¿Cómo es un día típico?

- ¿Qué planes de futuro tienes?

■ Me llamo…
■ Tengo… años.
■ Sí, hace… años.
■ Un día conocí a… Me ayudó mucho. Encontré trabajo como…
■ Por lo general, estás… Buscas… En la calle hay problemas muy graves como…
■ A ver, en el futuro me gustaría viajar/conocer otros países/tener nuevas experiencias.

Nuestro planeta
9

Environment

You are going to have a conversation with your teacher about problems currently facing the planet. Your teacher could ask you the following:

- What environmental problems are there in your region?
- What should we do to protect the environment?
- What shouldn't we do?
- What do you do for the environment?
- What are you going to do for the environment in the future?
- What global problems concern you?

Remember that you will have to respond to an unexpected question that you have not yet prepared.

 1 You are going to hear Helen taking part in the above conversation with her teacher. Listen to part 1 of the interview and match the beginnings and ends of her sentences.

> ¿Qué problemas hay con el medio ambiente en tu región?

> ¿Qué se debe hacer para proteger el medio ambiente?

1 El mayor problema es…
2 También hay muchos…
3 Otro problema…
4 Se debe usar más el transporte público…
5 También se debe plantar más…
6 Se debe apagar las luces y desenchufar…

a …es que hay mucha basura.
b …atascos.
c …árboles y proteger la naturaleza.
d …los electrodomésticos.
e …que hay mucha contaminación.
f …y reducir la contaminación.

> desenchufar = to unplug

2 Listen to part 2 of Helen's conversation and fill each gap with the correct word(s) from the box.

| por ejemplo | se debe | fui | me ducho | cogí | compro | opino | reciclo | siempre | qué |

– ¿Qué no se debe hacer?
– A ver… No se debe malgastar agua, **(1)** ▢ mantener el agua limpia. No se debe tirar basura al suelo. **(2)** ¡▢ feo! ¿Qué más? No se debe consumir demasiada energía. No se debe encender todas las luces **(3)** ▢.
– ¿Qué haces tú para proteger el medio ambiente?
– A ver… **(4)** ▢ papel y vidrio y reutilizo lo más posible por lo general. Para ahorrar agua, **(5)** ▢ en vez de bañarme. Cuando voy de compras **(6)** ▢ llevo una bolsa y **(7)** ▢ productos locales. **(8)** ▢ que es muy importante. Ayer **(9)** ▢ de compras pero no compré mucho. **(10)** ▢ el autobús en vez de usar el coche.

 3 Here are two further questions that Helen is asked. What do the words in red mean?

> ¿Qué vas a hacer en el futuro **para proteger el medio ambiente**?

> ¿Qué problemas **te preocupan**?

4 *Now listen to part 3 of Helen's conversation. In which order does she use these phrases? What is the final unexpected question that Helen is asked?*

a Bueno… para mí hay muchos problemas serios en el mundo.
b El terrorismo por supuesto. A mí me da mucho miedo el terrorismo.
c Hay demasiada contaminación.
d Me gustaría ser voluntaria con Greenpeace porque opino que es un grupo importante.
e Me preocupa mucho el calentamiento global y también me preocupan la discriminación y el racismo.
f Creo que me voy a hacer miembro de un grupo ecologista.

5 *Now it's your turn! Prepare your answers to the task and then have a conversation with your teacher or partner.*

- Use the Grade Studio and your answers to exercises 1–4 to help you plan.
- Adapt what Helen said to talk about yourself but add your own ideas.
- Prepare your answers to the questions and try to predict what the unexpected question could be. The examiner might base this question on something you have already said, or ask something totally new!
- Record the conversation. Ask a partner to listen to it and say how well you performed.

Award each other one star, two stars or three stars for each of these categories:
- *Pronunciation*
- *Confidence and fluency*
- *Range of tenses*
- *Variety of vocabulary and expressions*
- *Using longer sentences*
- *Taking the initiative*
What do you need to do next time to improve your performance?

⭐ GradeStudio

Make sure you cover the basics.
- Use **simple structures** such as *voy* (I go), *compro* (I buy), *reciclo* (I recycle), *reutilizo*, (I reuse), *es* (he/she/it is) and *hay* (there is/are).
- Use **simple connectives**. Look at how Helen uses *y* (and), *o* (or) and *también* (also).
- Use **no** to create **a simple negative**, e.g. *No hay muchos espacios verdes.*

To reach Grade C, show that you can:
- Use **adjectives** correctly, such as *mucho* and *demasiado*, e.g. *Hay mucha basura. Hay muchos problemas.*
- Use *se debe/no se debe* + infinitive, e.g. *Se debe apagar las luces.* (We should turn off lights.)
- Use a **range of tenses**. Helen uses:
  - **the present tense** to say what she does to help the environment, e.g. *Siempre llevo una bolsa y compro productos locales.* (I always take a bag and buy local products.)
  - **the preterite** to say what she did yesterday, e.g. *Ayer fui de compras pero no compré mucho.* (Yesterday I went shopping but I didn't buy much.)
  - **the near future tense** to say what she is going to do, e.g. *Me voy a hacer miembro de un grupo ecologista.* (I am going to become a member of an eco group.)

To increase your marks:
- Use more **complex opinion-giving expressions**, such as *Opino que…/Creo que…* (I think that).
- Use *para* + infinitive (in order to): *Para ahorrar agua, me ducho en vez de bañarme.*
- Borrow these expressions from Helen: *El mayor problema es que…; Otro problema es que…*

Read the text and put these topics into the order of the text.

    a   Doing voluntary work abroad
    b   Helping the environment at home
    c   Rubbish in the streets
    d   Pollution in Manchester
    e   Operation 'clean up'

Amy

Me llamo Amy y vivo en Manchester. Mi ciudad es muy grande y para mí el mayor problema es la contaminación. Mucha gente va en coche o en moto todos los días así que hay demasiado tráfico y muchos atascos. No hay muchos espacios verdes en Manchester. Yo creo que primero se debe plantar más árboles y también se debe usar más el transporte público.

Otro problema en Manchester es que hay mucha basura. Para proteger el medio ambiente, no se debe tirar basura al suelo. El sábado pasado fui a limpiar las calles con un grupo de Scouts. Tuve que recoger basura con unas pinzas. Vi muchos papeles en el suelo. Trabajé mucho pero lo pasé bien y después cenamos juntos. Para mí es importante ser una persona responsable y por eso me hice miembro de Greenpeace.

Opino que hay demasiados problemas en el mundo. Me preocupan mucho el medio ambiente y el calentamiento global. Ahora, me ducho en vez de bañarme. Apago las luces y nunca utilizo bolsas de plástico. También reciclo vidrio, papel y plástico.

En el futuro, me voy a hacer voluntaria. Voy a viajar y a conocer otras culturas. Me encantaría ayudar a los demás.

así que = *and so*
tuve que recoger = *I had to pick up*
pinzas = *pincers, tongs*

Find these phrases in Spanish in the text.

    1   …for me the main problem is…
    2   There are not many green spaces…
    3   I think that first we must plant more trees…
    4   Another problem in Manchester is that…
    5   In order to protect the environment…
    6   For me it's important to be…
    7   I am very worried about the environment and global warming.
    8   Now I shower instead of taking a bath.
    9   …I never use plastic bags.
   10   I am going to do voluntary work.

Read the text again. Make a list of the verbs in the preterite. There are seven of them. Which of them is in the 'we' form?

leer 4 *Read the text again and answer the questions in English.*

1 What is the main problem in Amy's city?
2 What does Amy think is the main cause of this problem?
3 What does Amy suggest should be done to improve Manchester? (2 details)
4 What did she do last Saturday?
5 What happened at the end of the day?
6 Why did she become a member of Greenpeace?
7 Name four things she does to protect the environment.
8 What is Amy going to do in the future? (3 details)

escribir 5 *You might be asked to write about the environment as a controlled assessment task. Use the Grade Studio to help you prepare your account.*

⭐ GradeStudio

Make sure you cover the basics.

- Use **simple structures** correctly, e.g. Amy uses *vivo* (I live), *es* (it is), *hay* (there is/are) and *no hay* (there is/are not).
- Join your sentences with **connectives**. Look at how Amy uses *y* (and), *pero* (but), *también* (also) and *o* (or).

To reach Grade C, show that you can:

- Use **the present tense**. Amy talks about Manchester and what she does to protect the environment: *Hay demasiado tráfico y muchos atascos. Apago las luces.*
- Use **the preterite**. Amy says what she did: *fui...* (I went...) and *vi...* (I saw...).
- Use **the near future tense**. Amy says what she is going to do: *Voy a viajar.* (I'm going to travel.)
- Use **(no) se debe** + infinitive to talk about what people must and must not do. Amy says: *Se debe usar más el transporte público. No se debe tirar basura al suelo.*

To increase your marks:

- Use *para* + infinitive (in order to...), e.g. *Para proteger el medio ambiente, no se debe...*
- Use *me encantaría* + infinitive (I would love to...), e.g. *Me encantaría ayudar a los demás.*
- Use different **opinion-giving phrases**. Amy uses *Yo creo que primero se debe...* (I think that first of all, we must...), *Opino que...* (I think that...) and *Para mí...* (For me...).

escribir 6 *Now write a full account of your views on the environment.*

- Adapt Amy's text and use language from Module 9.
- Structure your text carefully. Organise what you write in paragraphs.

escribir 7 *Check carefully what you have written.*

- spelling and accents (near-cognates spelt correctly, including any accents: *contaminación, tráfico, planeta?*)
- verbs (infinitive used after *(no) se debe, para, en vez de...?*)
- correct accents (on regular verbs in the preterite: *trabajé?*)

General summary of your view on the environment

Where do you live?
What environmental problems are there in your area?

Main paragraph

What have you done to help the environment?
How environmentally friendly are you at home?
What do you think should be done about environmental problems?

Conclusion

What would you like to do in the future to help the environment or tackle other world problems?

 Read these pieces of advice on helping the environment and decide which part of our lives they will affect. Write the number followed by the correct letter. (3 marks)

1 ¡Es estúpido malgastar agua!

2 ¡Es importante usar gasolina sin plomo!

3 ¡Es bueno usar papel reciclado!

> ⭐ Think laterally – what do you do with the things mentioned in each of the texts? For example, if food is mentioned, you use it for eating!

a eating   **b** writing   **c** washing   **d** running   **e** driving

 **Read these comments in a magazine by a homeless person and identify the four places he sometimes spends the night. Write the four correct letters. (4 marks)**

1 "No tengo un sitio permanente para dormir. A veces duermo en la entrada de una tienda grande."

2 "Si no llueve paso la noche en el parque de la ciudad."

3 "Es demasiado caro dormir en un albergue juvenil así que prefiero dormir en la estación de tren."

4 "Mi lugar favorito es el sótano de un bloque de oficinas porque hace calor allí."

> ⭐ All the answer options are mentioned in the text, but they are not all places that the person sleeps in. Use other words, including negatives, to eliminate the places that he chooses not to sleep in.

a town park   **c** youth hostel   **e** road underpass

b office block basement   **d** shop doorway   **f** train station

 Read what Pedro and Conchita write on a blog about global issues. Write down who has the opinions that follow. Write P (Pedro), C (Conchita) or P+C (Pedro and Conchita). (4 marks)

Me preocupa el planeta sólo un poco hoy en día. Primero tenemos que ayudar a la gente pobre que no tiene comida. No doy dinero a una organización internacional, porque los empleados de la organización recibirán más que la gente pobre. Eso no es justo, en mi opinión. Es muy importante consumir menos pero, por ejemplo, no quiero escribir en las dos caras de una hoja de papel. Prefiero usar papel reciclado.
Pedro, Barcelona

Proteger nuestro planeta es el problema más grave que tenemos ahora. Cuando doy dinero a un grupo ecologista internacional estoy segura de que ayudaré a todo el planeta. Me gusta ayudar a la gente. Cuando compro productos de comercio justo puedo mejorar la vida de las personas que tienen hambre y que no tienen dinero.
Conchita, Madrid

> ⭐ Read the questions first, as they may help you to understand the texts. But before answering them it is important to read both texts, as they each contain essential information. Pay careful attention to qualifiers (e.g. *sólo, un poco*) and negatives (e.g. *no es justo*).

1 Who thinks saving the planet is today's biggest problem?

2 Who wants to bring an end to poverty and hunger?

3 Who is in favour of contributing to an international organisation?

4 Who doesn't write on both sides of sheets of paper?

4

Listen to Roberto talking about the environment in his town and answer the questions in English. (4 marks)

1 What does Roberto like about his town?
2 What does he not like in his neighbourhood?
3 What is going to improve in the future?
4 How does he help the environment?

⭐ Try to pick out the key words in the statements. Sometimes a speaker will talk about things in the plural form, e.g. *las casas* (the houses) rather than *mi casa* (my house). This is because he is talking about things in general, but it may make some words more difficult to understand.

 5

Listen to Alicia talking about recycling bins. Which bin do they have in (1) the shopping centre, (2) the restaurant and (3) the street? Write down the correct letter for each place. (3 marks)

a paper   **d** cans
b plastic   **e** batteries
c glass

⭐ You will hear the items in the same order as the questions but the answer options will be in random order.

 6

Listen to this reporter interviewing Beatriz, Ricardo and Manuela about the environment. Write down what each person thinks should be done to help. (3 marks)

1 Beatriz
2 Ricardo
3 Manuela

⭐ A question asking what someone *does* or what should be *done* usually needs a verb and a noun in the answer, e.g. 'recycle (verb) paper (noun)'. Keep your answers as simple as possible so that you express yourself clearly.

 7

Listen to this reporter interviewing a homeless person. Answer the questions below by writing down the letter which indicates the correct answer. (4 marks)

1 What will happen if Marta doesn't get somewhere to stay?
    a She will go to another town.
    b She will start taking drugs.
    c Her health will get worse.

2 What will happen if Marta doesn't get a job?
    a She will beg on the streets.
    b She will steal.
    c She will go home to her family.

3 What has helped her to cope with homelessness?
    a drinking alcohol
    b talking to volunteers
    c looking after a dog

4 What would she like to do in the future?
    a learn to drive
    b help other homeless people
    c travel to other countries

⭐ Remember that some ideas may be mentioned even when they are not relevant to the correct answer. Negatives or other expressions will enable you to eliminate these.

Palabras

Cambios medioambientales · *Environmental changes*

El aire y el agua están muy contaminados.	*The air and water are very polluted.*
En nuestra ciudad hay mucha basura.	*There's a lot of rubbish in our town.*
Hay demasiado tráfico.	*There's too much traffic.*
Hay muchas fábricas.	*There are lots of factories.*
Hay muchos atascos.	*There are lots of traffic jams.*
La sequía es un problema.	*Drought is a problem.*
Mucha gente va en coche o en moto todos los días.	*Lots of people use their car or motorbike every day.*
No hay espacios verdes.	*There are no green spaces.*
No llueve mucho.	*It doesn't rain much.*
Se debe…	*We must…*
Es necesario…	*It is necessary to…*
comprar productos ecológicos	*buy green products*
consumir menos energía	*use less energy*
plantar árboles	*plant trees*
proteger la naturaleza	*protect nature*
reciclar papel y vidrio	*recycle paper and glass*
reducir la contaminación	*reduce pollution*
usar el transporte público	*use public transport*
No se debe…	*We mustn't…*
malgastar el agua	*waste water*
tirar la basura al suelo	*throw rubbish on the ground*
Vivo en…	*I live in…*
un barrio industrial	*an industrial neighbourhood*
el centro de…	*the centre of…*
una ciudad turística	*a touristy city*
una ciudad histórica	*a historic city*
¿Qué problemas hay en tu región?	*What problems are there in your region?*
El mayor problema es que…	*The biggest problem is that…*
¿Qué se debe hacer para proteger el medio ambiente?	*What must we do to protect the environment?*
Creo que es necesario…	*I think it's necessary to…*
Para mí…	*In my opinion…*
Opino que…	*I think that…*
También se debe…	*We must also…*

Piensa globalmente · *Think globally*

Me preocupa(n) más…	*I'm most worried about…*
El mayor problema es…	*The biggest problem is…*
El peor problema es…	*The worst problem is…*
la destrucción del ecosistema	*the destruction of ecosystems*
la contaminación del aire	*air pollution*
la basura	*rubbish*
el calentamiento global	*global warming*
las especies amenazadas	*endangered species*
la sequía	*drought*
Para ahorrar agua, es mejor…	*In order to save water, it's better to…*
Para consumir menos energía, es mejor…	*In order to use less energy, it's better to…*
Para evitar la basura, es mejor…	*In order to avoid waste, it's better to…*
Para luchar contra el calentamiento global, es mejor…	*In order to fight against global warming, it's better to…*
Para reducir la contaminación del aire, es mejor…	*In order to reduce air pollution, it's better to…*
Para usar menos gasolina, es mejor…	*In order to use less oil, it's better to…*
andar	*walk*
apagar las luces	*turn off the lights*
bañarse	*have a bath*
comprar productos de países lejanos	*buy products from faraway countries*
comprar productos locales	*buy local products*
ducharse	*have a shower*
encender las luces	*turn on the lights*
hacerse miembro de un grupo ecologista	*join an eco group*
ir en bici	*travel by bike*
llevar una bolsa a la compra	*take a bag when you go shopping*
pedir muchas bolsas de plástico	*ask for lots of plastic bags*
usar (más) el coche	*use the car (more)*
ver la televisión	*watch TV*
en vez de…	*instead of…*

Voluntarios *Volunteers*

Si apadrino a un niño, …	*If I sponsor a child, …*
Si compro productos de comercio justo, …	*If I buy fair trade products,…*
Si doy dinero a Oxfam, …	*If I give money to Oxfam, …*
Si me hago voluntario/a, …	*If I become a volunteer, …*
Si reciclo y reutilizo, …	*If I recycle and reuse, …*
ayudaré a los trabajadores	*I will help the workers*
ayudaré a otras personas	*I will help other people*
cuidaré el medio ambiente	*I will look after the environment*
daré al niño la posibilidad de sobrevivir	*I will give the child a chance to survive*
mejoraré la sociedad	*I will improve society*
¿Por qué quieres trabajar como voluntario/a?	*Why do you want to work as a volunteer?*
el terrorismo	*terrorism*
la discriminación	*discrimination*
el racismo	*racism*
la pobreza	*poverty*
el hambre	*hunger*
los sin techo	*the homeless*

Sin techo, sin derecho *No roof, no rights*

las personas sin casa/sin techo/sin hogar	*homeless people*
vivir en la calle	*to live on the streets*
Te quedaste sin casa hace unos años, ¿verdad?	*You found yourself homeless a few years ago, didn't you?*
Sí, hace (cuatro) años.	*Yes, (four) years ago.*
¿Cómo saliste de esta situación?	*How did you escape from that situation?*
Un día conocí a…	*One day I met…*
Me ayudó mucho.	*He/She helped me a lot.*
Encontré trabajo como…	*I found work as a…*
Ahora trabajo para una organización humanitaria.	*Now I work for a humanitarian organisation.*
¿Cómo es un día típico?	*What is a typical day like?*
Por lo general, estás solo.	*Generally, you are alone.*
Andas mucho.	*You walk a lot.*
Buscas comida o dinero.	*You look for food or money.*
En la calle hay problemas muy graves como…	*On the streets there are very serious problems, such as…*
el consumo de alcohol	*alcohol consumption*
el consumo de drogas	*drug-taking*
la violencia	*violence*
¿Qué planes de futuro tienes?	*What plans do you have for the future?*
En el futuro me gustaría…	*In the future I'd like to…*
conocer otros países	*get to know other countries*
tener nuevas experiencias	*have new experiences*
viajar	*travel*

Te toca a ti A

Match up the texts to the correct hotel.

a Club Verano **b** HOTEL IMPERIAL **c** Hotel Margaritas

1

Me alojé en un hotel que era magnífico.
Tenía tres plantas y 91 habitaciones. Había
un bar y un restaurante. También tenía varias
tiendas y una peluquería. Fue una experiencia
fantástica.

2

*Pasé unas vacaciones muy románticas
en este hotel de lujo en la zona
residencial de la ciudad. Tenía bares y
restaurantes. También tenía una piscina
al aire libre y una cancha de tenis.
Fuimos alguna vez al centro de fitness.*

3

Mis vacaciones en México fueron estupendas. Me quedé en un hotel
que era muy bonito. El hotel estaba en la costa. Tenía una piscina,
una sauna y un gimnasio. También había un bar. Estaba muy bien
equipado. Lo mejor del hotel era que tenía una discoteca genial.

**Write out these dialogues in the correct order. Start with the green
sentence each time.**

1 a ¿En qué puedo ayudarle?
  b ¿Quiere una habitación con baño o sin baño?
  c Para cinco noches, del 21 al 26 de junio. ¿Cuánto es, por favor?
  d Con baño, con balcón y con vistas al mar, por favor.
  e ¿Para cuántas noches?
  f Son 280€.
  g Quiero reservar una habitación doble.

2 a Williams.
  b El restaurante está abierto hasta las 22:00 horas.
  c ¿Su apellido, por favor?
  d Vale. Una habitación doble con balcón. Aquí está su llave.
  e ¿Cómo se deletrea?
  f W-I-L-L-I-A-M-S.
  g Tengo una reserva para esta noche.
  h Dígame.
  i Gracias. ¿Hasta qué hora está abierto el restaurante, por favor?

Match the descriptions to the holidays. There is one holiday too many.

1 En agosto fui de vacaciones solo. Mi hotel estaba en la montaña. No era muy animado. Era muy tranquilo. El primer día hizo frío y llovió un poco, pero después hizo sol. Generalmente descansé y medité. Escribí mi blog y leí mucho. **Manuel**

2 El verano pasado fui de camping a Achiltibuie en Escocia porque me gustó la idea del turismo sostenible. Pasé una semana allí. El camping estaba en la costa. Era muy cómodo y no era caro. Generalmente hice windsurf y vela en la playa. ¡Fue muy divertido! El último día, primero di una vuelta en bicicleta. Luego salí en barco y por fin tuvimos una fiesta en el camping. Para mí Escocia es un lugar de vacaciones ideal. ¡Fue genial! **Isabel**

3 Mis vacaciones fueron inolvidables. Mi hotel de lujo estaba en la montaña. Hice alpinismo todos los días. Un día hice caída libre y tuve miedo. ¡Qué horror! Una noche fui a una clase de flamenco y me gustó bastante. Por las tardes, nadé en la piscina del hotel. El jueves, monté en bici y visité un castillo. Era del siglo XVI – impresionante. **Nuria**

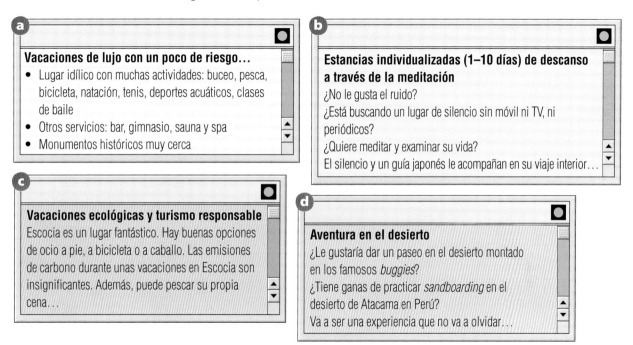

a

Vacaciones de lujo con un poco de riesgo…
- Lugar idílico con muchas actividades: buceo, pesca, bicicleta, natación, tenis, deportes acuáticos, clases de baile
- Otros servicios: bar, gimnasio, sauna y spa
- Monumentos históricos muy cerca

b

Estancias individualizadas (1–10 días) de descanso a través de la meditación
¿No le gusta el ruido?
¿Está buscando un lugar de silencio sin móvil ni TV, ni periódicos?
¿Quiere meditar y examinar su vida?
El silencio y un guía japonés le acompañan en su viaje interior…

c

Vacaciones ecológicas y turismo responsable
Escocia es un lugar fantástico. Hay buenas opciones de ocio a pie, a bicicleta o a caballo. Las emisiones de carbono durante unas vacaciones en Escocia son insignificantes. Además, puede pescar su propia cena…

d

Aventura en el desierto
¿Le gustaría dar un paseo en el desierto montado en los famosos *buggies*?
¿Tiene ganas de practicar *sandboarding* en el desierto de Atacama en Perú?
Va a ser una experiencia que no va a olvidar…

 Write down the letters of the four sentences that are true about the texts in exercise 1.

a Nuria stayed in the city.

b Manuel's holidays were quiet.

c Isabel went shopping every day.

d Nuria was scared when she went sky-diving.

e It rained throughout Manuel's stay.

f On her last day, Isabel went for a bike ride.

g Nuria enjoyed her flamenco lesson.

h Isabel's campsite was comfortable but expensive.

 Write an account of this holiday.

April, Lanzarote, with parents
2 weeks
water sports, beautiful beach
guest house – comfortable
generally sunny

☺

En… fui a… con…

Pasé… allí.

Durante las vacaciones hice… La playa era…

Mi pensión estaba en la costa. Era muy…

Generalmente hizo…

¡Fue…

Te toca a ti A

leer 1 Match up the questions and answers.

1 ¿Qué vas a hacer hoy?
2 ¿Cómo vas a ir a la Alhambra?
3 ¿A qué hora abre la Alhambra?
4 Y después ¿qué vas a hacer?
5 ¿Quieres venir conmigo?

a A las ocho y media.
b Voy a ir a pie porque hace buen tiempo.
c Luego voy a comer algo.
d Voy a visitar Granada. Primero voy a ir a la Alhambra. Voy a dar un paseo y voy a sacar fotos también.
e Sí, va a ser interesante.

leer 2 Read the advert and then answer the questions below in English.

1 What can you see in the museum?
2 On what day is the museum closed?
3 What time does the museum open in the morning?
4 What time does it open in the afternoon?
5 What time does it close in the evening?

Venga al Museo de Bellas Artes de Sevilla, en Sevilla
Impresionante colección de arte español de la época medieval a la moderna.
Abierto: Martes a domingo: de 10:00 a 13:00 de la mañana y de 14:00 a 20:00 de la tarde

leer 3 Write out the words in the word snakes with the correct punctuation. Then match the sentences to the pictures.

1 Deprimerplatovoyatomarcalamares.
2 Porfavormefaltauncuchillo.
3 Desegundoplatovoyatomarjamónserrano.
4 Porfavormefaltauntenedor.
5 Elvasoestásucio.
6 Porfavornohayaceite.
7 Depostrevoyatomarhelado.
8 Nohayvinagre.

leer 4 Read the text. What opinion does Juan have of the restaurant? Write P (positive), N (negative) or P+N (positive and negative).

En pleno centro de Sevilla hay uno de los bares de tapeo más típicos de la ciudad. De precio está muy bien, es muy barato. Cuando pides una bebida te ponen una tapa. Las mejores eran las de calamares fritos. Lo malo es que un era bar pequeño.
Juan

Comida: 8
Calidad del servicio: 8
Ambiente: 10
Calidad / Precio: 7

 1 *Match the sentences to the symbols.*

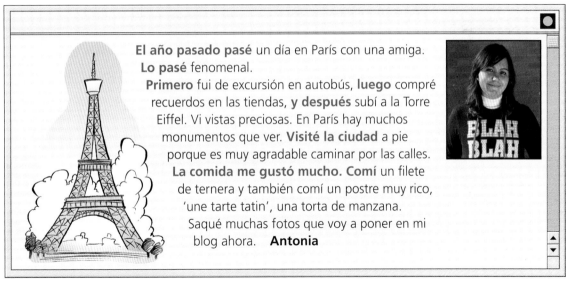

1 No me gusta nada viajar en avión. **Tengo miedo**.
2 Me gusta mucho mi independencia y por eso, **prefiero ir en coche**.
3 Cojo siempre el autocar **porque es barato** y puedo leer o escuchar música.
4 Normalmente cojo el tren… **porque no es caro** y por respeto al medio ambiente.
5 **Prefiero ir a pie** porque creo que de esta forma no contamino.
6 No me gusta esperar y prefiero llegar rápidamente, **por eso cojo un taxi**.

 2 *Translate the phrases in red above into English.*

 3 *Read the text and then answer the questions below in English.*

El año pasado pasé un día en París con una amiga. **Lo pasé** fenomenal. **Primero** fui de excursión en autobús, **luego** compré recuerdos en las tiendas, **y después** subí a la Torre Eiffel. Vi vistas preciosas. En París hay muchos monumentos que ver. **Visité la ciudad** a pie porque es muy agradable caminar por las calles. **La comida me gustó mucho. Comí** un filete de ternera y también comí un postre muy rico, 'une tarte tatin', una torta de manzana. Saqué muchas fotos que voy a poner en mi blog ahora. **Antonia**

1 Where did Antonia go?
2 How long did she spend there?
3 What did she do? (3 details)
4 How did she visit Paris?
5 What two things did she eat?
6 What is she going to put on her blog?

 4 *Write a passage about a day you spent in London. Use the phrases in blue in the text from exercise 3 to help you structure your text.*

Londres
1 día

(bought) souvenirs
(saw) Big Ben
(went to) Madame Tussaud's

fish and chips

Te toca a ti A

1 Copy out the sentences and complete them with the correct letters.
Then write each sentence in English.

Example: **1** Voy en bicicleta. – I go by bike.

1 Voy e _ bi _ icl _ t _.

4 Vamos en t _ _ n.

2 ¿Vas en au _ _ ca _?

5 Lucas y Ana María van _ pi _.

3 Juan va en c _ c _ e.

2 Copy out the sentences and complete them with the correct times.
Then write each sentence in English.

1 Tengo matemáticas a las…

3 Tenemos alemán a…

2 Tienen inglés a las…

4 María tiene dibujo…

3 Read the texts and complete the timetable with the missing subjects.

El lunes por la mañana tengo matemáticas e inglés antes del recreo y después tengo español a las once y dibujo a las doce. Por la tarde tengo geografía e informática.

Los miércoles tengo informática e historia antes del recreo y después tengo dos horas de geografía – desde las once hasta la una. Por la tarde tengo dos horas de educación física: a las dos y media y a las tres y media.

El martes por la mañana tengo historia a las nueve menos cuarto y tengo ciencias a las diez menos cuarto.

hora	lunes	martes	miércoles	jueves
08:45	matemáticas	C	informática	dibujo
09:45	inglés	D	historia	alemán
10:45	RECREO			
11:00	español	teatro	E	
12:00	A	matemáticas	F	
13:00	COMIDA			
14:30	geografía	religión	G	
15:30	B	español	educación física	

4 Write out your own timetable for Thursday and Friday in Spanish.

1 Read each opinion and complete the sentence with an appropriate adjective. Be careful with the adjective endings! Then change the sentence to give your own opinion.

Example: Me gusta mucho el español porque es <u>guay</u>.
Me gusta mucho <u>la geografía</u> porque es <u>divertida</u>.

1 Me gusta mucho el español porque es…
2 No me gusta nada el inglés porque es…
3 Odio las matemáticas porque son…
4 Me encantan las ciencias porque son…
5 Mi asignatura preferida es la música porque es…

aburrido   difícil   guay
práctico   útil   divertido
interesante   fácil
entretenido

2 Copy and complete the sentences with the correct words from the box.
Then write the sentences in English.

1 Me _____ las matemáticas porque no son difíciles.
2 Mi profesor de ciencias es bastante _____ .
3 Siempre llevo una _____ gris y una camiseta azul.
4 Las clases _____ a las ocho y media todos los días.
5 No voy al club de _____ porque no me interesa.

severo   ajedrez   empiezan
encantan   falda

3 Read José's text and find the Spanish for the phrases that follow.

Me llamo José y estudio diez asignaturas. Mi instituto es grande con muchos alumnos y por eso no me gusta nada. Hay muchas reglas. Por ejemplo, está prohibido llevar joyas. En clase está prohibido escuchar tu MP3 y no se permite mandar mensajes con el móvil. Lo bueno es que no llevamos uniforme y normalmente llevo vaqueros y una camiseta. En mi instituto hay acoso escolar. ¡Es terrible! Antes mi colegio era muy bueno pero ahora no.

1 lots of pupils
2 There are lots of rules.
3 You can't send texts.
4 There is bullying.
5 My school used to be good.

⭐ Remember to use a dictionary or the *Vocabulario* section when working through a text on your own. Note down any new words you find in a vocabulary book or your exercise book, in Spanish and English, so that you can revise them later.

4 Answer the questions about José's text in English.

1 How many subjects does José take?
2 Why doesn't he like his school? (2 reasons)
3 Name two school rules he mentions.
4 Describe what he wears to school.
5 What happens at his school that is really bad?

Te toca a ti A

escribir 1 *Answer these questions for the people below in full sentences.*

- ¿Cuántos años tienes?
- ¿De dónde eres?
- ¿De qué color son tus ojos?
- ¿Cómo es tu pelo?
- ¿Cómo es tu carácter?

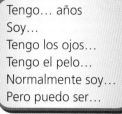

Tengo... años
Soy...
Tengo los ojos...
Tengo el pelo...
Normalmente soy...
Pero puedo ser...

Luis – 16

Mexicano

Normalmente: sincero, tolerante

Puedo ser: tranquilo pesimista

Angélica –14

Estadounidense

Normalmente: egoísta, un poco agresiva

Puedo ser: valiente, optimista

leer 2 *Read the text and write a clock time for each picture.*

Example: **a** 6.30 am

La vida en la isla es dura. Voy a describir un día típico (pero cada día es diferente). Me levanto temprano, a las seis y media de la mañana. Primero me visto y después desayuno porque tengo mucha hambre. Desayuno fruta a las siete menos diez. Me lavo los dientes quince minutos más tarde, a las siete y cinco.

Durante el día paso mucho tiempo en la playa, pero también arreglo mi dormitorio por la tarde, a las cuatro y media.

Por las tardes, Eugenio prepara la cena y ceno a las ocho y cuarto normalmente.

Me acuesto temprano – a las nueve y media.

1 Follow the lines to find the words and write them out.
Then match the English to the Spanish.

1	agre	mista	**a**	aggressive
2	ale	cero	**b**	brave
3	ama	roso	**c**	cheerful
4	ego	tido	**d**	friendly
5	gene	ísta	**e**	generous
6	introver	gre	**f**	introverted
7	maledu	pático	**g**	nice
8	opti	ble	**h**	optimistic
9	pesi	sivo	**i**	pessimistic
10	sim	liente	**j**	rude
11	sin	mista	**k**	selfish
12	va	cado	**l**	sincere

2 Read these texts and then answer the questions.

Tengo mucho sentido del humor y creo que soy amable. Mis amigos son muy importantes para mí. Me gusta mucho salir con ellos. Charlamos y nos divertimos. Salgo tres o cuatro veces a la semana. Me encanta hacer deporte y luego ir a la cafetería. *Aitor*

Normalmente soy creativo y no soy muy ambicioso. No me gusta nada trabajar. Prefiero navegar por Internet, mandar mensajes con mi móvil o jugar con mi ordenador. A veces cojo el teléfono de mi hermana y mando mensajes a sus amigas. Le da rabia cuando lo hago. *Magec*

No me gusta nada hacer regalos a la gente. No quiero gastar mi dinero así. Estoy ahorrando para mis vacaciones. Trabajo sólo para mí, no tengo ganas de gastar mi dinero en otras personas que no quieren trabajar. Yo sé que tengo razón. *Laura*

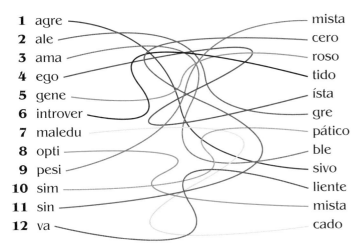

Who…

1 is saving for their holidays?
2 has a good sense of humour?
3 is selfish?
4 annoys their sister?
5 likes sport?
6 is lazy?

3 Read Alicia's diary and answer the questions below in English.

Querido diario:
Estoy en esta isla desde hace un año. Ahora en verano hace mucho calor durante el día. Hay fruta, huevos y pescado en abundancia.
Lo que más me gusta en la primavera es que hay muchos pájaros exóticos y tortugas gigantes.
El otoño es un poco duro, pero no tanto como el invierno. En invierno lo peor es que llueve mucho, ¡odio la lluvia! Además, los días son muy cortos.
Nunca me levanto. Paso todo el tiempo en la cabaña.

In which season does Alicia…

1 get the worst rains?
2 enjoy the wildlife around her?
3 find life most difficult?
4 find it easiest to get food?
5 never get up?

Te toca a ti A

1 Read the sentences and unjumble the jobs.

1. Viajo a veces en ambulancia. Soy **oimcéd**.
2. Corto y seco el pelo de varias personas. Soy **elupaequr**.
3. Miro las bocas y los dientes. Soy **setditan**.
4. Corro mucho en un estadio. Soy **suitflatob**.
5. Hablo por teléfono. Soy **espricanteico**.

2 Read the emails and answer the questions below.

Example: 1 Chuy

Estoy trabajando en una tienda de moda cerca de mi casa. Me gusta porque la ropa es muy barata. Lo peor es que tengo que trabajar los sábados. ¿Y tú? ¿Trabajas o estudias? El año pasado hice un curso de inglés. Me gustó pero el inglés es muy difícil. Prefiero trabajar. Un beso, *Leída*

Hola, ¿qué tal? Estoy mal porque ahora trabajo en una peluquería y mi jefe es muy pesado y serio. Todos los días tengo que lavar el pelo de los clientes y tengo que barrer el suelo. ¡Es tan aburrido! pero se paga bien. El año pasado trabajé en una zapatería. Lo pasé bomba pero gané poco. Un abrazo, *Chuy*

Who…

1. has a boss who is serious?
2. currently works in a shop?
3. studied last year?
4. prefers to work?
5. is paid well?
6. has to sweep the floors every day?
7. has to work Saturdays?
8. had a great time working last year?

3 Copy out the grid and fill in the missing verbs.

infinitive	present (I…)	preterite (I…)
trabajar	**A**	trabajé
estudiar	estudio	**B**
C	**D**	escribí
beber	**E**	**F**
hacer	hago	**G**

1 Match up the questions and answers.

Example: **1** b

1 ¿Qué has estudiado en el instituto?
2 ¿Cuál es tu correo electrónico?
3 ¿Qué es importante para ti?
4 ¿Por qué quieres ser dependienta?
5 ¿Qué experiencia laboral tienes?
6 ¿Qué cualidades tienes?

a Es Alice.Newton@gmail.com.

b He estudiado muchas asignaturas diferentes. Pero mi asignatura favorita es la historia.

c Porque me gusta mucho la ropa y hablar con los clientes.

d Pienso que soy muy alegre, responsable y respetuosa.

e Me gusta tener responsabilidades y trabajar en equipo.

f He trabajado como dependienta en una tienda de recuerdos.

2 Read the word snake and write out the sentence correctly.

Misprácticaslaboralesfueronbastantedivertidasporquetrabajéconniñosymijefeerasimpático.

3 Read the text and copy and complete it with the correct words.

mando
gustaría
telefónicas
parcial

paga   trabajé
pequeño
gustó   dieciocho
domingos

Me llamo Eugenia y tengo **(1)** ___ años. Vivo con mis padres en un piso bastante **(2)** ___ en Oviedo. Tengo un trabajo a tiempo **(3)** ___ en un hospital. Organizo los documentos de cada paciente, **(4)** ___ correos electrónicos y contesto llamadas **(5)** ___. Me interesa mi trabajo pero no se **(6)** ___ bien y tengo que trabajar los **(7)** ___. El año pasado **(8)** ___ en una clínica privada pero no me **(9)** ___. En el futuro me **(10)** ___ seguir con mis estudios para ser enfermera.

4 Copy Eugenia's text from exercise 3, changing key phrases, to write a letter from Simón. Include the information below.

Age: 16
Part-time job: in a hotel – pays well
Tasks: receives emails – talks to clients
Last year: worked in a restaurant – didn't like it
Future: would like to live abroad

dieciséis
Recibo correos electrónicos
Hablo con clientes
Trabajé en un restaurante

Te toca a ti A

1 A computer virus has jumbled up the letters in these adjectives. Use the English meanings to help you sort them out.

Example: **1** laom = malo

educational   informative   bad
entertaining   slow   exciting

1 laom

2 nolet

3 camoiteneno

4 odiacutev

5 enedintrote

6 farmivontio

2 Read the text and answer the questions below.

Me llamo Marisa y me gusta ir al cine con mis amigos. Me encanta ver películas de acción porque normalmente los efectos especiales son buenísimos. Odio las películas románticas porque son tontas y aburridas. A mi amigo Sergio le gustan las películas del Oeste pero en mi opinión son muy lentas y bastante violentas. También veo la televisión dos veces a la semana. Me gustan los concursos y las telenovelas pero prefiero ir al cine.

1 What does Marisa like to see at the cinema and why?
2 What does she say about the type of film she likes least?
3 What does her friend Sergio like?
4 Does she like this type of film? Justify your answer.
5 How often does she watch TV?
6 Does she prefer watching TV or going to the cinema?

3 Copy out the sentences and complete them with your opinions about films and television programmes.

1 Me gustan mucho las películas de ▮▮▮ porque son ▮▮▮ .
2 Odio las ▮▮▮ porque son muy aburridas.
3 Las telenovelas son más ▮▮▮ que los concursos.
4 Las noticias son menos ▮▮▮ que los programas de deporte.
5 Me encantan ▮▮▮ porque son ▮▮▮ .
6 Mi programa preferido se llama ▮▮▮ . ¡Es fenomenal!

182   ciento ochenta y dos

leer 1 *Find the odd one out in each list of sports.*

1	fútbol	tenis	equitación	baloncesto
2	natación	vela	windsurf	fútbol
3	pesca	baloncesto	tenis	golf
4	wakeboard	footing	snowboard	esquí
5	rugby	béisbol	billar	gimnasia

leer 2 *Read the text. Copy and complete the English sentences below with the correct information.*

Me llamo Jaime y mi deporte preferido es la vela. La practico todos los fines de semana con mi familia. La vela es un deporte bastante emocionante. A mí me gusta salir en nuestro barco de vela con mis hermanos, mi madre y mi padre. Mi padre tiene mucha experiencia.

El barco se llama *Felicidad* y tiene una radio-CD para poner música. A mí me encanta la música rock pero mi hermano prefiere la música rap. Normalmente en el barco comemos pan con jamón o queso.

En el futuro me gustaría trabajar en un barco. Me encantaría visitar y conocer otros países de Europa. El verano pasado hice un curso de vela y pasé tres días en un barco de vela de siete metros, donde aprendí muchas cosas nuevas. ¡Fue fenomenal!

1 Jaime's favourite sport is
2 He does this sport with
3 He describes his favourite sport as
4 His father has
5 His boat is called
6 His boat has
7 In the future he would like to
8 He learnt a lot when he

escribir 3 *Copy out these sentences about Jaime's text, choosing the correct ending.*

1 El deporte preferido de Jaime es **el voleibol** / **la vela**.
2 Practica este deporte con **sus amigos** / **su familia**.
3 La música preferida de Jaime es **el rock** / **el rap**.
4 En el futuro Jaime quiere **seguir estudiando** / **trabajar**.
5 El verano pasado Jaime hizo **un curso de vela** / **natación**.

escribir 4 *Now change the information given in bold in each of the exercise 3 sentences (and the name!) to write about a friend or family member.*

Example: **1** El deporte preferido de Matt es el fútbol.

1 Read the description and choose the correct bedroom.
Then write a description of the other bedroom.

En mi dormitorio hay una cama, un armario y una mesa. En las paredes hay pósters y en el suelo hay una alfombra. Mi cama está debajo de la ventana. Hay revistas encima de la cama. A la derecha de la mesa hay un armario. Hay un ordenador encima de la mesa. Hay una silla delante de la mesa. En mi dormitorio normalmente hago mis deberes o juego con mi ordenador. A veces veo la televisión. Me gusta mucho mi dormitorio. **Beyonce**

2 Unjumble these questions and then use the phrases in the panel to write answers to them.

¿ qué En casa tipo vives de ?

¿ está Dónde ?

¿ es Cómo ?

¿ Cuántos hay dormitorios ?

¿ fuera tu de hay casa Qué ?

¿ opinas tu Qué casa de ?

Mi casa es… También es…
Fuera hay…
Vivo en…
Está…
En mi opinión, mi casa es… porque…
Lo bueno es que tenemos…
Lo malo es que…
Hay…

3 Put this conversation into the correct order.

a Por supuesto… ¿Qué tal le quedan?
b Buenas tardes. ¿En qué puedo servirle?
c Sí, los tengo en negro, verde y azul.
d Me gustan mucho pero son demasiado pequeños.
e ¿Me los puedo probar en azul?
f ¿Tiene estos pantalones en otro color?

leer 1 Unjumble the words in bold, and then match them up to the correct symbol.

1 No hay muchos **selobár**.
2 Hay muchos **ettahbians**.
3 No hay red de **pottrensar** público.
4 Hay mucho **ártcoif**.
5 Hay una zona **lapnoeat**.
6 No hay muchos **sociapes** verdes.
7 Hay muchos **sritstua**.
8 Hay muchas **adniets**.
9 No hay muchas áreas de **cioo**.
10 Hay muchos museos y muchas **sagílera** de arte.

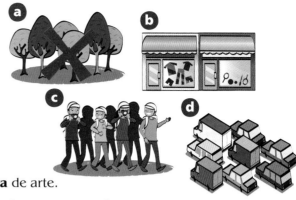

escribir 2 Write a description of these two places.

1 big city
✓ shops
✓ sports centre
✗ no trees
✗ no green spaces

2 small village
✓ historic
✗ no leisure possibilities
✗ no transport

> Vivo en un pueblo/una ciudad…
>   histórico/a, moderno/a, pequeño/a, turístico/a, grande, importante, industrial,…
> Lo bueno es que hay…
>   un centro comercial, un polideportivo, parques, una biblioteca, una pista de tenis, salas de juegos, bares, discotecas, restaurantes
> Lo malo es que no hay…
>   muchos árboles
>   muchos espacios verdes
>   red de transporte público
>   muchas áreas de ocio

leer 3 Read the text. Choose the correct information.

Nuestra actriz más internacional, Penélope Cruz, y su hermana Mónica han diseñado una colección especial de prendas para la marca *Mango* que consta de 25 piezas, e incluirá también algunos accesorios.
La moda de los famosos que crean sus propias colecciones para las firmas de ropa está más de moda que nunca.

la prenda = *the garment*
constar de = *to consist of*

1 Penélope and Mónica Cruz have designed…
   a a special collection for *Mango*.
   b all of *Mango's* clothes.
   c three collections for *Mango*.
2 The collection consists of…
   a bags.
   b accessories.
   c garments and accessories.
3 Celebrity endorsements are…
   a less common nowadays.
   b more and more popular.
   c less and less successful.

Te toca a ti A

 escribir 1 Unjumble the words in **bold** and write out the phrases correctly.

1 una lata de **tanú**.
2 una botella de **verezca**.
3 quinientos gramos de **estomat**.
4 un paquete de **cúraza**.
5 una caja de **steapsel**.

6 un paquete de **féac**.
7 una bolsa de **taapsta**.
8 un cartón de **helec**.
9 una barra de **nap**.
10 una docena de **shevuo**.

 leer 2 Match the sentences to the pictures. Then note down what each person doesn't eat.

1  Como frecuentemente pescado o pollo pero no como carne roja.

2  De vez en cuando bebo café pero nunca bebo té. Siempre como muchos huevos.

3  Para estar en forma bebo agua o zumo de naranja y nunca bebo limonada, pero me encanta comer caramelos.

4  Para estar en forma nunca como comida basura porque contiene mucha grasa. Como verduras pero odio la fruta.

a  **b**  **c**  **d**

 leer 3 Read the postcard. Are the statements below true (T), false (F) or not mentioned (NM)?

¡Hola! ¿Qué tal, amiga? Estoy en Barcelona y no me siento bien. Tengo gripe desde hace tres días y me duele mucho la cabeza. Tengo tos y estoy muy cansada. Fui al médico y tengo que tomar unas aspirinas y beber mucha agua.
Un abrazo,
Sandra

1 Sandra is in Spain.
2 Sandra has a temperature.
3 Sandra has had flu for three weeks.
4 She went to the doctor.
5 She has to take aspirin.
6 She must rest and not go swimming.

1 Read the sentence halves and match them up correctly. Then translate them into English.

Example: **1** c – You have to drink lots of water.

1 Tienes que beber   **a** este jarabe.
2 Tienes que descansar   **b** hospital inmediatamente.
3 Tienes que tomar   **c** mucha agua.
4 Tienes que ponerte   **d** en casa.
5 Tienes que tomar una   **e** esta crema.
6 Tienes que ir al   **f** aspirina.

2 Copy out the text and complete it with words from the box.

Nunca fumo **(1)** _____ porque es perjudicial para la salud.
A veces bebo **(2)** _____ porque es divertido. Mi bebida
preferida es la **(3)** _____. Nunca tomo drogas blandas y
nunca tomo drogas **(4)** _____ porque las drogas son muy
(5) _____. Creo que llevar **(6)** _____ es una tontería.

duras	alcohol
navajas	malas
cigarrillos	cerveza

3 Read the text and answer the questions in English.

Me llamo Nadia y **vivo** en Guadalajara en México. Creo que
llevo una vida bastante sana porque **me encanta** practicar
deporte. Mi deporte preferido es la equitación porque me
encantan los caballos. También **me gusta** hacer footing.
Normalmente como mucha carne o pollo y me gustan las
zanahorias y los guisantes. **Odio** la fruta pero a veces como
un plátano porque contienen muchas vitaminas. Para llevar
una vida más sana **voy a comer** más pescado y **voy a
beber** menos Coca-Cola porque es muy mala para la salud.
Nunca voy a fumar porque es una tontería.

1 What does Nadia think of her lifestyle?
2 Which sports does she like doing?
3 Name two vegetables she likes to eat.
4 What kind of food does she not like at all?
5 Why does she sometimes eat a banana?
6 Describe two things she will do to be healthier.

4 Write a paragraph like Nadia's. Try to use
the verbs in **bold** in her text, but with your
own information or opinions. Remember to
write about what you are going to eat and
drink to lead a healthier life.

> ⭐ Remember that **me gusta** and **me
> encanta** change to **me gustan** and **me
> encantan** with plural words or with more
> than one item:
>
> Me gusta el tenis.
> Me gusta**n** los guisantes.
> Me gusta**n** el tenis y el fútbol.

Te toca a ti A

1 Write out these sentences correctly and then translate them into English.

1 sireciclo y reutilizo cuidaré el medioambiente

2 si compro productos de comercio justo ayudaré a los trabajadores

3 si apadrino a un niño daré al niño la posibilidad de sobrevivir

4 si me hago voluntaria mejoraré la sociedad

5 si doy dinero a Oxfam ayudaré a otras personas

2 Match each object with the time you think it would take to decompose.

¿Sabes cuántos años tienen que pasar para la degradación natural de las cosas que tiramos al suelo?

1	pañuelo de papel	**a**	de 3 meses a 2 años
2	periódico	**b**	de 1 a 5 años
3	cigarrillo	**c**	4 000 años
4	chicle	**d**	de 3 a 12 meses
5	cáscara de fruta	**e**	3 meses
6	encendedor de plástico	**f**	100 años
7	vaso de vidrio	**g**	5 años

pañuelo de papel = *tissue*
cáscara = *peel/skin*
encendedor = *lighter*

3 Find the answers to these questions and write out the whole conversation in order.

- ¿Cómo te llamas?
- ¿Cuántos años tienes?
- ¿Te quedaste sin casa hace unos años, ¿verdad?
- ¿Cómo saliste de esta situación?
- ¿Qué planes de futuro tienes?

A ver, en el futuro me gustaría viajar y conocer otros países. Me encanta tener nuevas experiencias.

Me llamo Elena.

Sí, hace dos años.

Un día conocí a una chica que me ayudó mucho.

Tengo diecinueve años.

1 Complete these sentences in English.

1 Finca Bellavista is located…
2 They use… and… energy. (two types)
3 They reuse…
4 There is a… and a community garden.
5 Although you are immersed in nature, it is possible to…

Casas sostenibles en los árboles en la Finca Bellavista, Puerto Rico.

La Finca Bellavista se encuentra en las montañas de la costa sur del Pacífico. Estas casas utilizan energía hidroeléctrica y solar, y reutilizan agua. Hay un centro de reciclaje y un jardín comunitario.

Incluso estando inmerso en la naturaleza, es posible conectarse a Internet. Yo me conectaría sin duda, ¡no puedo vivir sin Internet!

2 Read the text and answer these questions in English.

1 What could you use the other side of a piece of paper for? (Mention one possibility.)
2 What are the two advantages of reusable coffee filters?
3 What do they suggest you do with toys when you have grown tired of them?
4 What can you do with clothes you have grown out of?
5 Which material can be useful if recycled?

Es importante reutilizar las cosas… Por ejemplo:

1 Al utilizar papel para escribir, no escribas sólo en una cara, utiliza el otro lado para notas, para dibujar…
2 Si en casa tomas café y utilizas filtros de papel, hay que comprar filtros reutilizables y lavables. Es más barato y produce menos basura.
3 ¿Te has cansado de tus juguetes? En lugar de tirarlos a la basura, puedes darlos a otros niños…
4 La ropa pequeña para ti, a lo mejor le puede servir a alguien más pequeño que tú.
5 También la madera puede ser reutilizada. Busca en tu zona algún sitio donde la recojan.

3 Match up the Spanish and English slogans.

1 ¡Elimina la pobreza y el hambre!
2 Todos los niños tienen derecho a ir al colegio.
3 Los hombres y las mujeres deben ser iguales.
4 Vamos a mejorar la salud de las mujeres del mundo.
5 ¿Sufrir el SIDA? ¡No!
6 Un mundo mejor para todos

a Equal rights for men and women
b Let's improve women's health!
c A better world for all
d Stamp out poverty and hunger!
e AIDS? No way!
f All children have the right to go to school.

Gramática Basics

The present tense

What is it?

You use the present tense to talk about the things in the present. Use it to talk about:

- – What usually happens: Siempre **escucho** música pop.   (I always **listen** to pop music.)
- – What things are like: La playa **es** grande.   (The beach **is** big.)
- – What is happening now: **Vivo** en Bournemouth.   (I **live** in Bournemouth.)

How does it work?

Regular verbs

- To form the present tense you replace the infinitive ending (-ar, -er or -ir) with the present tense endings like this:

	escuchar (to listen)	**comer** (to eat)	**vivir** (to live)
yo	escuch**o**	com**o**	viv**o**
tú	escuch**as**	com**es**	viv**es**
él/ella	escuch**a**	com**e**	viv**e**
nosotros/as	escuch**amos**	com**emos**	viv**imos**
vosotros/as	escuch**áis**	com**éis**	viv**ís**
ellos/ellas	escuch**an**	com**en**	viv**en**

Stem-changing verbs

- Stem-changing verbs have the same endings. However, the middle of the verb (the stem) changes when you are talking about **I**, **you** (singular), **he/she**, and **they**. There are three common groups.

	o → ue	**e → ie**	**e → i**
	p**o**der (to be able)	qu**e**rer (to want)	p**e**dir (to ask)
yo	pu**e**do	qui**e**ro	p**i**do
tú	pu**e**des	qui**e**res	p**i**des
él/ella/usted	pu**e**de	qui**e**re	p**i**de
nosotros/as	podemos	queremos	pedimos
vosotros/as	podéis	queréis	pedís
ellos/as/ustedes	pu**e**den	qui**e**ren	p**i**den

- Other examples of stem-changing verbs are:

u / o → ue

ju**g**ar	(to play)	→	ju**e**go	(I play)
d**o**rmir	(to sleep)	→	du**e**rmo	(I sleep)
enc**o**ntrar	(to meet/find)	→	encu**e**ntro	(I find)
v**o**lver	(to return)	→	vu**e**lvo	(I come back)

e → ie

emp**e**zar	(to begin)	→	emp**ie**zo	(I start)
ent**e**nder	(to understand)	→	ent**ie**ndo	(I understand)
p**e**nsar	(to think)	→	p**ie**nso	(I think)
pref**e**rir	(to prefer)	→	pref**ie**ro	(I prefer)

e → i

s**e**rvir	(to serve)	→	s**i**rvo	(I serve)

Things to remember for a C grade

- **Use the correct ending:** The verb ending is the important part. This tells you 'who' the sentence is about.
- **Talk about yourself and others:** This will help to add variety to what you say, but check the endings of the verb are correct when you talk about other people.
- **Include time expressions where possible:** siempre *(always)*; a veces / de vez en cuando *(sometimes)*; nunca *(never)* normalmente *(normally)*; los sábados *(on Saturdays)*

Preparados

1 Fill in the gaps with the correct verb in the 'I' (yo) form.

1 Me llamo Mónica y vivo en Barcelona. *(vivir)*
2 Todos los días _____ con mis amigos por Internet. *(chatear)*
3 De vez en cuando _____ con el ordenador o con la Wii. *(jugar)*
4 _____ música por las tardes. *(descargar)*
5 No _____ mucho. *(leer)*
6 A veces barro el suelo y siempre _____ la comida. *(preparar)*

Listos

2 Complete the gap with the correct verb ending.
Then translate the sentences into English.

1 ¿Qué estudias en el cole? *(estudiar – tú)*
2 Normalmente _____ el coche los sábados. *(limpiar – nosotros)*
3 Mi madre no _____ mucho porque no le gusta. *(cocinar – ella)*
4 Mi padre _____ al fútbol conmigo. *(jugar – él)*
5 A veces _____ chocolates y caramelos. *(comer – nosotras)*
6 Siempre _____ en avión porque es fácil. *(viajar – ellas)*

limpiar = *to clean*
cocinar = *to cook*
viajar = *to travel*

¡Ya!

3 Underline the correct verb to complete each sentence.

1 Mis clases **empiezas / empiezan / empiezo** a las ocho.
2 Mis amigos y yo **necesitamos / necesita / necesitan** unos bolígrafos y una regla.
3 Mi amigo Carlos **bebes / bebe / beben** un refresco de cola todos los días.
4 Yo **prefiero / prefieres / preferimos** ir en bici.
5 A veces, en el recreo, nosotros **jugamos / juega / jugáis** al tenis.
6 Mi amiga Silvia **prefiero / prefieres / prefiere** las asignaturas prácticas.

Gramática · Basics

The present tense – irregular

What are irregular verbs?

Irregular verbs do not follow the normal patterns of regular *-ar*, *-er* and *-ir* verbs.
Many of the most common and most useful verbs in Spanish are irregular.

How do they work?

Irregular verbs

These verbs are only irregular in the 'I' form.

hacer	*(to make/do)*	→	ha**g**o	*(I make/do)*
poner	*(to put)*	→	pon**g**o	*(I put)*
salir	*(to go out)*	→	sal**g**o	*(I go out)*
coger	*(to take)*	→	co**j**o	*(I take)*

They otherwise follow a regular pattern. For example:

	hacer *(to do)*
yo	ha**go**
tú	hac**es**
él/ella	hac**e**
nosotros/as	hac**emos**
vosotros/as	hac**éis**
ellos/ellas	hac**en**

● Other verbs have more irregularity.

	ir *(to go)*	**tener** *(to have)*
yo	voy	ten**g**o
tú	vas	t**ie**nes
él/ella	va	t**ie**ne
nosotros/as	vamos	tenemos
vosotros/as	vais	tenéis
ellos/ellas	van	t**ie**nen

To be

There are two verbs for to be: 'ser' and 'estar'.

● 'Ser' is used for what does not change.
    Soy inglesa.   *(I am English.)*
    Es alto.   *(He is tall.)*

● 'Estar' is used for locations and things that are temporary.
    ¿Dónde **está** el parque?   *(Where is the park?)*
    La habitación **está** limpia.   *(The room is clean.)*

	ser *(to be)* [permanent states]	**estar** *(to be)* [locations, temporary]
yo	soy	estoy
tú	eres	estás
él/ella	es	está
nosotros/as	somos	estamos
vosotros/as	sois	estáis
ellos/ellas	son	están

● Look at the verb tables on page 216 for more irregular present-tense verbs.

★ **Things to remember for a C grade**

● You can't speak a language without knowing a range of verbs, and some of the most important verbs are irregular. Be prepared to **learn them**.

● Try to talk about **other people** as well as **yourself** using irregular verbs.

● Sometimes **just the 'I' form** is irregular. Knowing this will help you to talk about yourself and other people correctly.

Preparados

1 Unjumble the 'I' form of the verb shown. What does the sentence mean in English?

1 Por la mañana **o v y** al instituto en bicicleta. *(ir)*
Por la mañana **voy** *al instituto en bicicleta.*

2 **l o a s g** a las ocho y media. *(salir)*

3 Si llueve, no voy en bicicleta, **c o o j** el autobús. *(coger)*

4 **g o n e t** geografía los martes. *(tener)*

5 Después del colegio **y o v** al club de ajedrez. Me gusta mucho. *(ir)*

6 Los domingos **g o h a** natación. *(hacer)*

Listos

2 Fill in the gaps with the correct verb. Choose from the ones in the box, then write the sentences in English.

sale   va   ~~hago~~   haces   vas   vas   es

1 Hago mis deberes después del colegio.

2 Me gusta la biología porque ▓▓▓▓▓ divertida y también es fácil.

3 Cuando nieva, ¿▓▓▓▓▓ esquí?

4 Si llueve, ¿▓▓▓▓▓ de compras o ▓▓▓▓▓ al cine?

5 ¿A qué hora sale el tren? ▓▓▓▓▓ a las ocho diez.

6 Generalmente mi hermano ▓▓▓▓▓ en moto porque es rápido.

¡Ya!

3 Complete these sentences with the correct form of the verb.

1 Salgo a las ocho. *(salir)*

2 Cada noche yo ▓▓▓▓▓ mis deberes. *(hacer)*

3 Mis padres ▓▓▓▓▓ mucho. *(salir)*

4 Yo ▓▓▓▓▓ en autobús pero tú ▓▓▓▓▓ en tren. *(ir)*

5 Mis amigos y yo ▓▓▓▓▓ natación cada sábado. *(hacer)*

6 Mis padres ▓▓▓▓▓ una casa muy bonita. *(tener)*

4 Choose between 'ser' and 'estar'. Underline the right verb.

1 Bilbao **<u>está</u> / es** en el norte de España.

2 **Es / Está** delgado y alto.

3 El aseo no **es / está** limpio.

4 Normalmente cojo el autobús porque no **es / está** caro.

5 **Soy / Estoy** en Francia.

6 ¿Por dónde se va al supermercado? – **Es / Está** muy cerca.

Gramática Bonus points

Reflexive verbs

What are reflexive verbs?

We use reflexive verbs to describe actions that we do to ourselves, for example, washing, showering, getting dressed.

Reflexive verbs have an extra part called a reflexive pronoun.

How do they work?

- In the **infinitive**, the pronoun is shown at the end of the verb (duchar**se**).
- In the **present tense**, the pronoun is put in front of the verb and changes depending on who you are talking about (**me** duch**o**).

	ducharse *(to shower)*	despertarse *(to wake up)* [stem-changing]
yo	**me** ducho	**me** desp**ie**rto
tú	**te** duchas	**te** desp**ie**rtas
él/ella	**se** ducha	**se** desp**ie**rta
nosotros/as	**nos** duchamos	**nos** despertamos
vosotros/as	**os** ducháis	**os** despertáis
ellos/ellas	**se** duchan	**se** desp**ie**rtan

Verbs you are most likely to see and use

Here is a list of reflexive verbs in the 'I' form that you could use in your writing and speaking assessments.

'I' form	English	Infinitive
me acuesto	I go to bed	**acostar**se
me afeito	I shave	**afeitar**se
me despierto	I wake up	**despertar**se
me ducho	I shower	**duchar**se
me lavo	I wash	**lavar**se
me lavo los dientes	I clean my teeth	**lavar**se los dientes
me levanto	I get up	**levantar**se
me peino	I comb my hair	**peinar**se
me visto	I get dressed	**vestir**se

 Things to remember for a C grade

Using reflexive verbs will add variety to what you say and help to increase your mark. But it is also easy to make mistakes with them so try to remember these things:

- Remember to include the reflexive pronoun (*me, te, se,* etc.). Don't just leave it out.
- Remember that the pronoun changes depending on who you are talking about.

Preparados

1 Complete these sentences with the correct form of the verb.
Choose from the list of verbs in the box.

~~me despierto~~   me ducho   me peino   me acuesto   me afeito
me levanto   me lavo los dientes   me visto

1 Me despierto a las siete.
2 _____ a las siete y diez.
3 Luego _____.
4 Después _____.
5 No _____.
6 _____ a las once.

Listos

2 Write the sentences out correctly. Underline the reflexive pronoun
and then match up the Spanish with the English.

1 ¿Osducháisamenudo?

¿Os ducháis a menudo?
Do you shower often?

2 Mihermanasedespiertatemprano.

3 Normalmenteselevantaalasseisdelamañana.

4 ¿Aquéhoratevistes?

5 Nosacostamosalaunadelamadrugada.

6 Mispadresselevantanalassiete.

a What time do you get dressed?
b My sister wakes up early.
c My parents get up at seven.
d We go to bed at one in the morning.
e Normally she gets up at six in the morning.

¡Ya!

3 Choose the correct pronoun or verb form in each case.

Los fines de semana **(1)** *te / me* despierto tarde. Me **(2)** *levanto / levanta* a
las diez, veo la televisión y escucho música. Luego me gusta chatear un poco
con mis amigos. Mi mejor amigo, Javier, **(3)** *te / se* levanta a eso de las once,
pero se **(4)** *visto / viste* rápidamente y nos **(5)** *encuentro / encontramos* en
el parque donde jugamos al fútbol juntos. ¿Y tú? ¿Qué haces los fines de
semana? ¿A qué hora **(6)** *me / te* levantas?

Gramática Basics

The preterite

What is it?
The preterite tense is a verb tense used to talk about completed actions in the past.

Fui a la playa. *(I went to the beach.)*

Comió un bocadillo. *(He ate a sandwich.)*

How does it work?
Regular preterite verbs
- To form them, take the infinitive, remove *-ar*, *-er* or *-ir*, and add these endings.
  (The endings are the same for -er and -ir verbs.)

	visitar *(to visit)*	**com**er *(to eat)*	**sal**ir *(to go out)*
yo	visit**é**	com**í**	sal**í**
tú	visit**aste**	com**iste**	sal**iste**
él/ella	visit**ó**	com**ió**	sal**ió**
nosotros/as	visit**amos**	com**imos**	sal**imos**
vosotros/as	visit**asteis**	com**isteis**	sal**isteis**
ellos/ellas	visit**aron**	com**ieron**	sal**ieron**

Irregular preterite verbs
- The most common irregular verbs are:

	ser/ir *(to be/go)*	**ver** *(to see)*	**hacer** *(to do)*	**tener** *(to have)*
yo	fui	vi	hice	tuve
tú	fuiste	viste	hiciste	tuviste
él/ella	fue	vio	hizo	tuvo
nosotros/as	fuimos	vimos	hicimos	tuvimos
vosotros/as	fuisteis	visteis	hicisteis	tuvisteis
ellos/ellas	fueron	vieron	hicieron	tuvieron

Look at the verb tables to see some other preterite verbs once you feel confident with these.
- Some preterite verbs have **irregular spellings** just in the first person singular *(yo)*.

  sacar → sa**qu**é *(I got/took)*

  tocar → to**qu**é *(I played)*

  jugar → ju**gu**é *(I played)*

  llegar → lle**gu**é *(I arrived)*

 **Things to remember
for a C grade**

- **Understand them:** make sure you recognise them. In listening and reading you may need to understand if someone is talking about the past.
- **Use them:** they will help to increase your mark if you use them correctly in speaking and writing
- **Check for accents:** regular preterite verbs take accents for I forms and he/she forms – hablé / habló. But remember that irregular verbs don't need accents
- **Remember time expressions:** using a time expression about the past with a preterite verb will also help to increase your mark! ayer *(yesterday)*; la semana pasada *(last week)*; el fin de semana pasado *(last weekend)*; el año pasado *(last year)*

Preparados

1 Copy the sentences and write the correct 'I' (yo) ending for the verb in brackets.

  1 La semana pasada (*leer*) un libro muy bueno.
  La semana pasada leí un libro muy bueno.
  2 Ayer (*comprar*) un reloj y luego fui al cine.
  3 La semana pasada (*comer*) paella.
  4 (*tener*) una fiesta para celebrar mi cumpleaños.
  5 Ayer no (*hacer*) nada en casa.
  6 (*estudiar*) ocho asignaturas en el colegio.

Listos

2 You are working as a translator. Choose the correct verb to start each of the sentences and write out the rest of the sentence.

  1 I went to the bowling alley. (*ir – a la bolera*)
  Fui a la bolera.
  2 We bought a big dog. (*comprar – un perro grande*)
  3 He tidied his bedroom. (*limpiar – su dormitorio*)
  4 She played on the computer. (*jugar – con el ordenador*)
  5 We drank orange juice. (*beber – zumo de naranja*)
  6 I swam in the school pool. (*nadar – en la piscina del colegio*)

¡Ya!

3 Look at the list of phrases and decide if the verbs are in the present or the preterite tense? Then translate each verb into English.

  1 Desayuno a las diez.
  Present – I have breakfast.
  2 Primero fuimos al museo.
  3 Hace mucho sol aquí.
  4 Mi amigo compró unos recuerdos.
  5 Practiqué natación en el mar cerca de mi casa.
  6 Siempre hago mis deberes.
  7 En el colegio comemos a las doce y media.
  8 Anoche mis amigos fueron al cine.

Gramática Bonus points

Other past tenses

What are they?
Two other past tenses that you might come across or use are:

The imperfect – used for descriptions and background details.
El hotel era muy grande.   *(The hotel was very big.)*
La casa tenía garaje y jardín.   *(The house had a garage and a garden.)*

The **perfect tense** is used to describe what you **have done**.
He trabajado en equipo. (***I have worked*** *in a team.)*

How do they work?
- To form the **imperfect tense**:
  a) take the infinitive of a verb
  b) remove the infinitive endings *(-ar, -er, -ir)*
  c) add these endings (note that *-er* and *-ir* verbs take the same endings in the imperfect)

	estar *(to be)*	hacer *(to do)*	tener *(to have)*	vivir *(to live)*
yo	est**aba**	hac**ía**	ten**ía**	viv**ía**
tú	est**abas**	hac**ías**	ten**ías**	viv**ías**
él/ella	est**aba**	hac**ía**	ten**ía**	viv**ía**
nosotros/as	est**ábamos**	hac**íamos**	ten**íamos**	viv**íamos**
vosotros/as	est**abais**	hac**íais**	ten**íais**	viv**íais**
ellos/ellas	est**aban**	hac**ían**	ten**ían**	viv**ían**

- The verb 'ser' (to be) is irregular in the imperfect.

	ser *(to be)*
yo	era
tú	eras
él/ella	era
nosotros/as	éramos
vosotros/as	erais
ellos/ellas	eran

- The imperfect tense of **hay** (*there is*) is **había** (*there was/were*).
  Había mucha gente en la tienda.   *(There were a lot of people in the shop.)*
- To form the **perfect tense** take the present tense of 'haber' and
  add the past participle (ending in '-ido' or '-ado').
  He trabajado.   *(I have worked.)*
  He tenido.   *(I have had.)*

yo	he
tú	has
él/ella	ha
nosotros/as	hemos
vosotros/as	habéis
ellos/ellas	han

 **Things to remember
for a C grade**

- **Focus on the preterite:** learn the preterite first, as this is the main tense for you to talk about the past.
- **Learn some phrases in the imperfect:** It will help to improve your grade if you can include simple descriptions of things in the imperfect.
- **Recognise the imperfect and perfect tense:** You may come across these in your listening or reading exam, so it's important that you understand them.

Preparados

1 Complete the sentences with the 'he/she/it' part of these verbs in the imperfect.

1 Mi piso en Madrid *era* muy pequeño. *(ser)*
2 Antes _____ mucha pizza. *(comer)*
3 Mi jefe _____ muy simpático. *(ser)*
4 El chico _____ en la plaza. *(estar)*
5 En el hotel, _____ una piscina grande. *(hay)*
6 _____ un perro cuando era joven. *(tener)*

Listos

**2 Complete the sentences with the perfect-tense verbs in the box below.
Write down what each sentence means in English.**

~~he trabajado~~   he estudiado
he comido   ha vigilado   hemos hablado   ha servido

1 *He trabajado* como enfermera en un hospital.
2 _____ a los clientes.
3 _____ inglés y francés.
4 _____ ciencias y matemáticas.
5 _____ a la gente que nada en la piscina.
6 _____ una paella muy rica.

¡Ya!

3 Complete the sentences with one of the verbs in the imperfect.

~~era~~   había   estaba   tenía   eran   comían   hablaba   vivía

1 Mi profesor de inglés *era* genial.
2 En el colegio _____ una biblioteca pequeña.
3 Los profesores _____ antipáticos.
4 El camping no _____ restaurante.
5 El hotel _____ muy limpio.
6 Mis amigos _____ hamburguesas.

 This exercise has examples of 'ser' *(eran)* and 'estar' *(estaba)*.
● Use ser for things that are quite permanent (for example, the personality of your teachers).
● Use estar for situations that can easily change (for example, how clean something was).

Gramática [Basics

Talking about the future

What is it?

The near future tense is the most common tense in Spanish for describing future plans. It is used to describe 'what is going to happen' (for example, tonight, tomorrow, next week, etc.).

Voy a ir al cine.   *(I am going to go to the cinema.)*
Vamos a comprar un coche.   *(We are going to buy a car.)*

How does it work?

To form the immediate future, use a combination of three things:
ir (to go, in the present tense) + ***a*** + **verb** (in the infinitive).

yo	voy		comer, beber, jugar
tú	vas		practicar, tener, salir
él/ella	va	a	comprar, hacer, ir
nosotros/as	vamos		hablar, escribir, estudiar
vosotros/as	vais		escuchar, llevar, viajar
ellos/ellas	van		ver, mandar, chatear

Voy a comer patatas fritas.   *(I am going to eat crisps.)*
¿Qué **vas a comprar**?   *(What are you going to buy?)*
Mi amigo **va a jugar** al fútbol.   *(My friend is going to play football.)*
Vamos a ir al cine.   *(We are going to go to the cinema.)*
Vais a estudiar mucho.   *(You are all going to study a lot.)*
Mis padres **van a tener** una fiesta. *(My parents are going to have a party.)*

Other ways to refer to the future

You can also use two other expressions to talk about the future:

- **Querer + infinitive** *(to want to)*
  Quiero ir a la piscina este fin de semana.   *(I want to go to the swimming pool this weekend.)*
- **Me gustaría + infinitive** *(would like to)*
  Me gustaría ir a la playa.   *(I would like to go to the beach.)*

 Things to remember for a C grade

- **Talk about the future** alongside the present tense or the preterite. This will show that you can use a variety of language and help you to aim for a C grade.
- **Remember all the parts:** You need all three parts for it to be correct. Don't forget the '**a**'!
- **Use the future tense with time expressions** about the future.

mañana	*(tomorrow)*
la semana que viene	*(next week)*
el año que viene	*(next year)*
el fin de semana	*(at the weekend)*

- You can also use 'querer' and 'me gustaría' + infinitive to talk about the future.

Preparados

1 Write out the sentence in each word snake. Underline the infinitive and then match it to one of the pictures.

1 Mañanavoyacomerpaella

Mañana voy a <u>comer</u> paella.

2 Voyasacarmuchasfotosensevilla

3 Novoyamandarmensajes

4 ¿Vasaestudiarcomercioelañoqueviene?

5 Lasemanaquevienevoyairaladiscoteca

6 Elfindesemanavoyadormirmucho

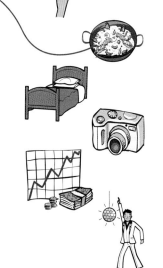

2 Rewrite the sentences from exercise 1 using 'quiero' or 'me gustaría' instead of 'voy a'.
1 Mañana me gustaría comer paella.

Listos

3 Read the text and underline all the verbs in the near future.

En el futuro, el mundo <u>va a ser</u> muy diferente porque la tecnología va a cambiar.
Por ejemplo, muchos coches van a ser eléctricos y vamos a tener un sistema de transporte público mejor.
Los institutos van a ser muy diferentes. Van a tener más ordenadores y los profesores van a dar clase a través de los 'podcasts'. Creo que voy a usar mi ordenador mucho más en el futuro.

¡Ya!

4 Each sentence has one part of the near future missing. Write out the sentence with all 3 parts.
1 I am going to buy a flat. / Voy comprar un piso.   Voy a comprar un piso.
2 My friends are going to go to the cinema. / Mis amigos van a al cine.
3 Today my father is going to cook. / Hoy mi padre a cocinar.
4 We are going to visit museums. / Vamos a museos.
5 Maite is going to study for her exams. / Maite va estudiar para sus exámenes.
6 They are going to go on the bus. / Van ir en autobús.
7 I am going to buy a necklace. / Voy a un collar.
8 Today we are going to play football. / Hoy vamos jugar al fútbol.

Gramática Bonus points

The future tense

What is it?

The future tense is used to describe what 'will happen' in the future or what things will be like. You need to be able to recognise this tense as you read or listen to Spanish.

En el futuro, mi colegio será diferente. *(In the future, my school will be different.)*

How does it work?

To form the future tense of most verbs, you take the infinitive of the verb and add the following endings (these are the same for *-ar*, *-er* and *-ir* verbs):

	ser *(to be)*
yo	ser**é**
tú	ser**ás**
él/ella	ser**á**
nosotros/as	ser**emos**
vosotros/as	ser**éis**
ellos/ellas	ser**án**

- Some verbs are irregular in the future tense. You need to use these '**stems**' instead of the infinitive, but the endings stay the same as for regular verbs.

decir	*(to say)*	→	**dir**é...
hacer	*(to do)*	→	**har**é...
poder	*(to be able to)*	→	**podr**é...
poner	*(to put)*	→	**pondr**é...
salir	*(to leave, go out)*	→	**saldr**é...
tener	*(to have)*	→	**tendr**é...
venir	*(to come)*	→	**vendr**é...

- The future tense of 'haber' is **habrá** *(there will be)*.

Things to remember for a C grade

Examiners will be impressed if you can use the future tense correctly, but make sure you can use the near future tense first (see page 200) as that will be more useful!

- If you use this tense, remember to add accents where they are needed.
- Use time expressions with this tense to impress examiners even more!

la semana que viene	*(next week)*
el año que viene	*(next year)*
en el futuro	*(in the future)*
en cinco años	*(in five years' time)*

Preparados

1 Match up the Spanish with the English.

1 En el futuro, seré instructor de esquí.   1 d
2 Hablarás muy bien español.
3 Ayudará a otras personas.
4 Tendrás experiencias muy positivas.
5 Reciclaremos más.
6 En el futuro, tendremos problemas.

a We will recycle more.
b You will speak Spanish very well.
c He will help others.
d In the future I will be a ski instructor.
e In the future, we will have problems.
f You will have very positive experiences.

Listos

2 Use the model to help you make your own resolution posters with the verbs below.

1 **reciclar** papel y vidrio
   Yo reciclaré papel y vidrio.

2 **apagar** las luces

3 **usar** el transporte público

4 no **usar** el coche

5 no **utilizar** bolsas de plástico

6 no **consumir** demasiada energía

¡Ya!

3 Write out the correct form of the verb indicated.

A: ¿Cuántos alumnos (1) *(ellos – estudiar → estudiarán)* español el año que viene?

B: Pues, no lo sé pero el colegio (2) *(él – tener)* más de quinientos alumnos en total.

A: ¿(3) *(haber)* un club de fotografía?

B: Sí. El club de fotografía (4) *(ser)* los lunes a la hora de comer.

A: Y tú, ¿(5) *(hacer)* algún deporte?

B: Si tengo tiempo, yo (6) *(jugar)* al béisbol los viernes o (7) *(nadar)* los martes.

Gramática   Bonus points

Poder, querer, deber + infinitive

What are they?

'Poder' (to be able to), 'querer' (to want to) and 'deber' (must) are verbs which can be used with infinitives. Use them when you want to express what you can do, what you want to do or what you must do.

Puedo jugar al fútbol.   (***I can*** play football.)
Quiero jugar al fútbol.   (***I want to*** play football.)
Debo jugar al fútbol.   (***I must*** play football.)

How do they work?

Use the present tense of '**poder**', '**querer**' and '**deber**' + **infinitive**.
Remember that for 'poder' and 'querer' sometimes include a stem change in the middle of the verb (see below).

	Poder (to be able to)	Querer (to want to)	Deber (to have to)	+ infinitive
yo	p**ue**do	qu**ie**ro	debo	ir
tú	p**ue**des	qu**ie**res	debes	hacer
él/ella	p**ue**de	qu**ie**re	debe	hablar
nosotros/as	podemos	queremos	debemos	comprar
vosotros/as	podéis	queréis	debéis	comer
ellos/ellas	p**ue**den	qu**ie**ren	deben	beber

'Se debe' and 'se puede'

The expression '**se debe**' translates literally as 'one must'.
The expression '**se puede**' translates as 'one can'.
Often, though, people say 'you must' or 'you can' to mean the same thing.
'Se debe' and 'se puede' are also followed by an infinitive.

Se debe escuchar en clase.   (*You must listen in class.*)
No se debe llevar maquillaje.   (*You must not wear make-up.*)
Se puede comprar un recuerdo.   (*You can buy a souvenir.*)

'Deberías'

You can use the verb deber in the conditional tense to mean 'should'.
Use it in the *tú* form (deberías) to give advice to someone:
Deberías comer menos chocolate.   (*You should eat less chocolate.*)
No deberías tomar drogas.   (*You shouldn't take drugs.*)

 Things to remember for a C grade

These structures will help to add variety to your Spanish and so will be very useful to get you up to a C grade.
Remember to check your infinitives:

- They always need to end in -*ar*, -*er*, or -*ir*.
- They don't always look like the verbs you most often use, for example, **jue**go (I play) but **ju**gar (to play). Check them if you think you might be using a stem changing verb.

Preparados

1 Translate these rules into Spanish using 'se debe'.

1 You mustn't wear make-up.   *No se debe llevar maquillaje.*

2 You mustn't run in the corridors.

3 You must do your homework.

4 You must wear uniform.

5 You mustn't eat chewing gum.

6 You can go out.

comer chicle

correr en los pasillos

escuchar en clase

escuchar música en clase

hacer los deberes

salir

llevar joyas / maquillaje / piercings / zapatillas de deporte

llevar uniforme

usar el móvil en clase

Listos

2 Fill in the correct parts of the missing verbs 'querer' or 'poder'.
Can you write the English for each sentence too?

1 *(He wants) ir al cine.*

Quiere ir al cine.

2 *(We can) comer chicle.*

3 *¿(You want) leer revistas?*

4 *(I can) escuchar música.*

5 *(We want) salir con amigos.*

6 *(They can) ver la tele.*

¡Ya!

3 Write a piece of advice for each picture in Spanish using 'deberías' (you should)
or 'no deberías' (you shouldn't).

1

Deberías comer más pescado.

2

3

4

5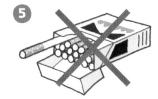

6

Gramática

Verbs for giving opinions

What are they?

There are lots of different verbs in Spanish for giving opinions.
Here are the ones that you will most often see:

me gusta	*(I like)*
me encanta	*(I love)*
me interesa	*(I'm interested in)*
prefiero	*(I prefer)*
odio/detesto	*(I hate)*

- Use them to say how you feel about something (with a definite article):
  Me gusta el baloncesto.　　　*(I like basketball.)*
  Me gustan los animales.　　　*(I like animals.)*
- Or to say you like to do something (with the infinitive)
  Me gusta jugar al baloncesto.　*(I like to play / playing basketball.)*

How do they work?

- Opinion verbs with pronouns:
  Change the pronoun depending on who you are talking about.
  Don't change the verb ending when it is followed by an **infinitive**:
  the verbs should always end in -a.

	Verb		+ infinitive
(a mí)	me	gusta	**ir**
(a ti)	te	encanta	**hacer**
(a él/ella)	le	interesa	**hablar**
(a nosotros/as)	nos	interesa	**comprar**
(a vosotros/as)	os	interesa	**comer**
(a ellos/ellas)	les	interesa	**estudiar**

¿Te gusta **nadar**?　　　　　　　　　*(Do you like swimming?)*
Nos encanta **ver** la televisión.　　*(We love to watch television.)*
Le interesa **ver** monumentos.　　*(He is interested in seeing monuments.)*

- Opinion verbs without pronouns:
  For these verbs, the verb endings change as normal depending
  on who you are talking about.

	Odiar *(to hate)*	**Preferir** *(to prefer)*	+ infinitive
yo	odi**o**	prefier**o**	**ir**
tú	odi**as**	prefier**es**	**hacer**
él/ella	odi**a**	prefier**e**	**hablar**
nosotros/as	odi**amos**	prefer**imos**	**comprar**
vosotros/as	odi**áis**	prefer**ís**	**comer**
ellos/ellas	odi**an**	prefier**en**	**beber**

Odio **hablar** por teléfono.　　*(I hate to talk on the phone.)*
Prefiero **beber** té.　　　　　　　*(I prefer to drink tea.)*

Things to remember for a C grade

- **Use a variety** of opinions in speaking and writing.
- **Look out for negatives** like '**no**' as you listen and read. They change the opinion completely.
- **Think about infinitives** and check that the ones you use are correct.

Preparados

1 Unjumble each inifinitive to complete the sentence.

1 Me gusta **a a n d r** en la piscina.   *nadar*
2 Me encanta **d i e u a r s t** matemáticas.
3 Me interesa **g j a u r** al tenis.
4 Me gusta **t a r o c** el piano.
5 Me encanta **h a c u e s c r** música.
6 Me interesa **e v r** documentales.

2 Now write each opinion in English

1 *I like swimming. / I like to swim.*

Listos

3 Write the opinions in Spanish. Remember to check that you have used the correct pronoun.

1 I like to play the guitar.   *Me gusta tocar la guitarra.*
2 He likes to swim in the pool.
3 We like to study Spanish.
4 They like to do sailing.
5 You all like to watch soaps.
6 Do you like to eat meat?

¡Ya!

4 Complete the missing verbs in each statement.

1 _____ la tele. *(I prefer to watch)*   Prefiero ver la tele.
2 _____ ciencias. *(he hates to study)*
3 _____ peras y uvas. *(we love to eat)*
4 _____ al fútbol. *(we prefer to play)*
5 _____ por Internet. *(she hates to surf)*
6 ¿_____ al aire libre? *(you like to work)*

Gramática Basics

Nouns and articles

Nouns

What are they?

Nouns are words that name things, people and ideas. You use nouns all the time!
You cannot speak a language without them.

How do they work?

In Spanish each noun has a gender: masculine or feminine.
Generally nouns ending in **-o** are masculine (**el** libr**o**).
Those ending in **-a** are feminine (**la** cas**a**).
Gender does **not** refer to whether a boy or a girl would have or use that item!
For example, *el vestido* (dress) is a masculine word.

- Some other endings will show you if a noun is masculine or feminine:
  - **Masculine:** nouns ending in: **-or** (actor, pintor), **-ón** (peatón, salchichón) and **-és** (escocés, estrés).
  - **Feminine:** nouns ending in **-ción** (tradición, educación), **-dad** and **-tad** (ciudad, libertad).
- To form the plural of nouns you normally add:
  -s to words ending in a vowel
  -es for words ending in a consonant

bolígraf**o**	*(pen)*	→ bolígraf**os**	*(pens)*
cas**a**	*(house)*	→ cas**as**	*(houses)*
actor	*(actor)*	→ actor**es**	*(actors)*

- Nouns which end in **-z** in the singular, end in **-ces** in the plural.

vez	*(time)*	→ veces	*(times)*

Articles

What are they?

Articles are used with nouns and mean 'the', 'a(n)' and 'some'.
You use definite articles **el** / **la** / **los** / **las** for 'the'.
You use indefinite articles **un** / **una** for 'a, an' and **unos** / **unas** for 'some'.

How do they work?

Articles change according to whether the noun is
masculine or feminine, singular or plural.

The...

el piso	*(the flat)*	→ **los** pisos	*(the flats)*
la casa	*(the house)*	→ **las** casas	*(the houses)*

A... / some...

un piso	*(a flat)*	→ un**os** pisos	*(some flats)*
un**a** casa	*(a house)*	→ un**as** casas	*(some houses)*

**Things to remember
for a C grade**

- **Try to use the correct articles** (el/la or un/una).
  Make them agree with the nouns they are with.
  This will help you to gain marks for accuracy.
- **Be aware of when articles are needed.** When
  giving an opinion you need to use articles in
  Spanish, even if you wouldn't use 'the' in English.
  Me encanta **el** inglés.   *(I love English.)*
  La geografía es genial.   *(Geography is great.)*
- Be aware of when articles are not needed. When
  talking about your profession in Spanish you don't
  need un/una.
  Soy médico.   *(I am **a** doctor.)*
  Es profesor.   *(He is **a** teacher.)*

Preparados

1 Fill in the gaps with the correct definite article.

1 El francés es interesante.   *El francés es interesante.*

2 Me gustan _____ matemáticas, _____ español y _____ geografía.

3 Mi hermana va a _____ discoteca.

4 _____ piso es muy grande.

5 Me duele _____ mano.

6 _____ foto es bastante buena.

Listos

2 Complete these opinions using the correct definite article.

1 Me gustan *las* manzanas pero prefiero *los* plátanos.

2 Me encanta _____ geografía porque es informativa.

3 Me gustan mucho _____ películas románticas.

4 No me gusta nada _____ zumo de naranja.

5 Me encantan _____ bicis pero _____ coches son más prácticos.

6 Odio _____ programas de deporte porque son aburridos.

¡Ya!

3 Complete the sentences with the correct definite or indefinite article.

1 En mi piso tengo *una* lavadora y *una* ducha.

2 En mi instituto hay _____ biblioteca pero _____ aulas son muy pequeñas.

3 En mi casa tenemos dos dormitorios, _____ cocina, _____ cuarto de baño y _____ salón bonito.

4 _____ pescado, _____ carne roja y _____ huevos contienen proteínas.

5 Me interesa _____ historia porque me gustan los edificios antiguos.

6 En mi opinión, _____ cigarrillos son muy malos.

Gramática Basics

Adjectives

What are they?

Adjectives are describing words. You use them to describe a noun, a person or thing and to give extra information.

How do they work?

● These are the common patterns of adjective endings.

Adjectives ending in:	Masculine singular	Feminine singular	Masculine plural	Feminine plural
-o/-a	baj**o**	baj**a**	baj**os**	baj**as**
-e	impresionant**e**	impresionant**e**	impresionant**es**	impresionant**es**
-or/-ora	hablad**or**	hablad**ora**	hablad**ores**	hablad**oras**
other consonants	azul	azul	azul**es**	azul**es**

● Adjectives of nationality ending in a consonant follow a different pattern.

Ending in **-s**	inglés	ingles**a**	ingles**es**	ingles**as**
	escocés	escoces**a**	escoces**es**	escoces**as**
Ending in **-n**	alemán	aleman**a**	aleman**es**	aleman**as**
Ending in **-l**	español	español**a**	español**es**	español**as**

● Some adjectives don't change and always take the masculine singular form. They are mostly:
   – Colours used with the words 'light' or 'dark' – *azul claro* (light blue), *rojo oscuro* (dark red).

 Things to remember for a C grade

● **Expand your vocabulary:** Learn the meanings of different adjectives. They will be tested in your listening and reading exams.

● **Get the endings right:** in Spanish adjectives have to 'agree' with the person or thing they describe. They may have different endings in the masculine, feminine, singular and plural.

● **Put them in the right place:** most Spanish adjectives come after the noun.
Una casa pequeña.   *(A small house.)*
Un edificio impresionante.   *(An impressive building.)*

Preparados

1 Underline the correct adjective.

1 Vivo en una ciudad **pequeñas / <u>pequeña</u>**.
2 Mis padres están **divorciados / divorciadas**.
3 Mi profesor de inglés es muy **antipáticos / antipático**.
4 Mi mejor amiga es **galés / galesa**.
5 Trabajo en una empresa **grandes / grande**.
6 Las chicas son **españoles / españolas**.

Listos

2 Write the correct colour adjective.

1 Llevo una gorra *azul (blue)*
2 Llevamos una corbata ▭▭▭ *(black)*
3 Me gusta el jersey ▭▭▭ *(red)*
4 Mi hermano tiene un móvil ▭▭▭ *(white)*
5 La lámpara de mi dormitorio es ▭▭▭ *(green)*
6 En el hotel las cortinas son ▭▭▭ *(orange)*

¡Ya!

3 Unjumble the personality adjectives that go in each gap. The English words below will give you a clue. Make sure you have written in the correct ending.

talkative   intelligent   lazy   ~~serious~~   optimistic   strict

1 Mi amiga María es bastante *seria*

2 Mis padres son muy ▭▭▭

3 Mi tía es un poco ▭▭▭

4 Mi abuelo es muy ▭▭▭

5 Nunca somos ▭▭▭

6 Siempre somos ▭▭▭

Gramática   Bonus points

Comparatives and superlatives

What are they?

You use **comparatives** to compare two things, for example, to say one is bigger, better, worse etc. than the other.

You use **superlatives** to compare more than two things and say one is the best, worst, biggest etc.

How do they work?

- The comparative is formed by using:
  - *Más* + adjective + *que*
    Juan es más alto que Julio.   *(Juan es taller than Julio.)*
  - *Menos* + adjective + *que*
    Marta es menos lista que Ana.   *(Marta is less intelligent than Ana.)*
  - *Tan* + adjective + *como*
    José es tan bueno como Luis.   *(José is as good as Luis.)*

  When using comparatives remember that the adjectives need to agree with the nouns they describe.

- The superlative is formed by using the correct form of the adjective with the following construction:
  - *el/la + más/menos + adjective*
    los/las + más/menos + adjective
    Mi hermana es la más alta.   *(My sister is the tallest.)*

- These are the irregular ones.

Adjective	Comparative	Superlative
bueno *(good)*	mejor *(better)*	el/la mejor *(the best)* los/las mejores *(the best)*
malo *(bad)*	peor *(worse)*	el/la peor *(the worst)* los/las peores *(the worst)*

Things to remember for a C grade

- **Use comparatives** to extend your opinions in your speaking and writing assessments. This will really impress the examiner!
- **Remember to make the adjectives agree** with the noun you are describing when you use comparatives.
  Mi perro es más alto que el tuyo.
  (My dog is taller than yours.)
  Tu amiga es más seria que tú.
  (Your friend is more serious than you.)
- For 'better' or 'worse', remember that you don't need to use 'más' or 'menos'

Preparados

1 Break up the word snakes to write sentences comparing two things.

1 MaríaesmásaltaqueJulia   María es más alta que Julia.

2 JoséesmenosatractivoqueAntonio

3 PaulinaesmásantipáticaqueFederico

4 Mihermanoesmásperezosoquemihermana

5 Mimadreesmásdelgadaquemipadre

6 Miamigaesmenosgordaquemiamigo

2 Now write each statement from exercise 1 in English.
  1 María is taller than Julia.

Listos

3 Write a sentence comparing each pair of things. Use the adjectives provided, but make sure they agree!

~~moderno~~   peor   caro   mejor   rápido   útil

1 el centro comercial + el cine *(modern)*   El centro comercial es más moderno que el cine.
2 los coches + las bicicletas *(faster)*
3 el inglés – las matemáticas *(useful)*
4 el ordenador + el libro *(expensive)*
5 la natación + la equitación *(better)*
6 los caramelos – el chocolate *(worse)*

¡Ya!

4 Identify which statement is a comparative (C) and which is a superlative (S) and then write the English.
  1 Este restaurante es el mejor de la ciudad.   (S) This restaurant is the best in the city.
  2 Mi casa es la más moderna.
  3 Tu coche es más rápido que mi moto.
  4 Mi perro es menos tonto que mi gato.
  5 Mi falda es la más bonita.
  6 Mis pantalones son los más feos.

Gramática Bonus points

Negatives

What are they?
Negatives are words which can be added to a sentence to make it a negative statement.
For example, 'I do **not** like history'. Use them when you want to say not,
nothing, never, nobody etc.

How do they work?
In Spanish the simple negative is 'no' and it goes immediately before a verb
(or before a reflexive pronoun or object pronoun).

No como.   *(I don't eat.)*
No me levanto temprano.   *(I don't get up early.)*

Other negatives consist of two or more words which go either side of the verb:

no ... nada   *(nothing / not anything)*
no ... nunca   *(never)*
no ... ni ... ni...   *(neither ... nor)*
no ... tampoco   *(not ... either)*
no ... ningún / ninguna   *(no, not any)*
no ... nadie   *(no ... nobody / not anybody)*

No bebo **nada**.   *(I **don't** drink **anything**.)*
No hacemos **nunca** deporte. *(We **never** do sport.)*
No tengo **ni** casa **ni** coche. *(I **don't** have **either** a house **or** a car.)*

- Sometimes, for emphasis, the negative expression can be placed before the verb
  and in this case 'no' is not used.
  Nunca vamos a ir allí.   *(We are **never** going to go there.)*

 **Things to remember
for a C grade**

- **Use simple negative statements** with 'no' in your
  speaking and writing. This will add variety to what
  you say and help you to gain marks.
  No bebo café.   *(I **don't** drink coffee.)*
- When you've done that try to **become familiar
  with one or two others** that will really impress the
  examiner. 'Nunca' (never) is a good one to use:
  Nunca bebo café.   *(I **never** drink coffee.)*
- **Make sure you can understand** some of the other
  negative phrases as they may come up in reading
  and listening exams and change the meaning of
  sentences.

Preparados

1 Make each statement negative.

1 Vivimos en el norte del país. No vivimos en el norte del país.
2 Tienen muchos problemas.
3 Mi hermana come mucha fruta y verduras.
4 Mis amigos de clase juegan al baloncesto los viernes.
5 Jaime se levanta a las ocho y media.
6 Mi madre compró unas botas nuevas.

Listos

2 Match up the correct sentence halves. Then write out the sentence in English.

1 c Juan doesn't wear uniform.

1 Juan no lleva...
2 María no tiene...
3 Ana no hace...
4 Miguel nunca…
5 Antonia no escribe...
6 Javier no viaja nunca...
7 Roberto no habla...

a ...nada para estar en forma.
b ...cuaderno ni bolígrafo ni regla.
c ...uniforme.
d ...hace ejercicio.
e …en avión.
f ...nunca correos electrónicos.
g …italiano ni alemán.

¡Ya!

3 Complete the gaps to form a negative phrase.

1 Elena ▢▢▢ come carne. *(never)* Elena nunca come carne.
2 No bebo ▢▢▢ por la mañana. *(nothing)*
3 En el colegio no hay ▢▢▢ biblioteca ▢▢▢ piscina. *(neither / nor)*
4 No come ▢▢▢ huevos. *(never)*
5 Mi hermano no escucha a ▢▢▢ *(no one)*

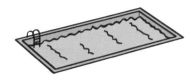

Gramática Basics

Verb tables

Regular verbs

Infinitive			Present	Near future	Preterite
hablar *(to speak)*	I	(yo)	habl**o**	Voy a hablar	habl**é**
	You	(tú)	habl**as**	Vas a hablar	habl**aste**
	He/she/it	(él/ella/usted)	habl**a**	Va a hablar	habl**ó**
	We	(nosotros/as)	habl**amos**	Vamos a hablar	habl**amos**
	You (pl.)	(vosotros/as)	habl**áis**	Vais a hablar	habl**asteis**
	They	(ellos/as/ustedes)	habl**an**	Van a hablar	habl**aron**
comer *(to eat)*	I	(yo)	com**o**	Voy a comer	com**í**
	You	(tú)	com**es**	Vas a comer	com**iste**
	He/she/it	(él/ella/usted)	com**e**	Va a comer	com**ió**
	We	(nosotros/as)	com**emos**	Vamos a comer	com**imos**
	You (pl.)	(vosotros/as)	com**éis**	Vais a comer	com**isteis**
	They	(ellos/as/ustedes)	com**en**	Van a comer	com**ieron**
vivir *(to live)*	I	(yo)	viv**o**	Voy a vivir	viv**í**
	You	(tú)	viv**es**	Vas a vivir	viv**iste**
	He/she/it	(él/ella/usted)	viv**e**	Va a vivir	viv**ió**
	We	(nosotros/as)	viv**imos**	Vamos a vivir	viv**imos**
	You (pl.)	(vosotros/as)	viv**ís**	Vais a vivir	viv**isteis**
	They	(ellos/as/ustedes)	viv**en**	Van a vivir	viv**ieron**

Irregular verbs

Infinitive			Present	Near future	Preterite
dar *(to give)*	I	(yo)	**doy**	Voy a dar	**di**
	You	(tú)	das	Vas a dar	**diste**
	He/she/it	(él/ella/usted)	da	Va a dar	**dio**
	We	(nosotros/as)	damos	Vamos a dar	**dimos**
	You (pl.)	(vosotros/as)	dais	Vais a dar	**disteis**
	They	(ellos/as/ustedes)	dan	Van a dar	**dieron**
decir *(to say)*	I	(yo)	**digo**	Voy a decir	**dije**
	You	(tú)	**dices**	Vas a decir	**dijiste**
	He/she/it	(él/ella/usted)	**dice**	Va a decir	**dijo**
	We	(nosotros/as)	decimos	Vamos a decir	**dijimos**
	You (pl.)	(vosotros/as)	decís	Vais a decir	**dijisteis**
	They	(ellos/as/ustedes)	**dicen**	Van a decir	**dijeron**
estar *(to be)*	I	(yo)	**estoy**	Voy a estar	**estuve**
	You	(tú)	**estás**	Vas a estar	**estuviste**
	He/she/it	(él/ella/usted)	**está**	Va a estar	**estuvo**
	We	(nosotros/as)	estamos	Vamos a estar	**estuvimos**
	You (pl.)	(vosotros/as)	estáis	Vais a estar	**estuvisteis**
	They	(ellos/as/ustedes)	**están**	Van a estar	**estuvieron**
hacer *(to do / to make)*	I	(yo)	**hago**	Voy a hacer	**hice**
	You	(tú)	haces	Vas a hacer	**hiciste**
	He/she/it	(él/ella/usted)	hace	Va a hacer	**hizo**
	We	(nosotros/as)	hacemos	Vamos a hacer	**hicimos**
	You (pl.)	(vosotros/as)	hacéis	Vais a hacer	**hicisteis**
	They	(ellos/as/ustedes)	hacen	Van a hacer	**hicieron**

ir *(to go)*	I	(yo)	**voy**	Voy a ir	**fui**
	You	(tú)	**vas**	Vas a ir	**fuiste**
	He/she/it	(él/ella/usted)	**va**	Va a ir	**fue**
	We	(nosotros/as)	**vamos**	Vamos a ir	**fuimos**
	You (pl.)	(vosotros/as)	**vais**	Vais a ir	**fuisteis**
	They	(ellos/as/ustedes)	**van**	Van a ir	**fueron**
poder *(to be able to)*	I	(yo)	**puedo**	Voy a poder	**pude**
	You	(tú)	**puedes**	Vas a poder	**pudiste**
	He/she/it	(él/ella/usted)	**puede**	Va a poder	**pudo**
	We	(nosotros/as)	podemos	Vamos a poder	**pudimos**
	You (pl.)	(vosotros/as)	podéis	Vais a poder	**pudisteis**
	They	(ellos/as/ustedes)	**pueden**	Van a poder	**pudieron**
poner *(to put)*	I	(yo)	**pongo**	Voy a poner	**puse**
	You	(tú)	pones	Vas a poner	**pusiste**
	He/she/it	(él/ella/usted)	pone	Va a poner	**puso**
	We	(nosotros/as)	ponemos	Vamos a poner	**pusimos**
	You (pl.)	(vosotros/as)	ponéis	Vais a poner	**pusisteis**
	They	(ellos/as/ustedes)	ponen	Van a poner	**pusieron**
querer *(to want / to wish)*	I	(yo)	**quiero**	Voy a querer	**quise**
	You	(tú)	**quieres**	Vas a querer	**quisiste**
	He/she/it	(él/ella/usted)	**quiere**	Va a querer	**quiso**
	We	(nosotros/as)	queremos	Vamos a querer	**quisimos**
	You (pl.)	(vosotros/as)	queréis	Vais a querer	**quisisteis**
	They	(ellos/as/ustedes)	**quieren**	Van a querer	**quisieron**
salir *(to go out)*	I	(yo)	**salgo**	Voy a salir	salí
	You	(tú)	sales	Vas a salir	saliste
	He/she/it	(él/ella/usted)	sale	Va a salir	salió
	We	(nosotros/as)	salimos	Vamos a salir	salimos
	You (pl.)	(vosotros/as)	salís	Vais a salir	salisteis
	They	(ellos/as/ustedes)	salen	Van a salir	salieron
ser *(to be)*	I	(yo)	**soy**	Voy a ser	**fui**
	You	(tú)	**eres**	Vas a ser	**fuiste**
	He/she/it	(él/ella/usted)	**es**	Va a ser	**fue**
	We	(nosotros/as)	**somos**	Vamos a ser	**fuimos**
	You (pl.)	(vosotros/as)	**sois**	Vais a ser	**fuisteis**
	They	(ellos/as/ustedes)	**son**	Van a ser	**fueron**
tener *(to have)*	I	(yo)	**tengo**	Voy a tener	**tuve**
	You	(tú)	**tienes**	Vas a tener	**tuviste**
	He/she/it	(él/ella/usted)	**tiene**	Va a tener	**tuvo**
	We	(nosotros/as)	tenemos	Vamos a tener	**tuvimos**
	You (pl.)	(vosotros/as)	tenéis	Vais a tener	**tuvisteis**
	They	(ellos/as/ustedes)	**tienen**	Van a tener	**tuvieron**
venir *(to come)*	I	(yo)	**vengo**	Voy a venir	**vine**
	You	(tú)	vienes	Vas a venir	**viniste**
	He/she/it	(él/ella/usted)	viene	Va a venir	**vino**
	We	(nosotros/as)	venimos	Vamos a venir	**vinimos**
	You (pl.)	(vosotros/as)	venís	Vais a venir	**vinisteis**
	They	(ellos/as/ustedes)	vienen	Van a venir	**vinieron**
ver *(to see)*	I	(yo)	**veo**	Voy a ver	**vi**
	You	(tú)	ves	Vas a ver	viste
	He/she/it	(él/ella/usted)	ve	Va a ver	**vio**
	We	(nosotros/as)	vemos	Vamos a ver	vimos
	You (pl.)	(vosotros/as)	veis	Vais a ver	visteis
	They	(ellos/as/ustedes)	ven	Van a ver	vieron

Vocabulario

español—inglés

A

el abanico   fan
el aceite   oil
acogedor(a)   cosy
el acoso   harassment, bullying
acostarse   to go to bed
actualmente   currently
actuar   to act
acuático/a   aquatic, water
adelgazar   to lose weight
además   moreover
adjunto/a   enclosed/attached
admirar   to admire
adorar   to worship
aeróbico/a   aerobic
la aerolínea   airline
aficionado/a   fan
agradable   pleasant
el agujero   hole
el ajedrez   chess
el albergue   hostel
la alegría   joy
alejarse   to go away
el algodón   cotton
la alternativa   alternative
el ama de casa (f)   housewife
amable   pleasant
el/la amante   lover
amar   to love
amenazado/a   threatened
la amistad   friendship
el amor   love
amplio/a   wide
anteayer   the day before yesterday
anteriormente   previously
el anuncio   advertisement
apagar   to switch off
aparcar   park
aparecer   to appear
el apartamento   apartment
apasionado/a   passionate
apasionante   exciting
apellidarse   to have as a surname
el apellido   surname
apetecer (me apetece)   to fancy
aportar   to provide
aprovechar   to make the most of
la aptitud   aptitude
apto/a   suitable
las armas   weapons
arreglar   to fix
el arroz   rice
el artículo   item
el ascensor   lift
¡qué asco!   how disgusting!
el asiento   seat
asistir a   to attend
el atasco   traffic jam
atentamente   sincerely

la atmósfera   atmosphere
las atracciones   attractions
atreverse   to dare
el aumento   increase
aunque   although
la autopista   motorway
avanzado/a   advanced
la azafata   air stewardess
el azafato   flight attendant (male)

B

el bachillerato   A-level equivalent
bailar   to dance
el baile   dance
el banco   bank
barrer   to sweep
el barrio   neighbourhood/district
el belén   crib
la belleza   beauty
el beneficio   benefit
el beso   kiss
la biblioteca   library
bienvenido/a   welcome
blando/a   soft
la bolera   bowling alley
el bollo   bun, bread roll
la bolsa   bag
el bolso   handbag
los bombones   chocolates
el bosque   forest
la botella   bottle
el buceo   diving

C

el caballo   horse
la cabaña   hut
la cadena   chain
caer   to fall
la caída   fall
la caída libre   free fall
la caja   box
la cajera   female cashier
el cajero   male cashier, cash point
el calentamiento   warming
callado/a   silent
el calor   heat
el calzado   footwear
cambiar   to change
caminar   to walk
el campeón   champion
el campeonato   championship
el campo   countryside
la cancha   sports court
cansado/a   tired
la cantidad   amount
el canto   singing
la capa de ozono   ozone layer
la capacidad   capacity, ability
el carbono   carbon
el Caribe   Caribbean
el/la carnicero/a   butcher

caro/a   expensive
la carrera   race, career
la carta   letter
el cartón   cardboard
casarse   to get married
la cáscara   peel
casi   almost
la casita   hut
el castillo   castle
la cena   dinner
cerca   close
el cerdo   pig
cerrado/a   closed
la cerveza   beer
la cesta   basket
charlar   to chat
el chat   chatroom
el chicle   chewing gum
el churro   Spanish fritter
el cinturón   belt
el circuito   circuit
el/la ciudadano/a   citizen
claro/a   clear
el/la colega   colleague
el comentario   comment
comenzar   to begin
el comercio   trade
la comida basura   junk food
la compañía   company
compartir   to share
la comunidad   community
la concha   shell
concluir   to conclude
el concurso   contest
conducir   to drive
el conejo   rabbit
conmigo   with me
conocer a   to (get to) know
conocido/a   known
el/la consejero/a   counsellor, adviser
el consejo   advice
constar de   to consist of
construir   to build
el/la contable   accountant
contribuir   to contribute
conveniente   desirable, convenient
convertido/a   converted
la copa   cup, wine glass
el corazón   heart
la corbata   tie
el cordero   lamb
el correo   mail
la correspondencia   correspondence
la corrida   bullfight
cortado/a   cut
cortar   to cut
un crack   an ace (slang)
el crucero   cruise
cuál(es)   which one/ones
la cualidad   quality
cualquier   any
la cucaracha   cockroach
el cuero   leather
el cuidado   care
la culpa   fault

Vocabulario

cultivar *to grow*
curar *to treat/dress (wound)*
curioso/a *curious*

D

dañar *to damage*
dar *to give*
decidir *to decide*
decir *say*
declarar *to declare*
la defensa *defence*
la deforestación *deforestation*
dejar *to let/leave*
delante *in front of*
el delantero *forward*
deletrear *to spell*
los/las demás *others*
demasiado/a *too/too much...*
dentro *inside*
dentro de... años *within... years*
deportivo/a *sports, sporty*
deprimido/a *depressed*
el derecho *right*
desafortunadamente *unfortunately*
desaparecer *to disappear*
el desarrollo *development*
el descanso *rest*
descargar *to download*
describir *to describe*
descubrir *to discover*
el descuento *discount*
desde *from*
desear *to wish*
el desempleo *unemployment*
desenchufar *to unplug*
desgraciadamente *unfortunately*
el desierto *desert*
deslizar *to slide*
desobediente *disobedient*
despacio *slowly*
destruir *to destroy*
la desventaja *disadvantage*
el detalle *detail*
el detergente *detergent*
diario/a *daily*
el dibujo *art*
la dificultad *difficulty*
dinámico/a *dynamic*
la dirección *address*
el/la director(a) *manager*
dirigirse a *to write to (formal)*
discreto/a *discreet*
la discriminación *discrimination*
diseñar *to design*
disfrutar de *to enjoy*
disponer de *to have*
distinto/a *different*
el dolor *pain*
el domicilio *home*
el dominio *mastery*
la duda *doubt*
el dulce *sweet*
durante *during*
durar *to last*

E

echar *to throw away*
el edificio *building*
egoísta *selfish*
el electrodoméstico *appliance*
elegir *to choose*
eliminar *to remove*
sin embargo *but, however*
la emisión *emission*
la emoción *excitement*
emocionante *exciting, moving*
emparejar *to match*
empezar *to begin*
el/la empleado/a *employee*
la empresa *company*
en seguida *immediately*
en vez de *instead*
enamorado/a *in love*
encantar (me encanta) *to love*
el encendedor *lighter*
encender *to turn on*
enchufar *to plug in*
encontrar *to find/meet*
enfadarse *to get angry*
enfermo/a *sick*
engordar *to fatten/get fat*
enseguida *straight away*
la enseñanza *education, teaching*
enseñar *to teach*
ensuciar *to get/make dirty*
entender *to understand*
entero/a *whole*
entonces *then*
el entorno *environment*
la entrada *ticket, entrance*
entrar *to enter*
entre *between*
entrenar *to train*
entretenido/a *entertaining*
la época *period, age*
equilibrado/a *balanced*
equipado/a *equipped*
el equipo *team*
la equitación *horseriding*
ese/esa *that ...*
esos/esas *those ...*
la escalera *stairs*
la escena *scene*
escolar *school*
escuchar *to listen*
la ESO *Obligatory Secondary Education*
el espacio *space*
la especie *species*
esperar *to wait/expect/hope*
el estadio *stadium*
el estado *state*
estadounidense *North American*
la estancia *stay*
el estilo *style*
estimado/a *dear (formal)*
la estrella *star*
estresado/a *stressed out*
el estribillo *refrain*
el evento *event*
evidente *clear, obvious*

evitar *to avoid*
la exclusión *exclusion*
la excursión *trip*
la explicación *explanation*
explicar *to explain*
explotar *to exploit*
el exterior *outside*
la extinción *extinction*
extranjero/a *foreign*
extraño/a *strange*
extremo/a *extreme*
extrovertido/a *extrovert*

F

la fábrica *factory*
la fauna *fauna*
la fecha *date*
la felicidad *happiness*
feliz *happy*
la feria *fair*
el filete *steak*
la finca *estate*
el fino *dry sherry*
la firma *signature*
la flor *flower*
la flora *flora*
la floristería *florist's*
el folleto *brochure*
el footing *jogging*
el formulario *form*
frito/a *fried*
los fuegos artificiales *fireworks*
la fuerza *strength*

G

gallego/a *Galician*
la galleta *biscuit*
el garaje *garage*
garantizar *to ensure*
la gasolina *petrol*
la gente *people*
la gestión *management*
el gesto *gesture*
gigante *huge*
golpear *to hit*
gordísimo/a *very fat*
la gorra *cap*
la grabación *recording*
gracioso/a *funny*
gráfico/a *graphic*
la granja *farm*
la grasa *fat*
gratis *free*
gratuito/a *free*
grave *serious*
griego/a *Greek*
gritar *to shout/scream*
el guante *glove*
la guerra *war*
el/la guía *guide*
la guirnalda *garland*
gustar (me gusta) *to like*

Vocabulario

H

el habitante *inhabitant*
habitualmente *usually*
hablar *to talk*
hacer *to do, to make*
hacer novillos *to play truant*
el hambre (f) *hunger*
harto/a de *sick of*
el hecho *fact*
la herida *wound*
la hermanastra *stepsister*
el hermanastro *stepbrother*
la heroína *heroin*
la hidroeléctrica *hydropower*
el hielo *ice*
la hierba *grass, herb*
el/la hincha *fan, supporter*
hindú *hindu*
el hipermercado *supermarket*
la hipoteca *mortgage*
el horario *timetable*
horroroso/a *horrible*
el huevo *egg*
humanitario/a *humanitarian*

I

igual *equal*
iluminado/a *lit*
la ilusión *illusion*
ilustrar *to illustrate*
importar *to matter*
impresionar *to impress*
imprimir *to print*
incluir *to include*
incluso *even*
inconsciente *unconscious*
la incorporación *incorporation*
increíble *amazing/unbelievable*
independiente *independent*
individual *single*
individualizado/a *individualised*
la industria *industry*
industrial *industrial*
infantil *infant*
influir *to influence*
inmerso/a *immersed*
inolvidable *unforgettable*
inseguro/a *insecure*
la instalación *installation*
la institución *institution*
intensivo/a *intensive*
intentar *to try*
el interés *interest*
interesar *to interest*
interior *inside*
introvertido/a *introvert*
la invitación *invitation*
el/la invitado/a *guest*
ir *to go*
la isla *island*

J

el jabón *soap*
el jamón *ham*
japonés/japonesa *Japanese*
el/la jefe/a *boss*
el jersey *jumper*
la jornada *working day*
el/la joven *young person*
las joyas *jewellery*
la joyería *jewellery shop*
el/la jubilado/a *retired person*
el/la jugador(a) *player*
el juguete *toy*
junto/a *together*
justo/a *fair*
juvenil *youth…, child…*

L

laboral *working*
el lado *side*
la lana *wool*
largo/a *long*
la lástima *pity*
la lata *tin, can*
la lavadora *washing machine*
la lavandería *laundry*
el lavaplatos *dishwasher*
lavar *to wash*
la lectura *reading*
lejano/a *distant*
la lenteja *lentil*
lento/a *slow*
levantarse *to get up*
la ley *law*
libre *free*
llamar *to call*
la llegada *arrival*
llegar *to arrive*
llenar *to fill*
llevar *to carry*
llover *to rain*
la lluvia *rain*
loco/a *crazy*
luchar *to fight*
el lugar *place*
el lujo *luxury*
lujoso/a *luxurious*
la luz *light*

M

maduro/a *mature*
la magia *magic*
el maíz *corn*
la maleta *suitcase*
malgastar *to waste*
mandar *to order, to send*
la manera *way*
la mano *hand*
mantener *to hold, to support*
la mantequilla *butter*
el mar *sea*
maravilloso/a *wonderful*

el marisco *seafood*
la mascota *pet*
matar *to kill*
el matrimonio *marriage*
mayor *bigger, older/eldest*
la media *average*
el medio ambiente *environment*
la meditación *meditation*
meditar *to meditate*
mejor *better, best*
mejorar *to improve*
memorizar *to memorise*
menor *minor, younger/ youngest*
el mensaje (de texto) *(text) message*
a menudo *often*
merecer *to deserve*
la merluza *hake*
el metro *metre*
la mezquita *mosque*
el miedo *fear*
el miembro *member*
mientras *while*
mil *one thousand*
la misa *mass (church)*
mismo/a *same*
el misterio *mystery*
la mitad *half*
mixto/a *mixed*
la moda *fashion*
modificar *to change*
el modo *way*
molestar *to bother*
el monasterio *monastery*
el monopatín *skateboard*
montar *to ride*
el montón *pile*
morado/a *purple*
morir *to die*
la moto *motorbike*
el motor *engine*
mover *to move*
el móvil *mobile phone*
el mueble *piece of furniture*
la muerte *death*
muerto/a *dead*
la mujer *woman, wife*
el mundo *world*
musulmán/musulmana *Muslim/Moslem*

N

nacer *to be born*
el nacimiento *birth*
nativo/a *native*
la naturaleza *nature*
navegar por Internet *to surf the net*
la Navidad *Christmas*
necesario/a *necessary*
la necesidad *need*
el negocio *business*
nevar *to snow*
la nevera *fridge*
la niebla *fog*

la nieta *granddaughter*
el nieto *grandson*
la nieve *snow*
ningún/ninguna… *no…*
ninguno/a *none*
la noche *night*
el norte *north*
las noticias *news*
la novela *novel*
la novia *girlfriend*
el novio *boyfriend*
nuestro/a *our*
de nuevo *again*
numeroso/a *numerous*
nunca *never*

O

la obesidad *obesity*
obligatorio/a *compulsory*
obtener *to obtain*
el ocio *leisure*
ocupado/a *busy*
ofrecer *to offer*
oír *to hear*
olvidar *to forget*
la oportunidad *opportunity*
la oscuridad *darkness*
oscuro/a *dark*
el otoño *autumn*
otro/a *other (sing.)*
otros/as *other (pl.)*

P

el padre *father*
los padres *parents*
pagar *to pay*
el pájaro *bird*
la paliza *pain (slang)*
las palomitas *popcorn*
el/la panadero/a *baker*
panorámico/a *panoramic*
el pañuelo *handkerchief*
la papelería *stationery*
parcial *partial*
parecer *to seem*
la pared *wall*
el paro *unemployment*
el partido *game, match*
el/la pasajero/a *passenger*
el pasatiempo *pastime*
pasear *to walk*
el paseo *walk*
el pasillo *corridor*
el pastel *cake*
la pastilla *pill*
el pavo *turkey*
peatonal *pedestrian*
el pescaíto *fried fish*
el pedazo *piece*
pedir *to request*
la pelota *ball*
la pena *sorrow*
pensar *to think*
la pensión *pension*
peor *worse*

perder *to lose*
perder peso *to lose weight*
la pérdida *loss, waste*
perdido/a *missed, lost*
perezoso/a *lazy*
perfectamente *perfectly*
el periódico *newspaper*
perjudicial *harmful*
el permiso *permit, permission*
permitir *to allow*
la persona *person*
el personaje *character*
personalmente *personally*
pertenecer *to belong*
peruano/a *Peruvian*
pesado/a *heavy, tedious*
a pesar de *in spite of*
pescar *to fish*
el peso *weight*
el petardo *firecracker*
el pez *fish*
la pieza *piece, item*
la pintura *painting*
el piso *floor, flat*
la pista *track*
el placer *pleasure*
el plan *plan*
planchar *to iron*
el planeta *planet*
la planta *plant*
plantar *to plant*
el plátano *banana*
el plato *dish*
pleno/a *full*
la población *population*
pobre *poor*
pobrecillo/a *poor (diminutive)*
la pobreza *poverty*
poner *to put*
porque *because*
el porro *spliff*
el portátil *laptop*
la postal *postcard*
el postre *dessert*
potable *drinking*
practicar *to practise*
práctico/a *practical*
precioso/a *precious, beautiful*
preferentemente *preferably*
el premio *prize*
la prenda *garment*
preocuparse *to worry*
la presencia *presence*
la presentación *presentation*
presentar a *to introduce to*
prestar *to provide, to lend*
la prevención *prevention*
principalmente *mainly*
privado/a *private*
probar *to test, to try*
prohibido/a *prohibited*
pronto *soon, early*
propio/a *own*
proteger *to protect*
provocar *to cause*
próximo/a *next*
publicado/a *published*
publicidad *advertisement*

pues *so*
el puesto *post, job*
el pulmón *lung*
la pulsera *bracelet*
el punto de vista *point of view*
puntual *punctual*

Q

quedar *to meet up*
quedarse *to stay, to find oneself*
quejarse *to complain*
querido/a *dear*
la química *chemistry*
quitar *to remove*
quizás *maybe*

R

¡Qué rabia! *How annoying!*
raro/a *strange, odd*
el rato *while*
de rayas *striped*
la razón *reason*
las rebajas *reductions, sale*
recibir *to receive*
recientemente *recently*
recomendable *recommended*
reconocer *to recognise*
recordar *to remember*
recorrer *to travel around*
el recuerdo *souvenir*
reducir *to reduce*
el refresco *soft drink*
el regalo *gift*
la regla *rule, ruler*
regular *regular, OK*
la rehabilitación *rehabilitation*
reír *to laugh*
la relación *relationship*
relajarse *to relax*
rellenar *to fill in*
renovable *renewable*
renovar *to renew*
repartir *to spread*
de repente *suddenly*
el/la reportero/a *reporter*
respetuoso/a *respectful*
respirar *to breathe*
el resumen *summary*
retirarse *to retire*
reunir *to gather*
reutilizar *to reuse*
el rey *king*
rico/a *rich, tasty*
el riesgo *risk*
el río *river*
la riqueza *wealth*
riquísimo/a *very rich/tasty*
rizado/a *curly*
un rollo *a drag*
romper *to break*
roto/a *broken*
el ruido *noise*

Vocabulario

S

saber *to know*
la sala *room, hall*
el salario *wage*
la salida *departure, exit*
salir *to leave, to go out*
saludable *healthy*
el saludo *greeting*
salvar *to save*
las sandalias *sandals*
la sangre *blood*
sano/a *healthy*
la sardina *sardine*
secar *to dry*
seco/a *dry*
la sed *thirst*
seguido/a *followed*
seguir *to follow*
según *according to*
segundo/a *second*
la seguridad *security*
seguro/a *sure, safe*
la selva *jungle*
sencillo/a *simple*
el senderismo *hiking*
sentado/a *sitting*
sentarse *to sit*
sentir *to feel*
la sequía *drought*
el servicio *service, toilet*
la sevillana *Spanish dance*
el SIDA *AIDS*
el siglo *century*
el silencio *silence*
simbolizar *to symbolise*
sin *without*
sino *but*
sin techo *homeless*
el sistema *system*
el sitio *site, place*
sobre *about, on*
sobre todo *above all*
sobrevivir *to survive*
la sobrina *niece*
el sobrino *nephew*
la sociedad *society*
socorrer *to rescue*

solamente *only*
solar *solar*
solicitar *to request*
la solidaridad *solidarity*
soltero/a *single*
sorprendente *surprising*
sostenible *sustainable*
sufrir *to suffer*

T

la temporada *season*
el tiburón *shark*
titular *leading, first*
la tortuga *turtle*
la tostada *toast*
traducido/a *translated*
el/la traductor(a) *translator*
traer *to bring*
el traje *suit, costume*
el tratamiento *treatment*
tratar *to treat*
a través de *through*
la travesía *voyage*
triste *sad*
la tristeza *sadness*
la trucha *trout*
el/la tutor(a) *tutor*
tuyo/a *yours*

U

usted/Ud. *you (formal)*
últimamente *lately*
último/a *last*
único/a *only, unique*
la urgencia *emergency*
urgentemente *urgently*
usado/a *used*
usar *to use*
el uso *use*
útil *useful*
la utilización *use*
utilizar *to use*

V

vacío/a *empty*
los vaqueros *jeans*
variado/a *varied*
el vaso *glass*
las veces *times*
el/la vecino/a *neighbour*
la vela *sailing*
vender *to sell*
venir *to come*
la ventaja *advantage*
ver *to see, to watch*
la vergüenza *shame*
¡qué vergüenza! *how embarrassing!*
el vestuario *changing-room*
la vez *time*
una vez *once*
el viaje *journey*
la victoria *victory*
la vida *life*
el vidrio *glass*
el viento *wind*
vigilar *to watch*
vigoroso/a *vigorous*
la vista *sight, view*
volar *to fly*
el/la voluntario/a *volunteer*
volver *to return*
la vuelta *return, tour*

Z

la zanahoria *carrot*
la zapatería *shoe shop*
la zona *area*

inglés—español

A

a lot of   *mucho/a/os/as*
about, of   *de*
active   *activo/a*
afterwards   *después*
all the time   *todo el tiempo*
almost   *casi*
also   *también*
always   *siempre*
and   *y*
anything, something   *algo*
to arrive   *llegar*
as well   *también*
at the end of   *al final de*

B

bad   *malo/a*
because   *porque*
to become   *convertirse en*
behind   *detrás de*
best   *el/la mejor*
better   *mejor*
black   *negro/a*
blue   *azul*
book   *el libro*
boring   *aburrido/a*
brilliant   *genial*
brother   *el hermano*
brown   *marrón, castaño/a*
but   *pero*
to buy   *comprar*

C

can, to be able   *poder*
car   *el coche*
to change   *cambiar*
to charge a mobile   *cargar un móvil*
to chat   *chatear*
cheap   *barato/a*
chess club   *el club de ajedrez*
chicken   *el pollo*
choir   *el coro*
cigarette   *el cigarrillo*
cinema   *el cine*
to clean   *limpiar*
clothes   *la ropa*
coffee   *el café*
to comb   *peinarse*
comfortable   *cómodo/a*
concert   *el concierto*
cool   *guay*
creative   *creativo/a*
to cross the square   *cruzar la plaza*
customer   *el cliente/la cliente*

D

daily routine   *la rutina diaria*
to dance   *bailar*

daughter   *la hija*
day   *el día*
the day after tomorrow   *pasado mañana*
the day before yesterday   *anteayer*
delicious   *rico/a*
design   *el diseño*
difficult   *difícil*
to do my homework   *hacer mis deberes*
to download   *descargar*
a drag   *un rollo*
during   *durante*
dynamic   *dinámico/a*

E

to earn money   *ganar dinero*
easy   *fácil*
egg   *el huevo*
energy   *la energía*
England   *Inglaterra*
English   *(el) inglés*
entertaining   *divertido/a*
environment   *el medio ambiente*
every day   *todos los días*
exciting   *emocionante*
Excuse me…   *Perdón…*
expensive   *caro/a*

F

fair   *justo/a*
fair, blond   *rubio/a*
fantastic   *estupendo/a*
to feel well   *sentirse bien*
few   *poco/a*
film   *la película*
finally   *por último*
first   *primero*
flu   *la gripe*
food   *la comida*
football   *el fútbol*
for…   *desde…*
For how long?   *¿Desde hace cuánto tiempo?*
for, (in order) to   *para*
free time   *(el) tiempo libre*
French   *(el) francés*
Friday   *el viernes*
from time to time   *de vez en cuando*
fruit   *la fruta*
fun   *divertido/a*

G

German   *(el) alemán*
Germany   *Alemania*
to get dressed   *vestirse*
to get up   *levantarse*
to go on an outing   *ir de excursión*
to go out   *salir*
to go to   *ir a*
to go to bed   *acostarse*

to go to the park   *ir al parque*
good luck   *buena suerte*
good-looking   *guapo/a*
great   *genial*
great!   *¡qué bien!*
green   *verde*
grey   *gris*
gym   *el gimnasio*

H

half a kilo of   *medio kilo de*
hand   *la mano*
hardly ever   *casi nunca*
hard-working   *trabajador(a)*
to hate   *odiar*
to have a cold   *tener un resfriado*
to have a fantastic time   *pasarlo bomba*
to have a wonderful time   *pasarlo fenomenal*
to have breakfast   *desayunar*
to have dinner/supper   *cenar*
he   *él*
healthy   *sano/a*
her   *su(s)*
here   *aquí*
his   *su(s)*
history   *la historia*
holidays   *las vacaciones*
how often?   *¿con qué frecuencia?*
to be hungry   *tener hambre*
to hurt   *doler*

I

I   *yo*
ICT   *la informática*
ill   *enfermo/a*
in   *en*
in front of   *delante de*
in order to   *para*
in the evening   *por la tarde*
in the morning   *por la mañana*

L

language club   *el club de idiomas*
last Friday   *el viernes pasado*
last summer   *el verano pasado*
last winter   *el invierno pasado*
last year   *el año pasado*
later   *más tarde*
lawyer   *el/la abogado/a*
lazy   *perezoso/a*
least   *el/la menos*
leather   *de cuero*
left   *izquierda*
less… than   *menos… que*
lesson   *la clase*
Let's see…   *A ver…*
library   *la biblioteca*
life   *la vida*

Vocabulario

to like *gustar (me gusta)*
to listen to music *escuchar música*
long *largo/a*
to lose weight *adelgazar*
(not) a lot *(no) mucho*
lunch hour *la hora de comer*

M

main course *el segundo plato*
market *el mercado*
to marry *casarse*
martial arts *las artes marciales*
match (football) *el partido (de fútbol)*
Monday *el lunes*
month *el mes*
monument *el monumento*
more *más*
more… than *más… que*
more or less *más o menos*
the most / the -est *el más…*
must *deber*
my *mi(s)*

N

nationality *la nacionalidad*
to need *necesitar*
neither *tampoco*
never *nunca*
next year *el año que viene*
nice, pretty *bonito/a*
night *la noche*
noise *el ruido*
normally *normalmente*
nothing *nada*
nothing else *nada más*
now *ahora*
now and then *de vez en cuando*

O

o'clock *en punto*
of course *claro que sí*
often *a menudo*
old-fashioned *anticuado/a*
on foot *a pie*
on time *a tiempo*
or *o*
our *nuestro/a*

P

patient *paciente*
to pay *pagar*
to phone *llamar por teléfono*
pink *rosa*
to play *jugar*
to play football *jugar al fútbol*
please *por favor*

por eso *so, therefore*
practical *práctico/a*
professional *profesional*
to protect *proteger*
public transport *el transporte público*
pupil *el/la alumno/a*

R

to read *leer*
to recycle *reciclar*
red *rojo/a*
red-haired *pelirrojo/a*
responsible *responsable*
to rest *descansar*
restaurant *el restaurante*
return (ticket) *(el billete) de ida y vuelta*
to ride a bike *montar en bicicleta*
to run *correr*

S

sandwich *el bocadillo*
Saturday *el sábado*
to save *ahorrar*
school *el instituto/colegio*
to send an email *mandar un correo electrónico*
serious *serio/a*
she *ella*
shop *la tienda*
shopping centre *el centro comercial*
short *bajo/a, corto/a*
to shower *ducharse*
shy *tímido/a*
to sing *cantar*
single ticket *el billete de ida*
sister *la hermana*
slim *delgado/a*
to smoke *fumar*
sometimes *a veces*
sort of… *tipo de…*
Spanish *(el) español*
to speak *hablar*
sport *el deporte*
to start *empezar*
starter *el primer plato*
straight on *todo recto*
strict *severo/a*
striped *de rayas*
strong *fuerte*
to study *estudiar*
stupid *estúpido/a*
to sunbathe *tomar el sol*
Sunday *el domingo*

T

to take *tomar*
to take photos *sacar fotos*
talkative *hablador(a)*
tall *alto/a*

text message *el mensaje de texto*
their *su(s)*
then *luego*
these *estos, estas*
they *ellos/as*
to be thirsty *tener sed*
this *este, esta*
Thursday *el jueves*
ticket *el billete/la entrada*
to tidy up *ordenar*
tired *cansado/a*
to *a*
toast *la tostada*
today *hoy*
tomorrow *mañana*
to travel *viajar*
tree *el árbol*
Tuesday *el martes*
to turn right *girar a la derecha*
twice a week *dos veces a la semana*

U

ugly *feo/a*
uncomfortable *incómodo/a*
useful *útil*
usually *generalmente*

W

to wake up *despertarse*
Wales *Gales*
to wash *lavar*
to waste *malgastar*
water *el agua (f)*
wavy *ondulado/a*
to wear/to carry *llevar*
the weather *el tiempo*
Wednesday *el miércoles*
week *la semana*
weekend *el fin de semana*
Well… *Pues/Bueno…*
what's more *además*
with *con*
to work *trabajar*
worse *peor*
worst *el/la peor*
to write *escribir*

Y

yellow *amarillo/a*
yesterday *ayer*
yesterday evening *ayer por la tarde*
you (sing.) *tú*
you (plural) *vosotros/as*
your (sing.) *tu(s)*
your (plural) *vuestro/a*